SOUTH AFRI

EDEN

James Stevenson-Hamilton (1867-1957)

SOUTH AFRICAN

EDEN

THE KRUGER NATIONAL PARK

1902-1946

James Stevenson-Hamilton
First warden of the Park

Introduction by Jane Carruthers Ph.D.

STRUIK

Struik Publishers (Pty) Ltd
A member of
The Struik Publishing Group
Cornelis Struik House
80 McKenzie Street
Cape Town 8001

First edition: Cassel & Company Ltd (London) 1937
Second edition: Cassel & Company Ltd (London) 1952
Third edition: Hamilton & Co (Stafford) Ltd (London)1956
Fourth edition: William Collins Sons & Co. Ltd (London) 1974
First published by Struik Publishers (Pty) Ltd 1993

Editor: Jane Carruthers
Managing editor: Valerie Streak
Designer: Neville Poulter
Cover designer: Alix Gracie
Cartographer: Angus Carr

Typesetting by Suzanne Fortescue, Struik DTP
Reproduction by Unifoto (Pty) Ltd, Cape Town
Printed by Kyodo Printing Co (Singapore) Pte Ltd, Singapore

ISBN 1 86825 343 0

ACKNOWLEDGEMENTS
Struik Publishers wishes to thank the photographic archives of the National Parks Board for its
kind co-operation in supplying photographs from the James Stevenson-Hamilton collection for
reproduction in this work and the South African National Museum for Military History for providing the photograph of Colonel Steinacker.

4

To Cinderella,
who became a princess

CONTENTS

6

7

FOREWORD

The reader of *South African Eden* is left to deduce for himself what sort of person my father was. The book makes no concessions to his enlightenment. The omission may have been due to my father's sense of modesty, but it is more likely that he simply did not want to make himself part of the public domain. Now, more than fifty years on, it is no longer necessary to maintain this veil of privacy. I should like, therefore, to introduce my father and to endeavour to sketch briefly his career until the opening chapter of *South African Eden*.

JAMES STEVENSON-HAMILTON WAS born in 1867 of Scottish parentage. He was the first of six children, of whom only three survived infancy. His father's family, who were Stevensons, were all accomplished soldiers. My grandfather was the oldest of five brothers; three of these were promoted to the rank of colonel and the other two became generals. It was thus the Stevensons who provided the impetus that was to set my father on course for his military career. However, if the call to arms came from the Stevensons, it was the ancient family of Hamilton – his mother's family – which endowed my father with his rich sense of history. The Hamiltons had occupied their lands at Fairholm since 1492 and the family papers bear witness to forebears who had become soldiers or administrators, or had led lives of varying degrees of usefulness. All contributed to the fabric of the genealogical tree, the codifying of which must have provided my father with hours of fulfilment.

On the death of her uncle, my grandmother, Eliza, inherited the Hamilton family estates. Under the Scots law of entail, possession of the estate of Fairholm had to be linked to the name of the family for all time. Thus it was that Hamilton was joined to her married name of Stevenson, and my father became Stevenson-Hamilton. Eliza was a gifted artist and she coached her young son to emulate her skills with pencil and paintbrush. My father's delightful watercolours of African scenes and the charm of his pen-and-ink drawings are testimony to the success of this early encouragement. My father was only eight years old when his mother died. His brother and sister were several years younger than he, and consequently James was thrown much on his own resources. He led a rather solitary life on the family's Scottish estate, and circumstances taught him from an early age to be resourceful and imaginative, qualities that were to stand him in good stead later in the African bush.

James went to Rugby, his father's old school. He had decided to make the army his career and in due course he entered Sandhurst Royal Military Academy. He passed out near the top of his class in 1888 and was commissioned into the 6th Inniskilling Dragoons, a well-known cavalry regiment, at that time stationed in Natal. In May of the same year he sailed from Southampton to Africa, where he was destined to live and work for much of the rest of his life.

After a month at sea twenty-one year old Stevenson-Hamilton landed at Durban. Six weeks later he was to have his first experience of active service, when, as a subaltern, he joined his regiment in Zululand where it was quelling an outbreak of violence.

In November 1890 the regiment returned to Britain, but by then my father had seen enough of Africa to know that he wanted to come back. It was, however, to be several years before an opportunity was to present itself, and when it did, he grasped it firmly. In 1898 he took a year's leave from his regiment and joined an expedition that was to bring him for the first time into contact with wild animals and to introduce him to the primeval Africa which he would later know and love so well.

My father's account of the expedition, whose objectives were to test the navigability of the Zambezi and to survey part of Barotseland, was published in 1953 under the title of *The Barotseland Journal of James Stevenson-Hamilton*. One member of the party died of dysentery and all suffered repeatedly from malaria, but the expeditition's purpose was fulfilled. In December 1899 my father was on his way home and had reached Tete, in Mozambique, when he learnt of the outbreak of war in South Africa. A ship took him to Port Elizabeth and from there he was able to rejoin the Inniskillings, who had already reached South Africa. He saw active service throughout the war, and soon after its end, in 1902, he met Sir Godfrey Lagden and made his momentous decision to accept the post of Chief

Ranger to the Sabi Game Reserve. It is at this point that the story of *South African Eden* begins and I will therefore trespass no further on the author's preserve.

Though in stature my father was short and lightly built, he was possessed of an obstinate streak and he was quite fearless. If he were to be in need of anything, he would have no compunction in approaching the man at the top. He had two other attributes which would be vital to his success, and which would not only distinguish him as an administrator, but would earn him the acclaim of the scientific world: he was an astute observer and he recognized the supreme importance of accurately recording his observations. The knowledge that certain of his methods of measurement are still practised by scientists in the Kruger National Park, in spite of widespread computerization, would give him immense satisfaction.

Like his father before him, my father kept a journal from the age of twelve. He confided to his diary almost every day his thoughts, the names of people he had met, and the sequence of daily events. The last entry is made a week before he died – at the age of ninety – in 1957. His journals provided him with a ready source of reference in compiling the reports required by his superiors, and they also furnished much of the material for the writing of *South African Eden*.

My father married late in life. He was almost sixty-three and my mother, at twenty-nine, was less than half his age. However, this was to be a highly successful marriage. My parents were wholly devoted to one another. My mother, who was Hilda Cholmondeley, had been studying art in London when she met my father on one of his regular leaves. She came out to South Africa in the charge of a chaperone and immediately took to life in the wilds, finding that it provided enormous scope for her artistic talents. My parents were married in Johannesburg in 1930.

We were three children, two girls and a boy, spaced at intervals of two years. Margaret, the eldest, died when she was four. This tragedy so distressed our parents that the decision was taken for my younger sister and I to remain in the healthy climate of Britain at the end of my father's next spell of leave. Our parents meanwhile returned to their idyllic life in the game reserve, leaving us at Fairholm with a nanny and in the care of my mother's family. We might have remained at Fairholm for much of our childhood, were it not for the threat of war in 1939. The possible dangers of wartime Britain were considered by our parents to outweigh those of the lowveld climate, and at the ages of six and four we were shipped out to South Africa with our nanny and our grandmother, who was some eight years junior to our father.

Despite the wilderness of the Kruger National Park, our early upbringing was formal. Nanny supervised the discipline of the nursery routine and it was her job to see that my sister and I were produced scrubbed and in clean clothes whenever visitors appeared – which seemed to us to be all too often. In general we were expected to be seen but not heard, and to speak only when spoken to. There were no children of our own age at Skukuza, and consequently no children's parties, but, perhaps surprisingly, we never felt any sense of deprivation due to this. Despite the rather stern code of behaviour, I can remember that we were perfectly contented children.

Affectionate – and understandably proud to have produced three children – our father was nevertheless a somewhat remote figure to us. He would disappear to his office at six every morning and he would reappear for meals. Breakfast and lunch were frequently attended by visiting guests, and at such times children's conversation was strongly discouraged. Dinner was a formal occasion from which children were banned altogether. It was during a much-prized half-hour at bedtime that Anne and I could usually expect to have our father's undivided attention. He would then enthral us with stories culled from his imagination, often bolstered by recitations from Lewis Carroll, many of whose works he knew by heart. As he spoke, he would illustrate the progress of his tale with a lively pencil and coloured chalk. These were magical moments.

As we grew older, however, the rules relaxed and in the camping season life assumed a new form. Camping invariably took place during the dry winter months, when my father would install his family and our retinue under tents in some otherwise remote area of the game reserve. He would then ride out on patrol with native rangers early every morning, leaving us to our own devices. We never knew what it was that he did, but he usually returned by midday. Anne and I had been taught to ride at an early age and we each had a pony. Often we would be taken for morning outings by our mother, a rifle supported in a leather bucket attached to her saddle. Trusty M'Gwelane would usually go ahead of the little party, slashing thorn branches from our path. The afternoons would normally be given over to fishing. It was a life of pack donkeys hung with tinkling bells, of hurricane lamps and canvas baths, and of playing in acres of river sand. At night we would sleep in the open around an enormous campfire under a brilliant panoply of stars, guessing at the sounds of the African bush. Although there were always Chinese

11

firecrackers at hand to scare off inquisitive lion, I cannot recall them ever being used in earnest.

Later, and long after our father had retired, Anne and I sometimes thought wistfully of how much greater would have been our appreciation of the privilege of living in the middle of the world's greatest wildlife sanctuary, and under the roof of its principal architect, had we been a little bit older at the time. It was at moments such as these that we wondered how it might have been had our father advanced his marriage plans by a few years.

In commending *South African Eden* to a new generation of readers, I would like to thank Dr Jane Carruthers, who has reshaped the index, corrected textual errors and added a set of extremely useful biographical notes. The selection of illustrations has been achieved with her guidance, and finally, she has written an introduction which will place the book firmly in a 1990s setting.

Fairholm, Scotland   *James C. Stevenson-Hamilton*
March 1993

INTRODUCTION

JAMES STEVENSON-HAMILTON'S *South African Eden* is a classic of Africana literature and the appearance of this new edition pays tribute to its enduring popularity. For more than fifty years readers of all ages have enjoyed the informative and elegant account of the author's long wardenship of the two game reserves – the Sabi and the Singwitsi[1] – which later became the Kruger National Park. *South African Eden* has, however, long been out of print, and although the delight of another generation of readers is a major reason for re-publication, it is not the only one. Exciting as it always is to glimpse an episode in our history and to gain an insight into the life and activities of a remarkable person, the great value of this book as we approach the end of the century is that it provides a focus for a dialogue between the past and the present. When he wrote the book in 1937, James Stevenson-Hamilton's aims were to change attitudes in favour of game protection, to provide an understanding of natural history, to legitimize the colonization of Africa in terms of conservation efforts, to entertain and also to record his own version of events. But while some of the reasons for writing the book still remain valid today, the interests and needs of the readership have changed and our appreciation of the contents of *South African Eden* is greatly enhanced with the passage of time. We are able to treasure the book not only because it is a delightful period piece, but also because there is now an historical context both to the man and his achievements. The re-publication of this work provides us with an opportunity to view it critically from the standpoints of the South African past generally and the history of nature conservation in particular.

HISTORICAL IMPORTANCE OF *South African Eden*
The conservation of nature is at present of global concern and circumstances are much altered since James Stevenson-Hamilton wrote this account. The author often refers to the two early game reserves as 'Cinderella', and the

story of *South African Eden* is indeed akin to a fairytale with a happy ending. It is a tribute to the efforts of many people to preserve something of primeval paradise in South Africa and it describes the opposition which had to be overcome to achieve this ideal. Stevenson-Hamilton vividly portrays the wide-ranging antagonistic forces, which included desultory officialdom, hunting interests, and a growing need of land for human settlement, agriculture and mineral exploitation. While this book clarifies what the struggle was *against*, it is only with the passage of time that we have been able to discern what it was fought *for*.

Those who were involved in the transformation of the two eastern Transvaal game reserves into the vast Kruger National Park lived at a time when natural resources were abundant by today's standards, and they could not have foreseen a future in which wilderness and intact ecosystems would become the earth's most precious resources. The idea of preserving such a wilderness area is the fundamental legacy of *South African Eden* and justifies the continuing relevance of the book.

Other aspects of the work, however, may appear rather dated to the modern reader, but they nevertheless show how priorities have changed and remind us that conservation principles are not immutable. For James Stevenson-Hamilton the preservation of certain species of wildlife was a critical issue; today the picture has changed dramatically and, due to their proliferation, thousands of animals are culled annually in the Kruger National Park. In the years after 1926 Stevenson-Hamilton found it difficult to attract visitors to the park; today accommodation is at a premium and even day visitors sometimes find themselves turned away. Indeed, increasing human pressure on recreational outlets has meant the burgeoning of accommodation and other facilities and this has altered the character of the park in many respects. While to a large extent scientists now manage the Kruger National Park, to Stevenson-Hamilton a strong administrative ability and a talent for public relations were more essential attributes for a game warden than a knowledge of wildlife. Most important, Stevenson-Hamilton's desire to leave his Eden to its natural fate is no longer feasible: increasing modernization requires active human mediation and the existence of a comprehensive wildlife and landscape management system.

When Stevenson-Hamilton wrote this book, one of his aims was to entertain the public with anecdotes of exciting encounters with large and dangerous mammals, particularly lion. But more than this, he had a firm belief in the value of literature as an educational medium, believing that it was ignorance which caused people to kill wildlife carelessly. Throughout his life Stevenson-Hamilton was a prolific writer and ardent teacher. He wrote numerous books and pamphlets, regularly contributed articles to academic and popular journals and accepted countless invitations to lecture. As a member of many international learned societies, he corresponded with protectionists and hunters all over the world. His views became widely known and he benefited from the exchanges of information which resulted. He was critical of those who did not read widely and also of those authors who presented wild animals as merely threatening and savage. Stevenson-Hamilton was dedicated to providing an understanding of natural history, enhanced by lively reminiscences of personalities and events. His principal achievement is that he redirected public interest away from reading hunting fables towards a desire to learn about the realities of wildlife. Above all, he engendered in others the concept of protecting nature.

TEXTUAL FEATURES OF *South African Eden*

Stevenson-Hamilton recorded meticulously his observations of human and animal life and these found a place in publications such as *Animal Life in Africa*, *The Low-Veld: Its Wild Life and Its People* and *Wild Life in South Africa*. In compiling *South African Eden* the author also made use of the journal which he kept every day and of the regular reports that he submitted to his superiors. These sources he augmented with information received from his rangers.

This may suggest that *South African Eden* is truly comprehensive and absolutely accurate, but although the book purports to be the full story of Stevenson-Hamilton's experiences in the Transvaal, it must be seen as a self-censored version because it was written for public consumption. There is an emphasis on achievements rather than on failures, and events or personalities that were distasteful to him, or that might have been offensive to others, have been omitted.

With the advantage of hindsight it becomes possible to elaborate on certain events and to explain some of the more difficult aspects of his career. Such knowledge makes Stevenson-Hamilton's work even more remarkable. His disillusionment with the calibre of most of the people who sought positions as game rangers is not mentioned, but of them he once said, 'All the flotsam and jetsam apply to me; I suppose they think it will be an easy life with not much to do except drink and so will suit them'. Of their dilatory attention to duties, or the occasional acts of disloyalty he experienced, there

15

is not a word. His private opinion of his superiors was seldom as complimentary as it appears here. Sir Godfrey Lagden was referred to in his journal as 'an old woman who won't push things ahead' and the officials in the Transvaal at the beginning of the century he considered to be 'a lot of blackguards'. Nor did his view of the actions of politicians mellow with the years, and what he took to be interference, ignorance, insult or political machinations on the part of various members of the National Parks Board upset him very much. Here one needs to be reminded of Stevenson-Hamilton's own obstinate streak – seen in the fact that at times the only pressure which kept him from resigning was that his continued presence thwarted those who longed for his departure. On many occasions he determined to remain in his post, because 'I know the rascals want to get rid of me'.

Moreover, nothing of his personal life, particularly the trauma of his retirement, is included. As time passed he was extremely loathe to relinquish his job, even when it became apparent to all – including himself – that his physical and mental powers were declining. He confided to his journal in 1946, the year of his retirement, that he yearned to die 'in harness'.

THE PROCLAMATION OF THE KRUGER NATIONAL PARK

Stevenson-Hamilton retired after forty-four years as a game warden, a career which began in 1902 as the 'Age of Wildlife Extermination' was ending. During the nineteenth century the spread of industrialization in Europe devoured much of the countryside; in Australia and New Zealand, settlers travelled into the interior with livestock, killing much of the fauna as they did so. In North America, large numbers of people moved westward and put pressure on areas which had hitherto been wilderness. With sophisticated weaponry and without effective restrictions of any kind, it did not take long for the huge herds of bison and the flocks of passenger pigeons, some numbering in their millions, to disappear altogether from America. Man, the ultimate predator, became increasingly capable of destroying whole species and of upsetting complex ecosystems, sometimes irreversibly.

As far as the Transvaal was concerned, in the nineteenth century wildlife was the basis of the early Voortrekker economy. After some years, declining wildlife numbers alerted attention to the necessity for conservation legislation and between 1846 and the end of the South African Republic in 1902 many such laws were passed. In 1889 the first Transvaal game reserve – the Pongola in the south-east – met with the overwhelming approval of the Volksraad and this small reserve was proclaimed in 1894. Owing to the presence of tsetse fly, herds of wildlife had managed to survive in the eastern Transvaal and many people considered this to be a suitable locality for another game reserve.

In 1888 the proposal came from a certain man by the name of Williams, who was farming near Bloemfontein, that a game reserve be created in the Barberton district. Shortly afterwards, J.A. Erasmus (a republican official) and G.F.J. Lottering suggested closing part of the eastern Transvaal as a 'wildkraal'. These proposals bore fruit in 1895 when the members of the Volksraad for Barberton and Krugersdorp, R.K. Loveday and J.L. van Wijk, formally asked the Transvaal Executive Council (i.e. President Kruger and his closest advisors) to proclaim a game reserve in the area between the Crocodile and Sabie rivers. On 17 September 1895 this motion was enthusiastically agreed to by the Volksraad and the Government was approached to make the proposal a reality. In the troubled circumstances of the Transvaal at that time – the Jameson Raid, drought and the rinderpest – the Government was tardy in doing so and had to be prodded into action by repeated reminders from Loveday. It was only on 26 March 1898 that President Kruger signed and published the proclamation, and only in September 1898 that the Executive Council agreed to appoint a game warden, although no appointment was made at that time. As the war-clouds gathered in October 1899 there was little indication of the prominent role that the Transvaal was yet to play in conservation in southern Africa and, indeed, in the world.

That the Transvaal became a world leader in nature conservation was primarily due to the efforts of James Stevenson-Hamilton, and the story of how this happened is recounted in *South African Eden*. The tale begins when Stevenson-Hamilton took up his appointment as warden of the Sabi Game Reserve in 1902; it goes on to relate how that reserve was extended northward and westward and how the Shingwedsi Game Reserve was proclaimed. In 1926 these reserves became legally entrenched when they were taken out of the hands of the Transvaal province and became the Kruger National Park in accordance with the National Parks Act passed by the parliament of the Union of South Africa.

Attentive readers of *South African Eden* may discern a distinct change in the tone of the book when comparing the eras before and after the establishment of the Kruger National Park. Before 1926 Stevenson-Hamilton was immensely happy and fulfilled. Not by nature gregarious, he gloried in the isolation forced upon him by his occupation, the opportunities for broadening his wildlife knowledge and the wide scope he was allowed for exercising his talents for efficient administration. When he left the army in 1902, his ambition had been to become a colonial administrator of a district such as Bechuanaland or Barotseland. Although the subsequent junior status he held as a civil servant in charge of the game reserves of the Transvaal sometimes irked him – especially when over the years he became aware of the successful careers of many of his contemporaries – he was, however, sufficiently perceptive to realize that he had in his charge the nucleus of one of the wonders of southern Africa.

It was after the union of the South African colonies in 1910 that Stevenson-Hamilton worked actively to secure the long-term existence of the reserves under his care by promoting their status from proclaimed game reserves of the Transvaal province to an entrenched national park similar to those in the United States of America. Such moves were inimical to him, for he was aware that in the process of such a change he would lose the authority and freedom of action he had so enjoyed, and would perhaps even forfeit his job, for there was no indication – let alone guarantee – that a newly formed National Parks Board would re-employ him. Nor, even if he were to be re-engaged, did he relish the thought of either the public invading what had until then been virtually his own wildlife sanctuary, or of having yet another level of administration above him.

Of course, the credit for the idea of the establishment of the Kruger National Park and the entire national parks system which exists in South Africa today cannot be ascribed to Stevenson-Hamilton alone, nor did he ever make such a claim. Many individuals, including politicians in colonial, provincial and central government circles, advocated such moves, as did wildlife protection bodies and even sportsmen's associations. Without wide support from private landowners and the general public the idea could never have gained acceptability. Credit must be given on the international front as well, where national parks were an established feature of many countries, and their economic benefits in terms of tourism and regional development had already begun to be appreciated.

The wider economic and socio-political circumstances of the 1920s in South Africa which favoured the establishment of a national park are not made clear in *South African Eden* and this background is thus briefly outlined here. The motto of the day was 'South Africa First' as Afrikaners and English-speakers sought common ground in the hope of burying past divisions and forging a united nation and a future free from British domination. It was a period of resurgent Afrikaner nationalism, evidenced by the coming to power in the 1924 election of the Pact government under Prime Minister J.B.M. Hertzog. The establishment of the Kruger National Park in 1926 formed part of a process which culminated in the loosening of South Africa's ties with Britain, as did the adoption of Afrikaans as an official language and the creation of a new national flag and anthem. In this situation, naming the park after an heroic Afrikaner figure, the former president of the South African Republic, Paul Kruger, touched a receptive chord and ensured the passing of the National Parks Act.

CHANGING CONSERVATION PHILOSOPHIES

If knowledge of the socio-political context of the time deepens our understanding of the complex reasons for proclaiming or deproclaiming game reserves, how much more crucial is it also to place the conservation philosophies expressed by Stevenson-Hamilton in *South African Eden* in a broader context. Stevenson-Hamilton's long career in the field spanned many transformations in protectionist ideologies. For most of his life he remained abreast of changes – sometimes he was even in advance of them – and it was only in his later years that he became inflexible and less able to move with the times.

A history of nature conservation in southern Africa has still to be written, and when it is, the figure of James Stevenson-Hamilton will loom large. But he is only one piece of an intricate tapestry which has its origins far back in time. For many centuries before white colonization, indigenous communities had taken advantage of the wide variety of wildlife of the subcontinent. The relatively large numbers of game compared to the small population of hunters, the methods of hunting employed, the largely subsistence nature of African economies, and perhaps also the exercise of certain conservation strategies, ensured that mass extermination of wildlife did not occur. White settlement, hunting with firearms and the introduction of a market economy changed the picture entirely and the number of wild animals declined steadily after Van Riebeeck's arrival at the Cape in 1652. This decrease in animal populations did not go unnoticed by the ruling authorities and legislation placing restrictions on hunting was frequently enacted but universally ignored. By the early decades of the nineteenth century the Cape was almost entirely denuded of its larger mammals.

Until this time, however, the wildlife of the interior had escaped almost unscathed, and when the first whites visited what came to be known as the Orange Free State, Natal and the Transvaal, they were astonished at its abun-

19

dance. But when a resource is abundant, its exploitation is conducted carelessly and often wastefully. It is only when that resource diminishes substantially that steps are taken to protect it, usually by those with economic and political power, who then restrict access to it. This pattern of events took place in the Transvaal after the establishment of the embryonic Boer republics. Because the economy of the early Transvaal depended on the exploitation of wildlife products, the first game protectionist legislation promulgated in the Transvaal was designed to confine the hunting of game to Boers, and to exclude both Africans and foreigners. These were utilitarian measures, and the restrictions – enlarged and altered from time to time by successive governments – were no more successful in limiting the slaughter of wildlife in the Transvaal than they had been in the Cape. The market for wildlife products proved irresistible and strong authority to enforce legislation was lacking. Soon the wildlife of the Transvaal was threatened with extinction.

Hunting restrictions are what we would today call 'conservation' tactics, in the sense that the concept entails the management and utilization of a resource so as to ensure its perpetuation. Conservation is frequently referred to as 'wise use' because the aim is to keep exploitation at a sustainable level – thus promoting the doctrine of 'sustainable yield'. An age-old device for protecting game, common in medieval Europe and even in the ancient world, is to declare certain areas of land altogether closed to hunting and in so doing to create the game reserve or game preserve. Preservation is different from conservation because the former aims to remove the human factor and allows for no strategy of utilization of the resource at all. It is interesting to note that from the 1860s onwards many private landowners in the Transvaal saw the need for such measures and established preserves on their farms.

Towards the end of the nineteenth century, the diminution of desirable wild animals in the Transvaal – due to both profligate hunting and the effects of the rinderpest – spurred the Transvaal government into joining the trend set by private landowners and led to its application of preservationist principles to wildlife on certain state land. Another factor to influence such measures was pressure from the large population of new immigrants in search of mineral wealth, who had brought with them from Europe, but mainly from Britain, ideas of sportsmanship and who established game protection societies to enable them to further their pleasure in hunting.

By 1899 there were four formal game reserves in the Transvaal – at Pongola, Groenkloof near Pretoria, Sabi and on the Springbok Flats – while hunting was prohibited in almost a third of the rest of the republic. Although welcomed by landowners and the sporting elite, these measures were not as enthusiastically received by the less affluent who depended on game for subsistence, and who saw the prohibitions as being deliberately designed to impoverish them further and thereby to force them into wage-earning labour.

THE IMPERIAL SPORTING ETHIC

After the end of the South African War in 1902 the Transvaal was ruled as a British colony. During this time ideas of the economic exploitation of game – whether for subsistence in the case of Africans or for the biltong and hide market in the case of poor whites – were anathema to the colonial regime with its well entrenched ideas of British 'sportsmanship'. Added to this was the scarcity of game animals and a growing international interest in game protection. In 1900 a conference was held in London at the conclusion of which a 'Convention for the Preservation of Wild Animals, Birds and Fish in Africa' was formulated, though for various reasons it was never ratified by all governments concerned.

It was at this stage of developments in the local and international game protection arena that James Stevenson-Hamilton accepted the position of warden of the Sabi Game Reserve in the eastern Transvaal. The function of the game reserve was to preserve certain species of animals – that is, antelope, which were desirable from a sporting point of view – and so to enable the herds to increase in numbers, free from the depredations of hunters. To this end Stevenson-Hamilton and his rangers pursued poachers relentlessly and exterminated anything regarded as 'vermin' that preyed upon the game. By definition, 'vermin' at that time included many species which today are regarded as magnificent and ecologically vital – animals such as lion, cheetah, leopard, wild dog and hyena, as well as raptors and reptiles. The presence of resident Africans within the game reserves was tolerated because, as squatters on Crown lands, they were a source of income and labour. The labour of prisoners detained as trespassers from Mozambique was also used to create the infrastructure of the game reserves.

When he took charge as warden, Stevenson-Hamilton realized that the area of the Sabi Game Reserve was too small to serve its purpose as an effective game nursery, and he accordingly lobbied for the reserve to be extended northward into state and private land. That this was accomplished without serious opposition was probably due more to the fact that the area comprising the reserve and its additional land was generally regarded as 'worthless', than to Stevenson-Hamilton's energy in promoting the issue. At that time the lowveld was unsuitable for prolonged occupation by humans or domestic stock owing to the presence there of endemic diseases, the innate lack of agricultural or mineral potential and the enervating climate.

STEVENSON-HAMILTON'S 'BALANCE OF NATURE'

After 1910 many of these ideas of 'worthlessness' began to change. In a united South Africa, land became more valuable and exploitation of all natural resources more attractive, the sporting ethic of the colonial elite was waning in influence, and efforts to overcome the effects of disease and climate were showing signs of success. It was then that Stevenson-Hamilton demonstrated that he was well abreast of new attitudes towards nature conservation. He began to ward off assaults on the physical integrity of the game reserve by cultivating friendships in high political and scientific circles and, more crucially, by disclaiming sporting or utilitarian needs in his campaign for nature protection. Instead, he began to refer to what he called 'a balance of nature' in which every species played a role, this being an early expression – perhaps the first in South Africa – of the view that every aspect of a natural habitat has its own right to existence, independent of human use. As early as 1912 he recorded his revulsion at the killing of lion and his fondness for hyena and birds of prey – not popular ideas at the time. The following year he wrote of his belief that nature has an inbuilt capacity for maintaining its equilibrium and that human interference should be minimal.

The First World War ushered in a new era and dealt the final blow to many outdated ideas which had lingered from the previous century. Increasing human population and modernization in terms of economic development and urbanization, became characteristics of South Africa. Although some of the new ideas were inimical to nature protection, paradoxically they nurtured a nostalgia for the past. It was this sentiment, coupled with a desire to experience primeval wilderness, which led to the replacement of outmoded preservation of wildlife with a new form of conservation – game-viewing. There was a new tendency too for growing urban populations to yearn for some form of escape from city pressures, and for many people game-viewing and its associated lifestyle provided that escape. Economic development now provided a measure of affluence which elevated whites above subsistence levels; for many this led to a new and sometimes sentimental attitude towards wild animals. In the 1920s the need to maximize the use of all land in the subcontinent, combined with the advantages of tourism and a growing awareness of economic factors, resulted in the introduction of a new form of wildlife conservation, where animals were indeed utilized for solely human ends, but this time not for food or sporting purposes.

ECOLOGY AND WILDERNESS

Wildlife conservation ideas continued to change in the 1930s and 1940s. Stevenson-Hamilton's simple 'balance of nature' became more fully understood as the science of ecology, and it is this discipline which reigns supreme in nature conservation circles today. The primacy of scientific principles and measurement and practice brooks no dispute, but it is in this respect that Stevenson-Hamilton began to fall behind emerging trends in the 1940s. He distrusted scientists and what he referred to as their 'theories', believing that no one could know more than the observant person on the spot and that experience was the only true teacher. His distrust of scientists and classroom knowledge stemmed from his encounters with veterinarians and agronomists who had, almost without exception, disagreed with his belief in the balance of nature and the need for wildlife protection. Stevenson-Hamilton complained that biologists did not conceive of nature as an entity, but, to use his metaphor, considered only individual trees and ignored the forest. His principal altercation with the scientific fraternity was over a point which is still a matter of debate, his fervent wish that the Kruger National Park should never become an institution akin to a zoological or botanical garden, but should remain as a wilderness.

Science has informed us greatly about the animals and plant species within the Kruger National Park and their ecological relationships with one another, but its state of wilderness is still its principal attraction. Today, nature conservation in South Africa must rise to the challenges of changing political, scientific and economic circumstances, and lessons can surely be gained from the wisdom contained in James Stevenson-Hamilton's *South African Eden*.

EDITORIAL POLICY

South African Eden was first published in 1937 and fresh editions appeared in 1952, 1956 and 1974. The present edition utilizes the 1952 version, which contained a concluding chapter written by Stevenson-Hamilton after his retirement. The author's lengthy introductory remarks have, however, been omitted and the information incorporated into the new introduction above.

A few episodes – digressions from the main thrust of the story – have also been omitted. Additions to the book include footnotes, a series of short biographies of people referred to in the text, a comprehensive index and two new maps.

Editorial intervention has been kept to a minimum and principally has involved modernizing and stream-lining the text. To this end punctuation has been simplified, obvious errors have been corrected, certain passages have been made clearer, and anachronistic or idiosyncratic spellings and inconsistencies have been altered in accordance with modern South African convention. Stevenson-Hamilton's references to 'police boys' (though in today's parlance they would be 'game rangers') have been retained as this was the term that was current at the time. In order to facilitate locating places mentioned in the book on modern maps of the Transvaal, place-names have been updated to conform with official usage. Currency, weights and measures have not been changed.

Jane Carruthers

PART ONE

❖

THE SABI GAME RESERVE

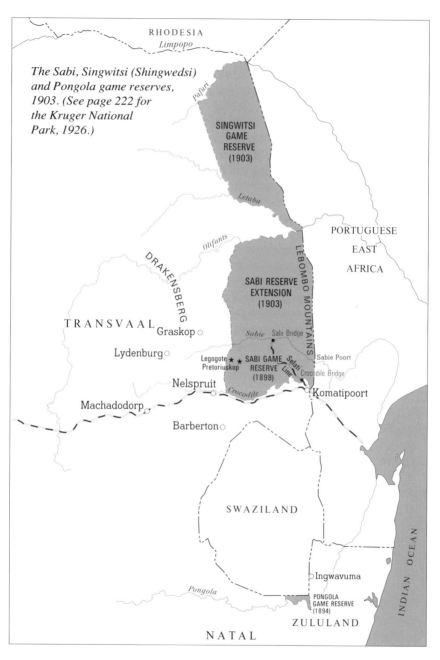

The Sabi, Singwitsi (Shingwedsi) and Pongola game reserves, 1903. (See page 222 for the Kruger National Park, 1926.)

RHODESIA

Limpopo

Pafuri

SINGWITSI
GAME
RESERVE
(1903)

Letaba

Olifants

PORTUGUESE
EAST
AFRICA

DRAKENSBERG

LEBOMBO MOUNTAINS

SABI RESERVE
EXTENSION
(1903)

TRANSVAAL

Graskop ○

Sabie   Sabi Bridge

Lydenburg ○

Legogote ★ ★
Pretoriuskop

SABI GAME
RESERVE
(1898)

Selati Line

Sabie Poort

Crocodile Bridge

Nelspruit

Crocodile

○ Komatipoort

Machadodorp ○

Barberton ○

SWAZILAND

Ingwavuma ○

Pongola

PONGOLA
GAME RESERVE
(1894)

ZULULAND

NATAL

INDIAN OCEAN

26

CHAPTER ONE
1902

FIRST IMPRESSIONS OF THE LOWVELD; NELSPRUIT; BARBERTON;
KOMATIPOORT; STEINACKER'S HORSE; MAJOR GREENHILL-GARDYNE;
SABI BRIDGE; MAJOR ROBERTSON; BILL SANDERSON

IT IS THE AFTERNOON of July 25, 1902. On the edge of the last escarpment
of the Drakensberg, overlooking the huddled welter of bush-clad ravines
and rocky terraces which compose the foothills, my little caravan has come
to a halt that I may for a while absorb the wonderful panorama of mountain
and forest which has just disclosed itself.

The sun, low in the west, is gilding the bare pinnacle of Legogote and is
lending fleeting shades of delicate pink to the three peaks of Pretoriuskop –
border beacons of the land of mystery beyond. Eastward, far as the eye can
see, stretches a rolling expanse of tree-tops; in the foreground a medley of
green, yellow and russet brown, but with increasing distance merging into a
carpet of blue-grey, which as it recedes, assumes an ever fainter hue, until at
last it blends with the dim haze of the horizon. Far away down the slope of
the mountain lies the lonely homestead of which I have been told:
Sanderson's farm, in its complete solitude and abandonment, a component
part of the surrounding wilderness.

Wildlife is just awakening from its afternoon siesta. Francolins are calling
all around, and from a nearby donga comes the sudden clatter of guineafowl.
Bush babblers are chattering among the trees, their cheerful din serving to
render yet less definable the vague sounds which here and there are beginning to rise from the distant forest. It is the voice of Africa, and with it
comes to me a sense of boundless peace and contentment.

But it is getting late, so I unwillingly come back to earth, mount and give
the order to proceed. The tired oxen seem to sense this to be the last stage of

their long day's trek, and the wagon jolts rapidly down the rough road, corrugated with deep ruts and dotted with large stones. Finally, amid the appropriate shouting and creaking of brake, we draw up before it is yet dark in
front of Sanderson's farmhouse. Except for a few guineafowl (remnants of a
tame flock) the place is quite deserted, and the house thoroughly cleared of
everything movable; but its walls and roof remaining intact, it provides a
welcome shelter of which we gladly avail ourselves.

The caravan was not an imposing one under the circumstances. A light
wagon, drawn by six emaciated oxen weakened by long and exhausting
transport work under active service conditions; three good ponies, all of
them old campaigners but 'unsalted' – that is, not immune from that curse of
Africa, horse sickness; a Cape 'boy', named Nicholas, as general factotum; a
Sotho youth from the Orange Free State as horse attendant; a driver and
leader for the wagon. Finally, a quaint old native known as 'Toothless Jack',
attired in a few nondescript and indescribably filthy garments, who on the
strength of his having formerly been one of Mr Henry Glynn's hunting boys
and so presumably knowing something about the country we were bound
for, had joined my retinue at Graskop.

During the night I reflected seriously on the circumstances hinted at
above. In brief, a complete stranger to everyone living there, white or black,
I was on the point of entering a country of which I knew practically
nothing, with instructions to convert it as soon as possible from its time-
honoured status of a hunter's paradise into an inviolable game sanctuary.
My mandate had been vague, general, and verbally conveyed to me by
people who were nearly as ignorant of the conditions prevailing as I was
myself. Except for a brief notice in the Government *Gazette* – unlikely to
have been seen by any of the local inhabitants – I had no visible authority
behind me. No special regulations for the game reserve had been drafted
and even the new game laws were not yet in being. Linguistically the party
was badly equipped to make the desired impression among the natives,
who, I had been informed, were still completely tribal and spoke no language but their own. I could hardly regard a few words of 'kitchen kaffir'
and a smattering of Sesotho picked up in Barotseland, as likely to be very
helpful among the Shangane, and my native followers were in this respect
nearly in as bad a case as myself. In fact, 'Toothless Jack' seemed to shine
as the sole asset of the party so far as rational intercourse with the local
inhabitants was concerned.

It seemed clear, therefore, that before making my official debut into the game reserve it would be expedient to gather a little more knowledge of local conditions than it had so far been possible to acquire. Information had hitherto been rather nebulous. On the journey by road from Machadodorp via Lydenburg and Graskop, while everyone had been eager to show how much he knew of the low country, most statements appeared mutually contradictory. Some had said that the reserve was full of game, others that Steinacker's Horse and the natives had killed everything. In fact, no one I met seemed to have any but a very vague secondhand acquaintance with the country. Only on one point were all agreed, namely, that it was a malarial death-trap, a veritable 'white man's grave' habitable only for about three months in each year. I was warned that I must on no account remain there later than the end of August, and that I ought at once to make suitable arrangements for the acquisition of some foothold on the top of the Drakensberg, to afford myself and my animals refuge until the following June. Having, however, had some years' experience of the upper Zambezi valley, I reflected that the lowveld could not, after all, be so very much worse, and that anyhow a game reserve could not well be supervised by anyone living the best part of a hundred miles away and visiting it only during three months of each year. So, on the whole, I thought (recalling a schooldays' tag) *fiat experimentum in corpore vili*[2] so far as residence was in question. Meantime I decided that my first move had better be to Barberton. This was the capital of the district wherein lay the game reserve, and was the residence of the magistrate with whom I should no doubt have many official dealings and with whom it was therefore important that I should be personally acquainted, and – if possible – on good terms. A certain Major McInerney had just been appointed to the position, and I had been warned that he was not altogether an easy man to get on with.

The next day, however, was spent in taking it easy and looking about. Sanderson's farm homestead was sited on a small plateau half-way down the hill, and the property so extended in both directions that it embraced parts of both lowveld and middle-veld. It was easy to see that in normal times it must have been a pleasant spot. There was a considerable plantation of orange and lemon trees, the remains of a corn-mill, a small store and many outbuildings. The view to the east was a magnificent one, and when the atmosphere was clear, it was possible to make out the outline of the Lebombo hills about seventy miles distant. One or two local natives turned up and I gathered that Sanderson was in camp somewhere near the Portuguese border, but that his return was expected shortly.

On the 27th I rode into Nelspruit station on the main line from Pretoria to Delagoa Bay on the Mozambique coast, about twenty-five miles along a fairly good wagon road, meeting on the way a number of local burghers returning to their farms, equipped with cattle, sheep and horses, provided through the Repatriation Department. In this part of the world the men had been allowed to retain their rifles as a 'defence against the natives', though rumour had it that the weapons were more likely to be required for use against any game that might have survived.

The wagon road led across bare-looking country, the only signs of habitation being an occasional corrugated iron shack; there were hardly any trees. This veld, in fact, had a bad reputation; it was said to be 'sour' and the only white inhabitants before the war had been people of the *bywoner,* or squatter, class. Today the same area is covered by the citrus plantations and the pleasant homesteads surrounding the White River township, with its sorting sheds, up-to-date hotel, railway station, club house and other social amenities.

Nelspruit is now a rapidly growing town, the centre of a district of the same name and of the citrus industry of the middle-veld. It possesses a good hotel, many stores, half a dozen garages and a full complement of officials, including a magistrate. But in 1902, apart from the railway station, there existed only two buildings, both of corrugated iron; to wit, a so-called hotel, the property of one Hansing, a German, and a store belonging to Mr Tom Lawrence, who there imparted to me my first reliable information about lowveld conditions. Prospects of adding to the transport did not seem particularly rosy. Cattle locally were dying of rinderpest and apparently all donkeys had been bought up by the Repatriation Department. Natives, too, had been so well paid in the transport service of the British army that at present they could not be induced to do any work at all. I met a Mr Grandy, recently demobilized from the Intelligence, who seemed to be the type of man I was seeking as assistant. Unfortunately, he had at the time some other and, to his mind, better opening in prospect. In those days, just after the conclusion of peace, the Transvaal was affected by one of the waves of deceptive prosperity which seem inseparable from such periods. Repatriation of the Boers was in full swing. Government money was flowing like water, and jobs were to be obtained everywhere. Few of them were, of course, anything but temporary, and the present boom was to be followed by a long and severe interval of depression, while the ruined colonies slowly struggled to their feet again. However, the meeting with Mr Grandy proved to be a fortunate one for me. In declining my offer of work he remarked, 'I know the very man for you – Harry Wolhuter – no one knows the game reserve better, or more about the game; but he is sure to have got another job; you may find him at Komatipoort'.

It was already clear that Komatipoort must be the next objective after Barberton. It was the only township actually abutting on the game reserve, and was also at present the headquarters of the mounted body of irregulars, concerning whose doings rumour had been so busy and about whom I was beginning to be rather curious.

The train dragged slowly along, up steep gradients and round the bases of mountains to Barberton, a journey of nearly four hours. Even then the town bore a depressing air of vanished prosperity. It had sprung into sudden life and fame as the scene of the first really big gold strike in South Africa. During a few short years people flocked to it from all parts of the world, and the new town was the centre of a vast, busy, and prosperous mining camp. Then came the discovery of the Witwatersrand goldfields and those of the Kaap paled into insignificance. The crowds of speculators, brokers, and others drifted away. The mines themselves – with few exceptions – did not fulfil early expectations and at the commencement of the South African War, practically only the Sheba was working profitably. Yet throughout its decline there was some factor in the atmosphere or the surroundings which nurtured optimism, and to this day there are old Barbertonians who still pathetically cherish the faith that some day their town will once more take a leading position among the prosperous cities of South Africa. It is a picturesque place tucked sleepily under the hills and facing the great expanse of the Kaap valley. The railway station a mile or so from the town was then quite isolated in the veld, following in this the general custom in the early days of railways in the Transvaal when they were considered to be not entirely respectable institutions. On the occasion of this visit, the town was crowded with mining and business people returning to their homes in the neighbourhood, with farmers being repatriated and with the officials of the scores of new departments just initiated by the civil government. Accommodation was difficult to find, and no bedroom at the Phoenix Hotel was tenanted by less than four people.

The magistrate, Major McInerney, proved to be a formidable-looking Australian, about six feet three inches high, clean shaven and the possessor of what is known as 'a cold grey eye'. However, he proved kind, helpful and sympathetic, and promised to do all he could to assist me in my coming task. As he pointed out, everybody was likely to be much too busy settling down during the next year or two to have time to think about shooting. The transport question was still unsolved. The British army, it was true, had two hundred and fifty donkeys standing idle, of which the officer in charge was only too anxious to be quit, but the authorities at Middelburg so far had refused permission to sell any of them.

Komatipoort, which I was to know well in the years to come, was reached after a wearisome train journey of over six hours, solaced, however, by the comfortable feeling that at least one would not be blown up, the constant possibility of which was the drawback to the full enjoyment of a railway journey during the South African War. This is one of the hottest places in South Africa, a fact due partly to its low site – only six hundred and twenty feet above sea level – and partly to its lying close under the Lebombo hills which shut it in from the south and east. It has always borne an evil reputation for malaria, and the cemetery, filled with largely unnamed graves, testifies to the mortality of the early days when men drank whisky 'to keep off the fever'. It is the border township with Portuguese East Africa[3] and originated in 1892, when a branch line to link up the Selati goldfields with the Pretoria-Delagoa Bay railway was commenced from a point just west of where the bridge crosses the Komati River.

A tin town quickly sprang into being, peopled by a miscellaneous crowd of sub-contractors and employees, traders and canteen-keepers, job seekers and loafers, with all the other nondescripts invariably found collected in former days on the scene of any new enterprise of this description. Whisky flowed like water. Some thousands of natives were employed on the construction and were paid mainly in game meat. The game, in fact, at that time numerous in the vicinity of the line, was exploited to the utmost. Many white men and natives made a living solely by killing buck to keep the working gangs supplied with meat, and trucks filled to the brim with carcasses of animals came down by every construction train returning to Komatipoort. These were the good old days of free hunting and no tiresome game laws.[4] Wild animals existed to be killed with as much profit as was possible to the killer, and biltong – then as now – commanded a good price and a ready sale. There were no hunting ethics whatever. If a man did not succeed in killing an animal he had fired at, the next best thing for his own glorification was to have wounded it. 'Well, I did not actually get anything today but I wounded a lot of them' was quite an ordinary remark to hear in a bar, even in 1902. One of the few hunters of the early Selati days who possessed the true sportsman's instinct was Mr H.F. Francis, a Natalian, who

32

also shone as one of the very few who ventured in pursuit of the lion as a hobby, and on foot.

The spacious days of the Selati railway construction, however, came to an abrupt close with the bankruptcy of the contractors and the prosecution of the promoters for being unable to account for about three-quarters of a million of the money put up by the public. The sub-contractors and, of course the natives, got no pay, so the latter philosophically threw down their picks and shovels and went home, and where they had left it, there the material was yet lying ten years later. A few of the 'old hands' still hung about Komatipoort buoyed up by the hope that some day and somehow the good days would return. Meantime they led a *dolce far niente*⁵ existence, much of it spent at the bar of the local canteen, where they always seemed to be able to get sufficient whisky on credit or otherwise. Despite the collapse of the branch railway which was to have converted it into a first-class junction, the place was still the last station in the Transvaal of the main line to Delagoa Bay and therefore remained the headquarters of the border customs. It also boasted a police station, the sergeant in charge of which was, after its proclamation in 1898, supposed to control the Sabi Game Reserve. Not that any practical supervision of the latter existed, and so long as he did not act too blatantly, the local sportsman suffered no annoying curtailment of his activities.

In 1902 Komatipoort was enjoying a second period of temporary prosperity. On a high bare ridge of the Lebombo overlooking the gorge where the Crocodile and Komati rivers, just united as the Inkomati, flow through into Portuguese territory, a thoughtful British army administration had caused to be erected groups of wood-and-iron cantonments, which, glaring white in the sun, were the first objects to strike the eye of the traveller as he left the train. There, perched high above the reach of malaria – or so it was fondly hoped – and far removed from all external cares and worries, lay the greater part of a battalion of British infantry. A guard-house faced that of the Portuguese across the frontier, and as the sentry of each 'Ancient Ally' met his opposite number at the end of his beat, it is said that, before turning smartly about, he expectorated contemptuously on the ground! Considerable expense must have been incurred in the erection of so many buildings in so inaccessible a spot and they remained there in fact for less than two years. The troops were all withdrawn before the end of 1902, and not long afterwards the huts were sold by auction for what they could fetch, which was not a great sum.

The commanding officer of the battalion was also the local commandant with an office in Komatipoort, and between him and the great Colonel Steinacker there raged an unending warfare. There was, for instance, the matter of the hippos. An almost tame herd of these animals had for long been preserved close to Komatipoort, and the commandant issued an order that they were on no account to be interfered with. Colonel Steinacker, not because he had any grudge against the hippos, but because he felt he should not be dictated to, at once issued a counter regimental order that his men were to shoot the lot immediately – an instruction which, to their credit, the corps decided to disregard.

Colonel Steinacker himself deserves passing notice. Whether he held the name he had been born to or not, he was at least rather a remarkable character, one of a type seldom to the fore except during periods of trouble and confusion, such as had recently afflicted South Africa. At the time of my first visit to Komatipoort he was absent overseas, attending with a detachment of his regiment the coronation of King Edward VII, so that I did not then have the privilege of meeting him. According to his own account a Bavarian by nationality and professing to have been at one time an officer of the Prussian Guard, he was reputed to have come originally to South Africa in 1889 in connection with a German filibustering attempt to obtain a footing in Pondoland. Later he gravitated to Natal, and on the outbreak of the South African War in 1899 is said to have enlisted in a corps known as the Imperial Guides. While with it he apparently carried out the duties of chief cook, but whether because the fare he provided was unsatisfactory to his clients or for some other reason, he soon severed his connection with the unit. Perhaps he felt that his genius and ambitions received inadequate expression in the stewing of potatoes and bully beef. Be that as it may, he had a sudden inspiration and, seeking out army headquarters, placed before the 'Great Ones' a plan for the raising of a small force, which, marching up from Natal via Swaziland, might haply blow up the Komati Bridge in front of the retreating Boer army and thus hinder them from saving their guns, stores and other equipment, which might thus more easily fall into the hands of the pursuing British.

The scheme was one that appealed to the Staff, and Steinacker was given the rank of temporary major with authority to raise a small band of picked men, who were to receive £1 per day and their rations. Accordingly, the newly appointed major, leading a little force known – no doubt most undeservedly – as the 'forty thieves', in due course set out on his adventurous journey. Unfortunately, this took longer than anticipated and by the time the railway line was approached, the Boer army was already at Komatipoort and therefore any attempt on the bridge at that place was not likely to prove a healthy operation for the adventurers. Obviously, however, something had to be done to save face. There was still no sign of the British advanced guard. The culvert at Malelane, twenty-five miles west of Komatipoort, the vicinity of which was clear alike of friend and foe, appeared to offer a solution and at least gave an opportunity of getting rid of a load of tiresome and dangerous explosives. It was true that Malelane lay now behind the Boer army and directly in front of the now closely approaching British, but the leader was one of those people who felt that any kind of action is better than none at all. So, having first climbed up a telegraph pole and cut the line, he then proceeded well and truly to demolish the culvert, after which the party faded away into the dim background of the limitless veld. Accordingly, when some time on the following day the first British made their appearance, they reported that the enemy had blown up the culvert on the main line of advance and that it would have to be repaired before any transport would be able to cross. The army was held up about two days in consequence, not that this made any real difference to the operations since the Boers had already thrown the heavy guns into the Komati River, and the commandos, with light transport, had marched away up the Selati line to the north.

Almost as soon as the British were established at Komatipoort, Major Steinacker and his followers appeared on the scene. Duly reticent about the affair of the culvert, Steinacker lost no time in approaching the general in command, when, with the eloquence and dignity which was his best stock-in-trade, he explained that he alone knew this part of the country 'as the back of my hand'. Therefore, since it was obviously necessary to raise and maintain a mounted force for the due guarding of the Portuguese frontier, he felt he was clearly the one and only person to be entrusted with this important duty. The vitally important nature of the work and the hazards connected with it – the wild and trackless country, unknown (except to himself); the deadly nature of the climate, rendering it impossible as a campaigning area for any but a few selected stalwarts under a determined leader – all received their due emphasis. The general, harassed with many cares and problems and impressed by the martial bearing and forceful arguments of one who seemed by his own account to be a born leader of men, looked on it as a happy chance that he had discovered an officer so apparently efficient if hitherto unknown. Clearly the right man in the right place; the hour and the man, in fact. Then and there Major Steinacker received a free hand to raise a mounted corps not to exceed three hundred in number, each member of which was, in view of the exceptional conditions, to receive a daily rate of pay of ten shillings, plus a special allowance of pickles, fresh milk, and whisky 'to keep off the fever'.

Thus originated the famous corps known as Steinacker's Horse, whose memory is still, thirty-five years later, so green in the land that the native name even now for any skerm or thorn zeriba, is a 'stenekese'. Within a few weeks all but a few of the regular troops had been withdrawn from the lowveld, and from that time until the end of the war in 1902 (and for a considerable period beyond that date), its commanding officer was, under martial law, the sole authority, wielding practically autocratic power throughout all the eastern districts of the lowveld between the Swaziland border in the south and the Letaba River in the north. Headquarters were established at Komatipoort but posts were strung all along the Portuguese frontier for over a hundred miles to the north, and southwards as far as Namaacha at the Swazi boundary.

The irregular British corps known as Steinacker's Horse attracted many adventurers to the lowveld during the South African War of 1899-1902. Here a group of officers is seen outside their headquarters at Komatipoort.

The question of rations was an easy one. The pickles and the whisky, together with the groceries, were drawn from a benevolent army commissariat; game provided the meat for all outposts, to which the other rations were adequately conveyed weekly by ox-wagon. The fresh milk question, too, was easily solved. Considerable numbers of cattle were in possession of local natives, and what better in the interests of the latter, than to collect the scattered herds within the sheltering aegis of the various posts of Steinacker's Horse, thus relieving the owners of any anxiety on account of possible enemy raids. There was the further consideration that the troopers could not be expected to sustain themselves on a meat diet consisting exclusively of game. It is true that, as it happened, no Boer stock-raiders ever entered the lowveld, but such an eventuality could hardly have been foreseen. Moreover, where any suspicion existed that a cattle owner had been holding or might hold communication with the enemy, it was merely common sense to detain his property as hostage for good behaviour.

Major, now Colonel, Steinacker varied his time usefully on recruiting trips between Lourenço Marques and Durban, places but a one day's sea voyage apart. He appointed his own officers and in this followed to some degree the example of other great captains of history in that his pockets always contained a small store of rank badges. Should he, therefore, take a fancy to an acquaintance, say in the Royal Hotel in Durban, or should one of his own men distinguish himself in any way, for instance by pre-eminence at a smoking concert, he was always in a position to present him with two stars, themselves hardly more to be prized than the accompanying impressive words, 'You may now regard yourself as one of my officers'!

Recruited largely from lowveld residents who were mainly of British birth but with a sprinkling of other nationalities, the rank and file of Steinacker's Horse were composed of excellent material, and the same may be said of some of the officers, though not unnaturally, discipline was perhaps hardly the strongest point of the corps. Major Greenhill-Gardyne of the Gordon Highlanders, who, as adjutant, practically commanded it during the frequent absences of his colonel, was able, assisted by one or two of the senior officers – veterans of the Cape Mounted Rifles – to convey to the regiment at least some outward resemblance to a military unit.

Major Gardyne was a keen sportsman with long experience of Indian shikar. From the moment he came to the lowveld he began to take a keen interest in wildlife preservation, the crying need for which he quickly grasped. He found that the game was rapidly being killed out. The local natives were busy with snares and dogs. The many outlying posts of the corps lived largely on buck meat and some of the officers were even sending away large quantities of biltong as a standby against possible lean times after the war. Risking unpopularity, he did much to put a stop to, or at least to check, the reckless shooting that had been going on, especially trying to prevent it within the game reserve. He achieved a considerable amount of success, and immediately on peace having been declared drew up for the civil government a most able exposition of the state of things existing with respect to game in the lowveld generally, adding some excellent and practical suggestions regarding the steps which ought to be taken for its permanent preservation. In fact, Major Gardyne's report, the outcome both of his personal experience and of his careful enquiries on the spot, proved one of the most helpful factors in determining policy during the early days of the game reserve administration.

The abandoned Selati line had proved useful to Steinacker's Horse, and a weekly train carrying supplies ran from Komatipoort to their large post at Sabi Bridge, fifty miles to the north and situated on the river of that name. The first time it went up, so thickly had the bush grown over the line in eight years of disuse that a gang of natives had to go in front of the engine cutting down saplings which were sprouting thickly on the permanent way!

At Sabi Bridge were stationed about twenty white men, with a number of native servants and police 'boys'. Several of the old huts, made of boiler plates and used by the former employees, were occupied, while many rondavels, or improved native huts, had been built. The outstanding feature was the rectangular blockhouse on the extreme point of the railway embankment overlooking the river, where the south end of the bridge should have found place. The bridge itself was represented by the foundations of its piers only, which the river covered when it rose in flood. There had been a wooden deviation bridge, but this had completely disappeared during a big flood in 1901 and now the only means of crossing was by wading knee-deep. The camp was encircled by a dense skerm, or thorn zeriba, as much to keep out dangerous wild animals as hostile human beings. In fact, since the Republican forces retreated up the Selati line in September 1900 (incidentally leaving the seven miles of permanent way between Komatipoort and the Crocodile River Bridge choked with abandoned rolling stock), the eastern lowveld had been far removed from the stress of warlike alarms. Except for the incident of their swashbuckling occupation of Bremersdorp in Swaziland and later undignified and hurried departure therefrom, Steinacker's Horse had experienced all the advantages, with few of the disagreeable drawbacks, of being on active service. As, years afterwards, an ex-member of the corps reminiscently and regretfully remarked to me, 'Ah, those were good days; every man with his own native to shoot him meat, and with his own case of whisky under the bed!'

In command at Sabi Bridge was Major Robertson whose career had been a varied one. Promoted from the ranks of the Fourth Hussars to a commission in the Royal Dragoons, he had transferred, as a captain, to the Inniskillings who were then in South Africa. Later, surrendering the pursuit of arms for that of gold, he had resigned his commission and sought Johannesburg in its early days. After that, he had held some agency post at Tete on the Zambezi River, and now, at well over fifty years of age, found himself with the grade of second lieutenant in command of a small detachment in a remote part of the Transvaal bush. After the end of the war he enlisted in the 'Boer' contingent which went to Somaliland in connection with the campaign against the Mad Mullah,* and with it served as a private, dying in South Africa a year or two later. He was occupying the blockhouse at Sabi Bridge, the front part of which, overlooking the river, was fitted with a firing platform converted into a veranda with a fine view both up and down the river for a mile in each direction.

The country all round Sabi Bridge was covered with dense *Acacia* bush, said in former days to have been 'red' with impala antelope, though unceasing persecution for more than ten years had made this only a tradition. On the railway journey of three hours from Komatipoort some game had been seen – a wildebeest or two, a steenbok and a few impala. First impressions on the whole were good. The game reserve only extended north as far as the Sabie River. The land on the other side belonged mainly to Johannesburg land companies having been surveyed into farms during the previous decade. None of these farms had, however, been occupied or used in any way and the country was said to hold a larger and better assortment of game than the reserve. Several shooting parties of British officers from Barberton and elsewhere had already enjoyed good sport.

A few days later I returned by train to Nelspruit and rode out to rejoin my resting caravan. Mr William Sanderson had in the meantime returned from Lebombo where he had been immured for the past year or more. He was a strongly built man of middle height, about fifty-five years old, and the possessor of one of the most patriarchal white beards I have ever seen. A Scotsman hailing from Edinburgh, he and his two brothers had emigrated as youths to Australia, but attracted by the early discovery of gold in the Lydenburg district in 1869 had transferred themselves to South Africa. After spending quite a short time at the diggings, they had drifted towards the lowveld, and finding hunting more congenial than gold seeking, in about 1871 they had settled on the excellent site which became their base. Both brothers had died – Bob having been killed by lightning – and Bill, who had been the eldest, was now the sole owner of the farm.

When the South African War broke out, the latter found himself in a dilemma. Having lived for so many years uninterruptedly in the Transvaal, with nearly all his friends and acquaintances among the Dutch population, himself, too, a burgher of the Republic, Sanderson did not want to fight against old friends. On the other hand, it was equally impossible to take up arms against his own flesh and blood. Moreover, he was no longer young and so he decided to be a neutral and to stay where he was, looking after his cattle, his little store, and his orange trees, in the hope that war's alarm would pass him by. Not for long, however, was this happy state to last. The fighting age in the Transvaal Republic was from sixteen to sixty, and presently the veldkornet sought him out, advised him that as a loyal burgher it was his duty to join up with the local levy, and, in short, commandeered him and hied him off to Ladysmith. Arrived in the camp of the besiegers, he was allotted a non-combatant post with the ambulance, but found his life an unpleasant one. Strangers for one thing accused him of being an 'Englishman', a calumny which he bitterly resented. So he sought out his friend Abel Erasmus, the native commissioner for the lowveld who held the rank of commandant in the local forces, and explained the position. Erasmus's influence was sufficient to get him sent back to Legogote to carry on the nominal duties of native commissioner during his own absence, and he promptly packed up and departed home rejoicing.

After this Bill Sanderson lived contentedly on the farm, paying small heed in that secluded spot to the untoward events which were rending the rest of the country. In fact, all went well with him until the British forces occupied Komatipoort in September 1900. Shortly after they had become well settled down, the Intelligence Department heard that an Englishman was marooned up among the Boers and was unable to get away. He was also reported to be possessed of a number of cattle and of several good horses, which were likely to be made use of by the enemy. A message was therefore sent to him that a force would shortly arrive to 'rescue' him, to which

Sanderson replied that he was quite happy where he was and only wanted to be left alone. This answer put a new complexion on things. Obviously this man must be a traitor and in direct communication with the enemy. Moreover, it was said that he had actually been on commando with the Boers and it was decided to remove him by force. Accordingly, the whole of Steinacker's Horse, having marched along the old Delagoa Bay road, made famous in Sir Percy Fitzpatrick's *Jock of the Bushveld*, passed Pretoriuskop and arrived early one morning at the farm. A few White River Boers were in the vicinity and some shots were exchanged, but there being no commando in the neighbourhood, these quickly made themselves scarce, and left the field clear. The unwilling Sanderson had to pack up his household goods, or as many as he could quickly get on his two wagons, collect his horses, cattle, and other livestock, and take the road. The rescuing party was eager to be off, as of course no one knew at what moment the enemy might appear in force. Their anxiety seemed justified, for as they were leaving, shots were fired from the hill above and in the general hurry some of the cattle got left behind or straggled, to be promptly pounced upon by a few Boers who were following up, and who looked on them now as spoils of war. When the landscape had become empty, these men – who were all neighbours – held a consultation. 'Here,' said they, 'is this skelm Bill Sanderson, whom we have looked on as one of ourselves, now gone over to the British, no doubt by arrangement: let us therefore make use of his property.' So they cleared up everything that had been left behind, thereafter occupying the house and using the corn-mill.

Meantime the unfortunate 'neutral' was having a difficult time. After some interrogation regarding his activities in the war, he was allotted a camping spot in a hot and malaria-stricken site close under the Lebombo mountains near the Sabie poort, and there kept more or less under observation. His best horses and rifles were commandeered by Steinacker's Horse under promise of compensation which, however, he said he never received. After a while news filtered through that the Boers were using his mill for grinding their corn, so another expedition was organized to blow the latter up, which was in due course done. He had therefore now returned minus a good deal of his property, including a good many of his cattle, to find a desolated home. So far as I know he was never recompensed. So much for trying to be a neutral, generally an impossible position in any zone of active hostilities, and one usually resulting in being ground between the two millstones of the contending parties.

*Bill Sanderson, lowveld pioneer and hunter, on the veranda of
his farmhouse near Legogote.*

I found Sanderson an exceedingly interesting man, to whom the game and
the lowveld generally were as an open book. He told me that in the early
1870s the White River country was covered with herds of eland and other
antelope while the adjoining lowveld, depopulated of its human inhabitants
by Swazi raids, was a veritable hunter's paradise – although, even at that
period, the elephant and the white rhinoceros had disappeared. The
Sanderson brothers were among the very earliest of the white hunters in that
part of the country, and in fact had only some half-dozen rivals in the field –
Abel Erasmus, David Schoeman, Henry Glynn the elder, and two or three
others. Every winter they would make an expedition into the tsetse fly country, taking with them donkey wagons, and setting off the certain ultimate
loss of their donkeys against their hunting profits in biltong and hides. Since
animals seldom succumb to nagana until after the first rains, they were
always able to draw the loaded wagons home before falling sick. Of course,

the more numerous the game shot, the greater the profit, but this never much exceeded the loss caused by the subsequent death of all the transport animals, and each succeeding year found the hunters vowing to increase next winter's bag. Buffalo were the most profitable game, and as they were numerous in the tsetse fly country, it was against them that the chief efforts were directed.

People who live this sort of life can hardly avoid becoming adepts at their trade and Sanderson looked the very type of the old pioneer hunter. His hunting stories, when he felt in the mood, were innumerable, and all well worth hearing. Professional hunters in the old days had no use for lion as game, the skins having then no marketable value. They were regarded merely as vermin, killers of creatures which should rightfully belong to the human predatory animal. When shot they were generally left where they fell. Not that it was a usual occurrence for the professional hunter in pursuit of herbivorous animals to encounter the king of the forest, since the report of firearms is enough to send that intelligent animal right out of the locality at once. Sanderson admitted to me that in his thirty years of hunting he had shot only six lions, which, indeed, was a considerable number as things were formerly reckoned. Many old experienced hunters never shot one at all, not from any unwillingness to face danger, but simply because they were not sufficiently interested to make the necessary special job of it that is necessary for success.

Among the real old-timers of the lowveld, of whom Bill Sanderson was typical, no characteristic was so prominent as was the pride which they took in their skill with the rifle. They were as proud of their shooting powers as any society belle of her personal attractions and were as jealous of their rivals in this respect as a young man might be of a competitor in love. You might asperse their morals, their personal appearance, even their honesty, and be pardoned; but to cast a slight on their marksmanship was an insult not to be forgiven. Men of both British and Dutch race were numbered among these old hands, and there was little to choose as to their relative abilities with the rifle. Their methods were not always such as recommend themselves to sportsmen. They had seldom regard either for sex or age, or for the number of animals they might kill. In fact, the main consideration was the largest number in the shortest time, with the least expenditure of ammunition, subject to it being often deemed unbecoming to fire at any but a running buck.

As he grew older Bill Sanderson, although still a fine shot, was scarcely so quick and accurate as he had formerly been, and of course became proportionately touchy on the subject. The kloofs seaming the hill slopes on his farm teemed with bushbuck and duiker, and up to the time of his death in 1913 he was accustomed to give annual shooting parties to his friends when the ravines would be driven out by natives and dogs, the guests being disposed at intervals on the hillside. It required pretty quick and accurate shooting, and a guest on his first visit was always told that the strict rules which had to be observed were: (1) only a rifle to be used, (2) only running buck to be shot at. The old man himself, accompanied by a small native boy, would take up his post on a flank at some distance, and when he shot a buck it was the duty of the youngster to run at once and find out exactly where the bullet had struck; let us suppose in the neck, for example. After the drive was over the guests would stroll up to congratulate their host on his success. 'A neat shot, Mr Sanderson.' 'Ay,' would be the reply, 'no a bad yin. I shot yon in the neck.' All would then walk up to the dead buck and sure enough the animal would have a wound in the stated part. 'Dear me, how could you tell at two hundred yards that you had shot it in the neck?' 'I suppose a man should hit where he aims, and I aimed at the neck,' would be the ready answer.

On one occasion, Wolhuter, happening to be at Legogote, wanted to try a new rifle. An empty bully beef tin was set up at a certain distance, and he put a bullet exactly through the middle of it. 'Now you have a shot,' he said, handing the rifle to Bill Sanderson. The weapon again duly spoke, and together they walked up to the mark. There was still but one hole. Sanderson carefully examined it, and without turning a hair remarked, 'Jist as I was thinking, clean through the same hole as your yin, Harry'.

Not long before the war he had captured alive a fairly large lion cub, which, after having kept it till it was nearly full grown, he had sold to Fillis's Circus. He had also once caught a young giraffe and later disposed of it to one Firmstone, an ex-officer of the Scots Greys, who formerly kept a store at Ingogo in Natal. Apparently its new owner was a man of short temper, for one day, becoming annoyed with it about something, he cut its throat, oblivious of the fact that at that time it might have been worth £1 000 delivered to the London Zoo!

There was no lack of company at Sanderson's during this visit. The house was full of dogs, monkeys and poultry, and there stalked solemnly about a full-grown *iNsingizi* or ground hornbill, a huge bird possessing an enormous beak, on which he occasionally would transfix any small fluffy chicken which he encountered, thereafter tossing it in the air and catching it cleverly in his gape. He was a most intelligent bird, going 'dead' when told and springing up again on the appropriate word. Flies in multitudes added yet more life to the environment, and effectually kept one awake and busy on a warm afternoon. Such was life on an old-fashioned lowveld farm.

CHAPTER TWO
1902

O N AUGUST 6, A DULL, chilly day and thus one very suitable for trekking, my caravan left Sanderson's for the game reserve to which I was now to make my official entry – by the back door, so to say. We crossed Pretoriuskop and went on through arid-looking country of the kind generally described as savannah, covered mainly with thin stunted *Acacia* forest, though larger trees, sometimes evergreen, lined the courses of the many dry spruits.

Following the back tracks of Sanderson's wagons, we headed straight for some prominent koppies about forty miles to the east as the crow flies. Viewed as a game reserve the country was disappointing. Even allowing for the time of year and the consequent lack of much water in the veld, one would have expected to see at least some indication of larger wildlife. Yet there was not even an old spoor to indicate that anything of the kind ever had existed there. Indeed it was not until the fourth day, our progress having been delayed by a broken *disselboom*, that we came across a few tracks of zebra, waterbuck and impala. The following morning I saw, in the flesh, a reedbuck ewe, a duiker and two jackal, and in the evening was much heartened by the appearance of a herd of nearly thirty impala. This was close to the group of koppies for which we had been making and which we now found to be on the Selati railway line.

Before the abandonment of the railway construction, several wood-and-iron gangers' cottages had already been completed, and in one of these dwelt an old Irishman named Butler, employed to keep the line in order for the weekly passage of the 'Steinacker' train. Except for a period spent in hospital recovering from an attack of blackwater fever, he had – he said – been working here continuously ever since the end of 1900, quite undisturbed by the war. He showed me the spoor of two lion, the first I had seen in the reserve, one apparently a fairly big one. The animals had crossed the line early the same morning. The 'boys' discovered the remains of an impala killed by a leopard, and during the night one of these and a hyena prowled around the camp. It began to feel more like Africa.

A rough wagon track followed the railway line all the way to Komatipoort, and after the caravan had proceeded a few miles in that direction, we encountered the weekly train to Sabi Bridge puffing along at a reckless fifteen miles an hour. I was riding some distance ahead accompanied by the two spare ponies, one ridden by the Sotho youth, John, the other following loose, and I pulled up while the train was passing. As it was doing so, at about fifty yards distance, shots rang out, and bullets whizzed all round. I felt at first rather hurt at what seemed a hostile demonstration, but concluded – no doubt correctly – that since we were standing behind fairly thick bush, the ponies had, from the moving train, probably looked like buck, and that consequently some of Steinacker's men, in accordance with custom, had fired a few light-hearted passing shots at them. Anyhow, my wagon following behind received no unpleasant attentions. The same evening I arrived at Steinacker's large post at Gomondwane about seven miles north of the Crocodile River, where I was hospitably received and my animals supplied with forage. The officer in command of this detachment, Captain Gray, was not, however, present, having established himself in a private camp at Lower Sabie, about a dozen miles to the north-east. Thither I rode on the following morning leaving the transport behind at the camp.

'Gaza' Gray, or M'stulela, the name by which he was known to the natives all over the lowveld, was a hard-bitten looking man of about fifty. Although hailing from the Eastern Province of the Cape, he had spent so long a time in the lowveld and adjoining Portuguese territory as a labour recruiter that he was a perfect linguist in the local dialects, possessing an unsurpassed knowledge of the natives, their ways, and their modes of thought. So much so, indeed, that he had acquired an uncanny reputation as *umthakathi*, or being possessed of occult powers, and was greatly feared. Gardyne had advised me to seek him out as soon as possible, as being the best man to advise me regarding local conditions and initial policy. He had a pleasant little camp of half a dozen well-built round huts, or rondavels, enclosed within a neatly made reed fence. This enclosure he kept sacred to himself and his personal servants. But outside, all day long alternately reposed and rioted a mingled crowd of natives belonging to both sexes, dogs, poultry, goats, sheep and donkeys. Towards evening a large herd of cattle was driven in from grazing, further to animate the scene.

We spent a whole day discussing plans. There was, Gray told me, still a fair amount of game along the Lebombo but it would not last much longer at the rate it was now being thinned out by the natives with snares and dogs. The whole country southwards to the Crocodile River was sprinkled with kraals, the inhabitants of which had – most of them – come into the game reserve since the beginning of the war from Portuguese East Africa and also from south of the Crocodile River with the object of being near the big game, which was finished in both the above-mentioned localities.

Before leaving Pretoria it had been impressed on me that the first difficulty would probably be with the natives, since these and the game could not be expected to exist together. I had already decided in my own mind that, so far as it might prove possible, the game reserve would have to be cleared of human inhabitants if a beginning was to be made at all. As a result of our talk, I decided to have all natives from the eastern and southern areas moved back whence they had come to be once more directly under their own tribal chiefs. I would then divide the reserve into districts, each under a white official who would have under him a small force of native police distributed in small posts, where they would be allowed to keep their wives and families and to raise crops, but not to have any other relations or friends as guests. Neither guns nor traps would be allowed. Certain routes through the reserve would be set aside and proclaimed, by which alone natives going to and from work at the mines and elsewhere would be allowed to travel. If approved by higher authority, the natives whom we had to move would be absolved from paying any tax for a year. The above were the general lines of administration then planned for adoption and, with additions and modifications, they have remained the basis of control ever since.

I made an arrangement with Gray under which, on condition that he was allowed to remain where he was and to graze his cattle in the game reserve, he consented to act as an honorary ranger, engaging native police, warning the natives to move before they had begun to plough and generally letting the new state of affairs as regards game preservation become well advertised. His sphere was to include all the reserve lying east of the Selati railway and between the Sabie and the Crocodile rivers. He stipulated that it should be in his power to withdraw at any time did more attractive employment come in his way. As a makeshift the scheme seemed as satisfactory as anything that could at the time be devised, and I had the feeling that at least a start had been made. Gray also explained that he was the owner of an old iron cottage, formerly used as a store and situated on the reserve side of the Crocodile River, which I was welcome to make use of as a temporary headquarters until I had settled definitely where I was going to live. There were several similar buildings scattered about the reserve; one at Gomondwane, and another at Sabie poort where Sanderson had been encamped. They had all been used before the war as trading stores, and it was clear that steps must be taken to prohibit the owners – all at present out of the country – from returning later to resume operations, since the native trade had to a great extent consisted in the exchange of cheap goods against game meat and skins of various kinds. I had, of course, no idea whether the Government would be prepared to support me in the carrying out of all the above ideas, but I hoped for the best, and thought it would at any rate be well to accomplish as much as possible without undue delay, and thus be in a position to present my superiors with accomplished facts.

The caravan moved to Crocodile Bridge immediately and the oxen were given at last the prospect of a good long rest in the midst of the excellent pasture found along the river banks. The place was but seven miles from Komatipoort and I was therefore in close touch with what was at present the centre of lowveld authority, for martial law still existed, and so far there had been no indication of the disbandment of Steinacker's Horse. All other temporary units had already been dispersed or were in process of being broken up, but it had been explained to army headquarters that the Portuguese frontier was in an unsettled state through lawless characters being at large and the native tribes disturbed. It was made clear that a strong armed force ought to be maintained in that remote part of the country. So for the time all was well so far as the corps was concerned. Indeed, the expectation seemed to be cherished that it would be retained as a permanent border guard.

In Komatipoort I met Wolhuter for the first time. He had just returned from the Olifants River, ninety miles to the north, where he was stationed, and Gardyne arranged an interview for me with him. At that time Harry Christopher Wolhuter, for so many years to be associated with me in the development and administration of the Sabi Game Reserve, was about twenty-seven years old. Tall and spare, with a heavy black moustache, a man of

*Appointed to the Sabi Game Reserve in 1902, Harry Wolhuter
was responsible for the Pretoriuskop section and remained at
this post until his retirement as head ranger in 1946.*

quiet determined manner and few words, he looked exactly what he was: a
typical farmer, bushman, and hunter of the best type. Born in the Cape
Colony, his family had emigrated while he was yet a small child to the
neighbourhood of Legogote. There the surroundings, coupled with his own
keen sense of observation, had not only taught him the principles of sound
farming and the care of domestic animals, but had given him an intimate
knowledge of all concerning the wild creatures of the lowveld and a complete familiarity with the native dialects and customs. He was a fine horse-
man and an almost perfect shot with the rifle. Of course, much of the above I
discovered for myself later, but at the time Gardyne confirmed and added to
what I had previously heard about him. Wolhuter, who at the beginning of
the war had taken his cattle into Portuguese country for safety, joined
Steinacker's Horse about a year later. Gardyne told me that he had been
greatly amused one day shortly afterwards to see a man who, as he put it,
had 'been born with a rifle in his hand', being meticulously taught aiming
drill by an instructor!

From my point of view this first interview with Wolhuter was not entirely a satisfactory one. With the exuberance of youth and in my growing enthusiasm for the success of the enterprise, I was inclined to overlook how things must appear to strangers. The new civil government was as yet only a name in the lowveld, and like other new and unknown things was viewed with suspicion. I had nothing but my own word and a hastily handwritten commission, which might or might not be genuine, to proclaim me other than an adventurer without any official or financial backing. In fact, I was at the moment even unable to give any indication as to what the salaries and other emoluments of my assistants were likely to be, all necessary disbursements up to date having been made from my own pocket. Fortunately I had known Major Gardyne in earlier days and he proved at this time a tower of strength to me, smoothing my path, imparting to me what he knew of the country and introducing me to all who were likely to be of assistance. In fact, had it not been for him, I do not believe that Wolhuter would even have considered my proposal – as it was, he pointed out that he had received several offers of good employment and that he would like a week to think it over. At the end of that time he decided to join me, conditionally on his being allowed to live at a camp (Mtimba) near Legogote, which was just outside the boundary of the reserve, but I felt instinctively that he was doing so with some misgiving. About the same time I engaged another man, who had been doing work for the British Intelligence in the Barberton district, said to be well acquainted as a hunter with the southern part of the reserve along the Crocodile River.

I now began to get in touch with the Native Affairs Department, under whom the reserve had been placed, and after some correspondence arranged for the payment of two assistants at £1 per day and horse allowance, as well as for the engagement of a certain number of native police at £2 per month each, to find their own food, this being slightly in excess of ordinary native wages in the lowveld at that time. This was so far satisfactory, but the pressing need was for some kind of special regulations to control the reserve, for legally I had no standing whatever and anything I might do would be by grace of Steinacker's Horse. Their chief being still absent, I found many of the officers as well as some of the lowveld residents, to be surprisingly sympathetic to the work of game preservation, which all agreed was long overdue. However, I do not think there were many who in their hearts believed it was going to be a permanency. The majority regarded it merely as an expedient designed to stop the present process of extermination, and to allow the area to be opened again for shooting in a few years' time.

Having talked over prospective arrangements with Wolhuter and communicated to him my rough idea of how the reserve was to be administered, I dispatched him to take over the northern and western portions, engage staff and move natives where necessary. Then, having borrowed two pack mules from Steinacker's Horse, I myself set off on August 21 to make a preliminary tour round my new domain.

We followed the course of the Mbyamiti River, at that time of the year merely a wide, dry sandbed, and on the second day struck the old wagon road from Delagoa Bay to Lydenburg which was still quite discernible in most places, though it had not been regularly used for more than twelve years. Game was scarce and wild, but we saw a few wildebeest, a couple of warthog and at night heard hyena, jackal and, on one occasion, a lion. The road passed Ship Mountain – or Mhukweni as the natives call it – a long, isolated, flat-topped hill consisting of huge boulders and rubble, with aloes and euphorbias growing among the stones. It conceivably bears some resemblance to the inverted hull of a wooden ship but to me the simile has always seemed a little strained. Northwards thence to the Sabie River the only game seen was a single reedbuck. Along the Sabie were many native kraals and consequently no signs of any wild animals. The people were Shangane with some Swazi affinities, under an old chief known as Mambatine. It was a little north of here and across the Sabie River that a detachment of Steinacker's Horse had been captured by the Boers in 1901, and their leader, the well-known Captain Francis, killed. Wolhuter had a narrow escape. He was sent by Francis with dispatches to Sabi Bridge and passed close to the koppies where the Boers were in hiding, but they let him go unmolested from fear of prematurely disclosing their presence.

After a march of some ten miles down the Sabie River, tracks of waterbuck and impala were noticed and a few of each kind were seen, all appearing exceedingly shy. About half-way to Sabi Bridge, and on my second night from Mambatine's, I experienced my first adventure in the reserve.

It was a very still night and the moon was due to rise shortly after midnight. We bivouacked on the top of the bank, about 150 yards from the river. As usual, I had pegged down a ground line of fairly thick rope to which my animals were tethered by rawhide riems; a roan stallion called Jorrocks at one end, next to him a little chestnut mare, then a gelding known as Charlie, and the two pack mules beyond. At each end of the horse-line, and a few yards away from it, a fire was lighted, my tiny bivouac tent being pitched by the one nearest the horses, while Toothless Jack and the young Sotho, John, lay down by the other one. About nine o'clock, my attendants having already composed themselves to rest and while I was myself just preparing to do so, there was a sudden and violent commotion on the horse-line. Not another sound, but the mules and the gelding were plunging for all they were worth, while the stallion and the little mare stood still and snorted. The mules tore up their end of the line and rushed wildly round, but the other end of the rope holding fast, in a moment the whole five animals were so tied up in a knot that none of them could move. At the same time the two men began shouting at the top of their voices, and I heard a very faint deep note coming from the outside darkness beyond them.

I had the sort of difficulty which always occurs at such moments in the ordinarily simple operation of undoing the slipknot which secured the front flap of the little tent. Then the rifle had got mixed up in the blankets, and by the time I had extricated it and got outside, Jack was already hurling burning brands into the darkness, and as he danced and yelled in the flickering firelight he looked like one of the figures in the Brocken scene of Faust. John, with commendable promptitude, had got to the horses which the attitude of the stallion had done much to quiet. I fired a few shots at random and then we got the animals a bit straightened out, secured the pegs more firmly and built up the fires. Meantime, Jack told me that before going to sleep he had sat up to put another log on the fire and as the flame sprang up, he had seen a big male lion standing looking at him, less than ten feet away. At the same moment the mules began to plunge and he threw a blazing stick at the lion, which then faded back into the night. We now all three mounted guard, each with a firearm, until the moon rose. It was perfectly silent outside, except that every now and then a screaming plover would rise as if disturbed, whereupon I would fire in the direction of the noise. One sensed the stealthy shapes gliding to and fro among the trees, their eyes fixed upon us, only waiting till all should again be quiet to make a second and perhaps a more successful attempt. Once the moon had risen we could see fairly well and thought it safe to turn in, in which belief we were justified, for everything remained perfectly peaceful during the rest of the night.

In the morning it was discovered that while one lion had come up on the side on which the mules were tethered, a second one had been creeping towards the horses, and when the alarm was first given was actually not more than four yards distant from them. We were lucky to have escaped so easily, and I learned cheaply the important lesson that when travelling in lion country with transport animals of any kind, one should never be without dogs and never fail to have built an efficient skerm or thorn zeriba to enclose the camp. I seldom again omitted these precautions and have to thank them for the almost complete immunity which I subsequently enjoyed in the course of hundreds of nights spent with transport animals in different parts of the game reserve.

On the above occasion I was indebted to the ground-line for the safety of at least the mules, and this was a safeguard which I continued invariably to exercise. A terrified horse, secured by a rope to a tree, can usually, by reining back, smash either his tether or the head-collar and then in all probability will charge through the surrounding fence straight into the jaws of a waiting lion. Dogs are a valuable protection but on wet, cold nights they may be curled up sound asleep when the lions come, as has happened several times within my experience. A man, whether mounted or on foot, can go anywhere and do almost anything he likes in the African bush by daylight with no more risk than he would have incurred elsewhere before the era of the motor car. But at night the situation changes, at least so far as one's transport animals are concerned. Few lions will touch a man even when he is asleep but his charges are always in the gravest danger, and it is not possible to take too much trouble in insuring their safety.

Nearing Sabi Bridge, more game – impala and waterbuck – was in evidence than before and we came upon a pack of African hunting dogs, remarkable looking animals. Their bodies are mottled with black, white and yellow blotches, and their bushy tails are white-tipped, but perhaps their most striking feature is the size of their round, upright ears. Upon being disturbed, they utter single hoarse alarm barks, jumping up and down in the grass the better to discern the intruder. *Lycaon pictus* – to give the animal its proper designation – is a dog only in name, in reality being further removed physiologically from the true dogs than either the jackal or the wolf. It is a unique species, the only one of the genus existing in the world today, and is now strictly confined to the African continent, though fossil bones show that in long past ages its range was a wider one. It is one of the speediest and most enduring of all the cursorial carnivora, although the drooping hindquarters, apparently straight shoulders and spindle-like limbs do not at once give that impression. Its prey includes impala, reedbuck, all the small antelope and wild pig, the females and young of waterbuck, kudu and even of such formidable fighters as the roan and sable antelope.

The method of hunting varies to some extent with the type of quarry. Where the larger antelope are concerned, such as waterbuck, they first cut out the females and young ones from the rest of the herd – at least, I have seen them apparently trying to do this. In all cases, once the chase has been started, they pursue relentlessly, loping with easy bounds some yards behind the hunted animal. Then each in turn makes a spurt, leaps at the flanks or hindquarters and drops back with a piece of the living flesh in his jaws, until covered with blood and with intestines hanging, the exhausted animal at last sinks down, when the pack at once rushes in to tear it to pieces in a few minutes. It is a gruesome business and once I surprised about ten of them surrounding a kudu cow, 'soiled' in a pool of water. The poor creature was in a terrible condition. The whole muzzle and face below the eyes had been torn clean away from the bone, as had the greater part of the hindquarters and the entrails were hanging to the ground. The dogs showed no inclination to dash in together at the living animal, but in a cool detached sort of way, trotted backwards and forwards round the edge of the pool, one or other from time to time darting in for a snatching bite at the kudu, which though drenched in blood, still kept its legs.

When a single wild dog has pulled down one of the smaller buck, or perhaps an impala lamb, he proceeds quite simply to devour it alive, taking no special steps to kill it, so long as he can deter it from running away. The rallying cry is a single plaintive note, frequently repeated at intervals of a second or two, and is easily mistaken by the uninitiated for the call of a bird. The larger males may stand thirty inches at the shoulder and weigh eighty pounds, so they are formidable brutes, but I have never known nor heard of a reliable instance of their displaying any aggressive tendency towards human beings. Before the days of intensive game preservation, wild dog in the Sabi country were seldom interfered with. The white hunters did not consider them worth the expenditure of a cartridge, while the natives looked on them rather in the light of benefactors in that they saved them the trouble of killing meat for themselves. Consequently they had greatly increased and multiplied and roamed about in packs of fifty or more, which seemed a serious menace to the continued existence of the game in its then depleted state. On this first occasion about twenty-five of them sprang up barking from among the long grass on the banks of a sandy spruit, before making off.

At Sabi Bridge I found old Major Robertson busily engaged in studying stars. He was just a little the worse for wear, having a few days previously settled a private difference with his sergeant in the time-honoured fashion, by knocking him out in two rounds, while the other ranks of the detachment formed the ring. As Major Robertson was turned fifty and the sergeant was a hefty young Australian of thirty or so, it was rather a good effort on the part of the former. Although the episode taken as a whole was not perhaps strictly in accordance with recognized military etiquette, yet it was not altogether out of keeping with the local conception of the fitness of things.

On the evening of my arrival my roan pony, Charlie, developed indications of the dikkop form of horse-sickness. In those days, before the discovery of a preventive serum, this disease was the curse of South Africa so far as equines were concerned. It appears in two forms, the first and more deadly known as dengsik and affecting the lungs. A mass of frothy mucus collects in the latter and in the last stage pours from the animal's nostrils, choking it in a few minutes. There are hardly any recoveries from this type, and none after the last stage has been reached. Dikkop, which is characterized by a swelling of the head and affects the heart, is also exceedingly fatal, though less so than dengsik, for from ten per cent to fifteen per cent of the animals attacked recover. Each type is merely a form of the same disease, and once a horse has got better it is immune for the rest of its life. In consequence, such 'salted' animals formerly had a very high market value and the purchaser usually demanded a twelve months' written guarantee. Horse-sickness, though present in greater or lesser degree almost everywhere at altitudes below four thousand feet in the wet season, was, and still is, so virulent in the lowveld as to persist throughout the year. In the summer months it is almost impossible to keep an unsalted or unimmunized horse alive, since only quite a small percentage show a resistive capacity. The disease can sometimes be evaded by stabling before sundown and not allowing the animals out till an hour or two after sunrise, but as conditions used to be in the lowveld this was rarely possible. Mules are slightly less susceptible than horses and donkeys bred in the country are practically immune, though imported animals sometimes die.

I was very concerned about Charlie who had gone through two years of the late campaign with me, and I sought out the farrier of Steinacker's Horse at Sabi Bridge to see if anything could be done. Since necessarily the corps was almost entirely mounted upon unsalted horses, their losses had been enormous during the previous summer, in spite of every precaution, such as building stables and looking after general health, and I thought the farrier might be a man of considerable experience. He advised a stiff dose of laudanum and this was duly administered, though I was inclined to regard it as in the nature of a kill or cure expedient. Anyhow, whether it was due to the medicine or whether he would have recovered naturally, the pony was much

*Stevenson-Hamilton on Charlie, the roan pony that recovered
from a particularly virulent form of horse sickness.*

better the following morning, even eating a little forage and picking about in
the veld. The head swelling had subsided and except for a slight stiffness of
the jaws, he seemed little the worse outwardly. Indeed within a couple of
weeks he was once more at work.

Having left my ponies and the mules in charge of Major Robertson, I
went down by trolley to Komatipoort, thence proceeding to Barberton and
Lourenço Marques; at the former to see the magistrate again and at the latter
to interview the Consul-General regarding the Portuguese border. I found
Major Baldwin, who had just been appointed, most sympathetic. He
promised to interview the Governor-General with a view to instructing all
Portuguese border officials to co-operate so far as possible, and also to see
what could be done towards getting the authorities to put an export duty on
heads and skins of game animals. I felt it important to establish early good
relations with our neighbours across the frontier, and in the years to come I
had on many occasions reason to be grateful to them for practical assistance
in connection with native poaching and in other ways.

I completed my first round of the reserve about a fortnight later without any special adventure, a strong skerm allowing us to sleep unconcernedly, although lion came on one occasion pretty close to the camp. I found Gray had collected a few police 'boys', and I took up more or less permanent quarters at Crocodile Bridge in the old iron shack. The flies therein were equalled only by the rats, with which the place positively swarmed, consequent no doubt on its formerly having been used as a mealie store. At night they steeple-chased about between the ceiling and the roof, making a terrific din as they scampered over the corrugated iron, sometimes seeming to fall down in heaps between it and the panelling and then scrambling up again, scratching, squeaking and rushing about without cessation. Eventually I got a cat and put her up in the roof, but the rats must have proved too much for her, as she deserted.

By this time, of my original attendants only John, the Sotho boy, and Toothless Jack, now in charge of the wagon, remained – the others, scared by the prospect of fever, having returned to the highveld. However, I was acquiring local natives as servants and police, and generally my mission – if not yet clearly understood – was beginning to be realized dimly. Of course it was looked on by all natives and by most white men as folly, and myself as rather a harmful kind of interfering lunatic. As one of my attendants remarked to somebody, 'Never have I travelled with such a white man; when he saw a zebra standing so close that I could have hit it with a stone, he only looked at it. Truly, he is quite mad!' But a beginning had been made. The reserve had been cleared of the natives, who had been moved to north of the Sabie and south of the Crocodile rivers respectively. The three areas into which the reserve had been divided were now each in charge of a ranger, and all game killing was definitely prohibited.

The next month or two was spent in touring the reserve in all directions and becoming thoroughly acquainted with its topography. Game was found only here and there. Pretoriuskop, later to become so covered with wildebeest that they looked like mobs of cattle scattered everywhere, then held but a few reedbuck and duiker. I paid several visits to Bill Sanderson, from whom I got a great deal of useful information as to past and present conditions. Abel Erasmus, the native commissioner who lived in the Lydenburg district had, up to the outbreak of the South African War, been the true king of the lowveld. Every year about May he would come down to his permanent lowveld camp below Bushbuck Ridge – about twenty miles north of the Sabie – to collect taxes and to hunt. His salted horses, ox transport and rifles were of the best, and he had the pick of the native trackers in the country. His native name was Mdubula, or 'he who shoots', and Sanderson himself had to admit that there was no better rifle shot even in the days when some dozen or less were considered to be in a class by themselves. In person he was tall and spare, with a flowing white beard more patriarchal even than Sanderson's own, as I had the opportunity of judging when I met him a year or two later.

Through his intimate knowledge of native ways and the great influence which he wielded, Abel Erasmus had been a valuable servant to the Republican Government, and indeed was responsible on one occasion for adding a considerable slice of territory to the Transvaal. The Swazi, by right of conquest, claimed all the country northwards from their own border as far as the Crocodile River. Their king had administered it in native fashion through a delegate ever since the conclusion of the native wars in the sixties of the last century. When the building of the railway to Delagoa Bay began to attract the attention of the Transvaal government to the lowveld, it became necessary to define the boundary of the Republic with Swaziland. Accordingly, Erasmus was appointed to represent the former, and he sent a message to Mbandzeni, who then ruled the Swazi, asking him to send a representative to meet him on a certain date near the suggested boundary line. Erasmus, with a couple of wagons and accompanied only by George Hutchinson, a trader, was careful to be on the ground some days before the fixed date, and he trekked as far as the Lomati River, which is about fifteen miles south of the Crocodile, and there established his camp. A day or two later one of Mbandzeni's principal chiefs arrived at the head of a regiment of several thousand Swazi warriors, who slowly approached the two solitary wagons on the hillside with all the pomp and circumstance of Zulu military display, feet stamping, assegais clashing against shields, and deep chants resounding in praise of their king.

Meantime Erasmus, alone and apparently quite unaware of their approach, sat on a chair in front of his wagons, stolidly smoking his pipe. Presently, the soldiers having halted at a little distance, by word of command the chief, with a considerable retinue, approached and gave the usual greetings, to which Erasmus, without moving from his chair, replied shortly. After a considerable pause he invited the chief to sit down and to send his followers out of earshot. He then called one of his servants and told him to open a case of gin, which he had caused to be placed in a handy position. He was well acquainted with this particular chief's main weakness, and as he

slowly handed him a mug well filled with the spirit, he watched with satisfaction the gleam in the old man's eyes. The gin duly disposed of, 'Now,' he
said, 'we can talk business. You like that drink?' An ecstatic roll of the eyes
and a wide grin being sufficient answer, he went on. 'Well, you know of
course that the Transvaal boundary runs through that hill,' pointing to a peak
about twenty miles still further to the south. The chief grew grave.
'Mdubula, you know as well as I do that the line between our people and
yours is the Crocodile River, which lies far to the north.' 'Ah,' replied
Erasmus, 'here is another mug of gin. I have twelve cases of it in my wagons, each case containing twelve bottles. They are all yours, but first you
must see clearly where the proper boundary lies.' As the second mug of gin
began to work and a pleasant glow to pervade his being, the chief began to
glance uncertainly first to the north and then to the south. Erasmus at once
proffered a third mug, and then after a few minutes silence, continued quietly: 'Now, do you recollect where the boundary lies?' 'Yes, Mdubula, I do. I
was forgetful, but now I remember well that the peak to the south is the
proper boundary.'

And so that matter was duly settled and confirmed. It is not related what
story was composed for Mbandzeni's benefit, but as that potentate never
happened to visit so remote a corner of his dominions, nor so far as is known
ever made any further enquiries into the matter, everything ended to the
satisfaction of all concerned. The Transvaal got the land and the chief the
twelve cases of gin, which no doubt he thought it prudent to share with his
indunas by way of hush money.

Perhaps the best known old-timer of the lowveld – according to
Sanderson the very first of all the hunters – was Henry Glynn the elder. He
operated chiefly between the Sabie and Olifants rivers, but also in
Portuguese territory, and it has been said that he killed more big game with
his own rifle than any of his local contemporaries, men whose main business
in life was shooting. He had died from fever while on his way home from a
hunting trip in the Portuguese country a good many years before the South
African War. His two sons, Henry and Arthur, continued to follow in their
father's footsteps, and up to 1899 were among the best known of the
lowveld hunters. They carried their activities as far as Beira, a popular hunting ground before the rinderpest, where, in about 1894, they accounted for a
large number of buffalo, which no doubt would anyhow have succumbed to
the disease a year or two later.

All these old hunters (Erasmus, the Glynns, Schoeman, etc.) were invariably equipped with the best and most modern of breech-loading firearms – in those days Westley Richards and Martini-Henry falling block, or double-barrelled Express rifles, firing black powder. Smokeless powder and magazine small-bore rifles had not yet come into use – happily for the game, which otherwise would no doubt have been entirely exterminated. These men were all magnificent shots, splendidly mounted, and quite ruthless in their methods, while the trekboers who came down in large numbers each year for the winter grazing, also shot everything they encountered.

Towards the end of the year, Colonel Steinacker unexpectedly appeared in Komatipoort. He had gone to England to attend the coronation without apparently having considered it necessary to obtain any superior authority for so doing. In consequence, his name had appeared in army orders as having ceased to command the regiment and his return had not been anticipated. It was therefore in the nature of a surprise when, one evening, he walked into the officers' messroom during the dinner hour. Major Webstock, who was in temporary command, managed to blurt out, after the first bewildered silence, something to the effect that it was very good of him to come and pay his old corps a visit. 'Pay you a visit!' was the reply, 'I have come to take command.' 'But, Colonel, your name was in army orders as having left.' 'Army orders! What the blanketty-dash do I care for army orders. My name has not yet in the *Gazette* been, and until it is, I am in command and you will all damn well know it!'

The next question was in regard to his pay. None had been drawn on his account for the past two months, and the regimental paymaster who refused to issue any without authority, was promptly confined to his quarters under close arrest. While thus in durance, the safe in his office was burgled and a considerable amount of cash stolen. Colonel Steinacker, pursuing the vendetta, then wanted to have him tried by court martial for having lost the money and would not be convinced that such a procedure did not fit in with strict ideas of justice. Meantime he had discovered, to his scandalized amazement, that much had changed since his departure five months before. He viewed the independent attitude and the unauthorized interference of the new civil government with a just resentment, which gradually turned to fierce indignation as his recommendations were disregarded and his protests ignored.

About this time it happened that Mr Hogge, the native commissioner for the whole of the Eastern Transvaal, wished to convene at Barberton a meeting with all the native chiefs of the lowveld. In that connection he sent a request to Steinacker's Horse, in default of there yet being any civil police, to instruct such as might be within their area to attend on a certain date. Colonel Steinacker personally replied that he would himself come to the meeting, and would bring with him such of his chiefs and indunas as he might consider advisable. Having stooped to make so considerate and generous an offer, he was naturally both angry and astonished to receive in reply a curt note to the effect that he personally was not wanted, and would he be so good as to warn the chiefs as requested. It was a gross insult and all natives were forbidden to attend the meeting under pain of summary arrest, which fortunately was still practicable under the not yet expired martial law. As a matter of fact, it did not really make much difference to the gathering, since the order affected only one chief of any importance – Mjonjela of Lower Sabie – but it was successful in definitely antagonizing the civil authorities who were slowly assuming control, even of the lowveld.

More or less concurrently with this episode Colonel Steinacker put forward a proposal that the corps should be kept on as a permanent frontier guard, and as a further inducement, a reduced estimate of only £100 000 per annum was tendered to cover the whole cost. This offer was passed on by the military authorities to the Government, and as a result I was asked to furnish a report as to local conditions, especially as to whether they appeared of such gravity as to justify the upkeep of so large an armed force. Although my own position was not sufficiently important to cause concern and I had not in any way obtruded myself, yet I was, at the time, the only local representative of the hated interlopers and was promptly put in my place by the arrest of as many of my newly enlisted police 'boys' as could be found and the clapping of them into gaol in Komatipoort, the provisions of martial law again proving very useful. I also had the privilege of a request to pay a call on the great man himself – whom I had not so far met – and thinking it as well to have a personal talk, I duly presented myself at the old Selati House in Komatipoort which he used as his headquarters. I entered a large room luxuriously furnished: well stocked book-cases lined the walls, the furniture was all of the best and a thick Turkey carpet covered the floor. (I was afterwards told, with how much truth I know not, that the temporary occupation of Bremersdorp had been responsible for much of this.)

After a not too prolonged period of waiting, Colonel Steinacker strode into the room, and at once in dignified manner beckoned me to sit down. Spare, even meagre in figure, and in height not much over five feet, he otherwise fulfilled, and even exceeded, all my preconceived ideas. The first

Colonel Steinacker, the colourful German character who assembled an irregular volunteer force to defend the lowveld from Boer incursions during the South African War of 1899 to 1902.

things about him that caught the eye were his tremendous moustachios, which were pendent quite ten inches on each side of his rather thin and bony face, and were, so to say, balanced by a long goatee, or imperial, which adorned his chin. He possessed bushy eyebrows, a large hooked nose and aggressive dark eyes. His uniform – which I believe was entirely of his own design – consisted of a staff cap, deeply encrusted with silver lace and encircled by a broad green band. He wore a double-breasted khaki frock-coat, padded and wasp-waisted which reached to his knees, adorned with rows of large silver buttons, and on his shoulders sat huge and solid epaulettes of the same material. A pair of long, soft leather brown boots, the heels adorned with box-spurs, met his neatly made riding-breeches at the thighs. Perhaps the most striking item of the equipment was the enormous sword, which might have fitted a *cuirassier* of the guard and was supported by a massive belt with two large, fringed, silver-laced tassels hiding all the upper part of the weapon.

Naturally I was speechless, and the conversation opened by the Colonel asking abruptly, 'Who is this damned fellow Hogge, who has been giving me all this trouble?' I said soothingly that I thought he was the native commissioner for this part of the world; but this was so far from impressing the Colonel, that smiling grimly, he at once announced his intention of converting 'hog' into 'bacon'. 'I will damn well let you all see who I am!' He went on to say that he understood that I intended going to live at Sabi Bridge, but as he now believed his corps was to be kept on, he intended sending a squadron there and feared I must seek some other habitation. Also, he said that since of course his men would have to exist on the game, he was afraid that my present ideas about preservation of the latter would not be fulfilled. As the interview did not appear likely to be a very fruitful one, I took my leave as soon as I conveniently could, with the growing conviction that the limelight which its commanding officer persisted in shedding on the corps, was not the best way of attaining his expressed object of prolonging its existence. A few weeks later martial law was finally abrogated and orders were received to call in all detached posts and concentrate at Komatipoort. This was for some reason regarded as an intimation that the regiment was going to be sent to Somaliland, where a campaign was contemplated against the Mad Mullah, and Colonel Steinacker accordingly sent a wire to army headquarters, in which he whole-heartedly placed all his transport at the disposal of the authorities for the purposes of the campaign. Yet another rude shock! The cold reply came, asking him by what authority he was assuming the disposition of His Majesty's property, and he was left to brood over the ingratitude of those whom he had so faithfully served through several strenuous years of war. The fact was that the new commander-in-chief knew nothing of Colonel Steinacker's personality and record, and the general officer at Middelburg, his immediate chief, had unfortunately never been much impressed by either.

Gardyne, who had recently returned from a shooting trip in Portuguese East Africa, during which his duties as adjutant had been performed by Captain Cunliffe of the Inniskilling Fusiliers, returned to his own regiment. A detachment of the newly formed South African Constabulary having taken over the police work, Steinacker's Horse ceased to function and was soon after finally disbanded, a staff officer from Middelburg coming down to be present at the sale of the horses.

Although its existence had become an anomaly for the last few months, on the whole the influence of the corps in regard to game matters had been for good, especially latterly, and I had much to be grateful for to them, both personally and otherwise. But for their presence I believe I should have found things much worse than actually was the case. The Shangane tribesmen regarded the game reserve as their special preserve and were, from natural aptitude and long usage, man and boy of them, in one way or another hunting experts. What they did not know about the various methods of compassing the destruction of wild animals was not worth knowing. Snares of every conceivable pattern and dogs were the methods employed. Some of the former were designed for, and were capable of, hoisting an animal of the size of a buffalo by one leg, there to hang suspended for an indefinite period until someone visited the trap, while others caught the foot in a cunningly devised ring of sticks to which a heavy log was attached. For small animals, falling log traps were in favour, but iron gins were also used whenever obtainable. Dogs bailed up the larger antelope, not a difficult matter, since most of them (especially waterbuck) when pursued usually sought a pool of water, there to stand at bay, and of course were easily dispatched in this situation by assegais. Warthog were chased to ground in antbear or porcupine holes, where the dogs held them earthed until their masters arrived to dig them out.

Given full opportunity, the lowveld natives were even more destructive to game than the white men. Before the advent of the latter their activities were limited by the fact that it was distinctly dangerous to venture very far from the kraals except in considerable armed parties, and even thus the constant terror of Swazi raids kept them from travelling far afield in pursuit of game. After the white hunters had begun to come regularly to the lowveld each winter and the Government – in the person of Abel Erasmus – had commenced to assert its authority, the Shangane, though thus freed from fear of their enemies, were unable to do much game killing until the summer, when the white men had departed to the highveld. The reason for this was that the Boers generally, and Erasmus, the native commissioner, in particular, were strenuous in limiting native hunting activities, not from any altruistic motives towards the fauna, but because the more game the natives killed the less would be left for themselves. To a great extent Steinacker's Horse had filled the gap during the war. It is true that its members and their 'boys' took a heavy toll, but on the other hand, the natives were to some extent restrained, and no doubt the presence of the corps deterred stragglers from the commandos, who otherwise might have visited the lowveld intent on hunting, from doing so. During the last twelve months, indeed, Major Gardyne's influence did a lot of good, and a certain measure of protection, at least within the reserve itself, was instituted.

Many of the lowveld residents serving in the corps were excellent sportsmen, and did their best to hinder unnecessary slaughter, whether on the part of their comrades or of the natives. Among these were the brothers Willis, 'Pump' and 'Clinkers', J. C. Travers, Neville Edwards, J. Banjer and of course H. C. Wolhuter and others. Unfortunately, all did not stand on the same plane. In fact, the corps included among its members several typical 'hard cases', whose method of livelihood before the war, by courtesy called 'native recruiting', included highway robbery on natives returning from the Johannesburg mines to Portuguese territory. A condition of war is that it draws together for a time into the closest companionship all sorts and conditions of men, who temporarily have to subordinate their individuality to a certain pattern of conduct, just as they discard their varying civilian garments for a uniform pattern of dress. Discipline, even where it may be of an elastic type, cannot but compress the members of any corporate body subject to it within a definite standard of behaviour beyond which it is dangerous to stray; while public opinion, as expressed by comrades-in-arms, may be an even more effective deterrent. It is fair to say that none of these 'hard cases' were of either South African or British birth, and after the war they mostly vanished from the picture so far as the lowveld was concerned.

Colonel Steinacker himself continued to haunt Komatipoort, scene of his former glory, for several months, usually wearing his uniform, and on special occasions the sword. But all his cattle having died from the new disease, east coast fever, he too drifted off, and after a few spasmodic efforts to get his wrongs redressed through the medium of the press, sank finally from public view.

CHAPTER THREE
1902 TO 1903

BEGINNINGS OF CONTROL; AGREEMENT WITH LAND COMPANIES; MOVE TO
SABI BRIDGE; CAMP ON SABIE; THOMAS DUKE; SELATI RAILWAY; JULES
DIESPECKER AND OTHERS; TRIP TO PORTUGUESE EAST AFRICA; BUSH
RIDES; DE LAPORTE

IT WAS NOW BECOMING possible to take stock of what had already been
done and to shape further plans. The mist of uncertainty had dissolved
and the way could be seen fairly clearly, provided the Government would
allow a free hand.

Dual control had disappeared for the time being with the disbandment of
Steinacker's Horse but there existed a widely spread conviction that a permanent border guard (probably drawn from the South African Constabulary)
would take its place. Along the frontier, at any rate north of the Sabie River,
it was obvious that some kind of supervision would be desirable. The country lay far from any railway or white settlement, and if left unadministered
might soon become an Alsatia. Border banditry would be resumed, within a
year or two the biltong hunters would again appear, and between their
unhindered efforts and those of the natives from Portuguese territory, all
game would quickly vanish. The opinion was universal among the better
class of lowveld residents that this area ought to be added to the game
reserve. It was in many ways more suitable than the old one, for the country
was more open and contained a larger and more varied assortment of big
game. The conviction grew in my mind that every effort must be made to
have this fine faunal area proclaimed and the staff increased to carry on the
necessary policing.

Any divided authority must mean chaos. Unfortunately, about half of the
several hundred large farms into which it had been surveyed were privately

owned, and these, nearly everywhere, were interspersed with the government ones throughout the area. Any general system of protection, therefore, would have to be prefaced by the consent of the landowners. Clearly the quickest and best way to set about obtaining this would be through private interviews; were the initial efforts left to be made through official channels, the tree itself might be cut down before the fruit was ripe. None of the farms was occupied by settlers, the greater part of the country was uninhabited and it had been proved devoid of any payable mineral deposits. Game preservation seemed the best, indeed the only practical, use to which at present it could be put.

There were a number of other matters to be settled, all of them indicating my early temporary return to civilization. So far, much that I had done had been *ultra vires*; there were no special regulations to support me and I possessed no judicial or other power, such as that of arrest, under the civil law. Martial law, although it had hit me once or twice, on the whole had been a useful ally, and a good deal had so far been done in its name, even to apprehensions for poaching! Now it was dead and something must be found quickly to take its place. This had been brought home to me when I requested the Barberton magistrate to have posted up certain handbills embodying various restrictions in connection with the game reserve, which in fact were practically identical with those subsequently adopted. His terse reply was to ask in what way I proposed to give effect to them!

A strenuous fortnight in Pretoria and Johannesburg followed. A set of regulations was drafted to be placed before the Legislative Council as soon as possible, and steps were taken to confer judicial powers upon the warden of the game reserve by creating him *ex officio* Special Justice of the Peace. Without the power to try locally the poaching and other offences committed in the reserve, cases had to be sent on foot to the magistrate's court either at Barberton or at Lydenburg, involving in each case an absence of over a fortnight for the police escort and witnesses. The new regulations were also designed to confer powers of arrest and detention within its boundaries upon the white and native members of the reserve's staff. In furtherance of the extension project I called separately upon the manager of every land company owning property in the Sabie-Olifants area. Mr Pott of Henderson's Consolidated, himself an old hunter and a keen sportsman, was responsible for effecting most of the introductions to other managers, as well as for many valuable hints and advice as to how to approach each individual.

The success achieved surpassed my highest expectations. Practically every land-owning company agreed to the suggestions put before it. These were to the effect that, in return for the safeguarding by the reserve staff of the fauna and flora, the prevention of prospecting and the collection on their behalf of any rents due from native tenants, the companies undertook to hand over, for a period of five years to government control, all their land in the Sabie-Olifants area. Within that period they would not make any use of it, nor sell, let, or give any rights to third parties. Each company signed a separate agreement drawn up in identical terms and I was then and there able to take these to my chief, Sir Godfrey Lagden, and induce him to promise to take early steps to have the plan adopted. But the wheels of governmental machinery revolve slowly, and it was nearly ten months before the addition of these four thousand square miles to the reserve made its appearance in the *Gazette*.

In the meantime, under the authority given by the private owners so far as their land was concerned, and with the help of the new general game ordinance promulgated in October 1902, I was able to carry on more or less; though, but for the remoteness of the area, and for the fact that the farmers were not yet in a position to resume their annual winter grazing and hunting, it would have been a good deal 'less' than 'more'. I was also successful in getting another piece of ground included in the proposed extension. The western boundary of the old game reserve, between the Sabie and the Crocodile rivers, was rather ill-defined and therefore unsatisfactory. By extending it twelve miles to the west, the foothills of the Drakensberg were all taken in and the reserve gained an excellent bit of well-watered and relatively healthy country, suitable for such game as kudu and sable. The new western boundary as proposed concurred with easily recognized features throughout, following from the south, first the watershed of the mountains through Legogote (the Lion Mountain), then the North Sand River to the Sabie River, thence to the Olifants, first along a well-marked wagon road to the Selati railway extension, and finally a considerable river, the Klaserie. I thought in any case the strip to be added to the western boundary of the original reserve would form an ideal buffer between the latter and the settled country around White River.

In subsidiary matters it proved possible at last to arrange for the purchase of a number of transport donkeys from the Repatriation Department, which I proposed to distribute among the rangers, and for myself I bought a very good, entire grey salted horse from Colonel Johan Colenbrander of Rhodesian fame, who at that time had some kind of government contract for selling off British army horses no longer required. My animal was a war veteran, having been right through the campaign, first on one side and then on the other, bearing also a battle scar on one flank.

During my visit I met for the first time one who was later to be a close friend, Dr J.W. Gunning, Director of the Pretoria Museum and Zoological Gardens. By birth a Hollander and educated in Germany, he had been, during the war, the very popular guardian of the British officer prisoners at Pretoria, and had many amusing anecdotes to tell relating to escapes and other matters which had occurred while he was in charge of them. Just after the British occupation of the capital, and when he was once more to his great satisfaction back at work in the museum, a tall British private soldier, his uniform much stained from campaigning, walked in and said he wanted to look at flies. Dr. Gunning said he felt a little nervous, as he could not conceive how a British private could genuinely be interested in such things, so he spoke soothingly to him for a time until, to his intense astonishment, he discovered that he was conversing with Professor E.E. Austen of the British Museum, one of the greatest living authorities upon tsetse flies and nagana disease!

Dr Gunning had started the zoological gardens on his own initiative only about a year before the war. Beginning with a few caged birds and small mammals in his office at the museum, he had contrived to get a grant of ground and the approval of the Volksraad for a zoo. He had then rapidly built it up and had recently acquired the historic lioness named Beauty, which had been presented in 1899 by Cecil Rhodes to President Paul Kruger as a 'gesture', and returned promptly by the latter as 'not wanted'. She had then been sent to the London Zoological Gardens, and after the war had been dispatched a second time to Pretoria, where she was destined to live to a ripe old age as quiet and almost as tame as a domestic cat.

I was not very much disturbed by a plan which I learnt the Land Settlement Board had in view to acquire some portion of the game reserve for its own purposes, since the project seemed founded on a complete ignorance of all prevailing conditions. On the whole the visit had been very encouraging. The Government, if nervous of any rapid action, seemed anxious to make the reserve a success, and a great deal of sympathy and interest had been shown in every quarter where it was likely to be of value.

On my return I packed up and trekked to the Sabi Game Reserve, abandoning without regret the rat- and fly-infested quarters at Crocodile Bridge. The Sabi was much more attractive, wild and unspoilt, with hardly even a native inhabitant for fifty miles round. The veranda of the old blockhouse proved to be particularly cool and pleasant. With a direct river frontage, it caught every breeze which blew from the two prevailing wind directions, north-west and south-east, and I adopted it as my dining and general living quarters, sleeping in one of the boiler-plate huts immediately below the railway embankment. As an office I used a small grass-roofed rondavel situated close by, each of these being always at least five degrees hotter than the blockhouse veranda.

By Colonel Steinacker's orders, the store-room, stable and several other buildings had been demolished, and all corrugated iron and other removables taken away when the last train had come up about a month before. Instructions had been given to pull down the blockhouse also, but fortunately for me, time did not avail for this, and it proved to be intact. Moreover, it held no less than fifty-three bottles of the famous pickles – rations which must have proved in excess of the requirements necessary for staving off fever.

The first few days were busy ones. There were about half a dozen natives

Used by Steinacker's Horse during the South African War,
this blockhouse on the Sabie River became Stevenson-
Hamilton's first headquarters in the Sabi reserve.

71

available, who were kept fully employed in the necessary tasks of building a new stable, a kitchen at the back of the blockhouse, thatching the veranda with reeds and making sun-screens for it, besides digging and watering the much neglected vegetable garden down by the river. I had acquired, besides the grey stallion, a good little chestnut gelding bought from a British officer in Komatipoort, which, having lived for two years in the lowveld, might reasonably be assumed to be immune from horse-sickness. These, with my now salted roan Charlie, made up a stud of three. The roan, Jorrocks, and the little mare had been sent temporarily to Lydenburg to be, as was hoped, safe from the disease during its worst period; though, as a matter of fact, they both succumbed to it while there. There had also been lent me to look after during the absence overseas of the owner, a half-breed greyhound and two pointer bitches, called respectively Lil, Ruby and Di. The latter two were quite useless for the purposes for which they ostensibly existed, while the first-named was an excellent watch-dog and very plucky.

A few nights after our arrival, Major Robertson's 'familiar', a huge brindled tom-cat, came sidling down from somewhere on the roof, to be greeted with growls of fury from the two kittens, Tweedledum and Tweedledee, but though at first exceedingly timid, he soon settled down as part of the household. This animal was said to be wild on the father's side and probably was so, as he bore the distinctive striping of the African wild cat, and although quite gentle and otherwise domesticated, for the entire five years during which he remained with me – until a python swallowed him – he would never willingly allow himself either to be stroked or even touched by the hand.

The interior of the blockhouse, which was used as a store, was full of the nests of the large black and yellow mason-wasps. These solitary insects build nurseries of clay which are firmly attached to a wall or other flat upright surface, and a certain number of grubs having been first paralysed by a sting, are placed inside to be fed on by the wasp grub. The nest is then sealed up and the mother's responsibility ceases; the young wasp, having reached the necessary stage of development, eventually finding its own way out. It was also interesting to watch from the veranda the big fish eagles sailing up and down the river, each one nearly always attended by one or two ridiculous little birds screaming and demonstrating, until, having treated them with haughty contempt for a time, at last the larger bird seemed to have had enough of it, and accelerating his pace, would quickly leave them behind. Whereupon, satisfied that their young were safe, the aggressors would then turn and make off whence they had come. If game was scarce, snakes at least were plentiful at that time of year, and during my daily rides in the bush, black mambas were more often seen than not. Usually they glided with great swiftness up the nearest large tree where they were easily dispatched with the shotgun I always carried. Hyena were numerous and came into camp almost every night. The carcasses of the horses which were continually dying during the occupation by Steinacker's Horse had doubtless collected these scavengers from far and near, and during the first year of my occupancy they were exceedingly troublesome. No skin or rawhide rope could safely be left lying about after dark. One night, indeed, a particularly daring one having walked up the ten wooden steps leading to the blockhouse, abstracted and made off with a bundle of about a dozen jackal and other skins which were hanging on the veranda.

The much reduced state of the antelope and other herbivora, consequent upon the unremitting persecution to which they had been exposed during many years (a persecution from which the predatory creatures, especially the larger ones, had been to a great extent free), had for the time upset the balance of nature. The preyers had been given a relative numerical advantage over the preyed upon, which could not, as I then believed, but result in a progressive decrease in the numbers of the latter. A few lion had been killed from time to time by Francis and some other white men, and very occasionally by natives. Leopard had been trapped now and then, but wild dog had hardly been interfered with at all and existed in quite disproportionate numbers. Judged by later standards, lions were scarce but nevertheless were more numerous in proportion to the big game than at a subsequent period. However, the assertion with which I was met on my first arrival to the effect that they periodically formed a continuous line and marched right across the reserve, devouring everything that came in their path, was scarcely justified by facts. Crocodile simply swarmed in the Sabie and other rivers. Therefore, although the ideal of a sanctuary is undoubtedly to preserve every form of wildlife existing within it from man's attack, and thus so far as may be possible allow the fauna as well as the flora to develop as they would under nature's guidance only, and as though man did not exist as a disturbing factor on earth, yet, as things then existed, such a course was seemingly impracticable. I thought the carnivora should be reduced not only to their proper relative proportion numerically, but at first even to a lower figure, in order to give the other animals a chance to get well ahead. At a later stage, when in fact the balance had become a more just one, it was nevertheless the case that lion were actually (though not relatively) more numerous in the game reserve than they had been in the early days. Then the very understandable fears of neighbouring stock farmers rendered it still necessary to continue the campaign against them, right up to the period when the reserve became a national park. Thereafter the lions, instead of being considered a menace – their existence providing merely a convenient weapon in the hands of opponents of the sanctuary – suddenly acquired immense popularity with the sight-seeing public and became its greatest asset. However, this is looking very far ahead, and at the beginning it was the policy to keep all carnivorous mammals, reptiles, and to a lesser extent predatory birds, within reasonable limits, having, of course, due regard to the continued existence of every species.

During Christmas week 1902 Wolhuter and I went into camp about five miles down the Sabie. This river, typical of most of the perennial streams which drain this portion of the Transvaal from west to east, runs at the bottom of a fairly deep and wide valley, clad with dense *Acacia* thorn-bush. Immediately bordering on the wide fringe of tall and almost impenetrable reeds which shut in the stream on either side, tall evergreen trees find soil for their roots, their dense shade offering a welcome solace to the wayfarer on a hot day. The stream itself, about two hundred feet in width, normally runs swiftly over a boulder-strewn bed, from time to time discharging itself noisily over rock bars, and anon running out into deep, still pools, the haunt of many crocodile and occasionally of hippopotamus. In places the river divides itself into channels enclosing long islands densely clad with evergreen trees, which form so thick a canopy that the sun is shut out and no grass or other ground vegetation can find life. There are but few places whence from the banks the stream itself is readily visible, so dense is the protecting reed barrier.

Little rain having so far fallen, the impala were still drinking, perforce at the river, which, so far as may be possible, they avoid doing when water is to be found elsewhere, from fear of crocodiles and the easy ambushes which the reeds afford to their land enemies. December is the lambing time, when the rams and ewes run separately, each herd of the latter accompanied by their offspring, which after about a week are able, more or less, to keep up with their mothers. As is the case with other gregarious wild animals, the parturient female goes away by herself to bring forth her young in some secluded spot, not to rejoin her companions until the little creature is strong enough to accompany her. It is amazing how fast the infant grows in the first few days of its life, and a prudent provision of nature that it should be so, since it is at this period that all the natural enemies of the game animals, especially wild dog, are most active in their pursuit. Whether the opinion sometimes expressed that while lying in its form and still too young to get about, the young creature has not yet acquired the distinctive scent or odour of its kind, is correct or not, it is difficult to say. It could be fully in accordance with nature's protective methods if it were so, since otherwise these helpless little things would be at the mercy of every roaming carnivore that came along, from a lion to a jackal. The mother feeds about in the vicinity, ready to afford any assistance that may be in her power, and I remember on one occasion how a gallant waterbuck cow completely put to flight a cheetah which attempted to seize her little calf, then just able to walk.

As we halted on the bank preparatory to finding a suitable site for a camp, there was a tremendous commotion in the reeds followed by a loud splash in the river, and Wolhuter, who being the nearer was able to get a glimpse of the cause, said it was the biggest crocodile he had ever seen. Thus warned, we gave very strict injunctions to the natives with regard to watering the animals while we remained in this camp, and we were constantly on the lookout for the reptile making a sudden and unexpected appearance, but we saw nothing more of it at that time.

One day Wolhuter went off for a walk accompanied by a couple of attendants, while I elected to stay in camp and try my luck at fishing. Just below the camp lay the deep, still pool, fed by a gentle stream into which our crocodile had disappeared, and abutting on it a small platform of level rock, with a space around free from reeds and trees, which gave room for the play of rod and line. I was using a small spoon bait, and hoping to secure a tiger fish, had linked it on a light steel trace. At about the fourth cast the rod bent nearly double, the reel screamed, away went the line, and far down stream a silvery shape leapt out of the water, once, twice and then again. My heart seemed to lose a beat as the line slackened; but all was well, and away the fish dashed, this time upstream, while I frantically reeled in. Again and again was the same performance repeated, each furious run ending in nerve-shaking leaps. I thought the creature would never tire.

In most African streams one is handicapped when a heavy fish has been hooked, by dense surrounding vegetation, negativing all hope of following along the bank, while crocodile, of course, prohibit any attempt to wade. Therefore all the playing must be done from one spot. When a tiger fish of any size is first hooked, his early rushes are so fierce and prolonged that no check is possible, notwithstanding the very strong tackle which is used. Even if the line and steel cast stand the strain, the top of the rod will probably break, while the mouth is so hard and bony, that it is always rather a matter of luck if the hook will hold.

On the present occasion, after twenty thrilling minutes, I managed to land my fish, and I need not tell any angler how pleased I felt. At once a headlong scurry to the camp with my prize, and a frenzied search for the scales ... just under nine pounds – the first and, as it proved, the largest, tiger fish I ever caught! For the information of those who may not be personally acquainted with this handsome fish, *Hydrocynus vittatus*, the following is its description as written long ago in my book *Animal Life in Africa*:

> Of slender and graceful build, covered with large silvery scales, ornamented on his sides with horizontal black stripes, his fins and tail of orange red, his personal beauty is as striking as his boldness and courage. His mouth is armed with truly formidable teeth, set well apart, and fitting into sockets in the opposite jaw. They are conical, sharp as needles, and, in large specimens, fully a quarter of an inch long. His character is in keeping with his outward appearance, for his habits are essentially predatory, and were it not for the crocodile, he would be the chief tyrant of the waters which he makes his home. In all probability, too, he amply revenges himself upon the newly hatched reptiles for the toll which the larger ones exact from his species ... It is said that in large rivers, like the Zambezi, they will exceed thirty pounds in weight, but the largest I ever saw caught there scaled sixteen.

I went on to say that the biggest one recorded from the local rivers up to that date had been fourteen pounds, and in fact I have never heard that this has since been surpassed, though tiger fishing is a popular sport on the Transvaal lowveld.

Wolhuter returned in his usual unobtrusive manner. What followed is rather typical. He at once asked me if I had got anything, upon which I eagerly displayed my catch and gave him a long and minute account of the struggle. He listened quietly, admired the size of the fish, which he said was the biggest he had seen caught in the Sabie River, congratulated me on my success, and then went away to clean his rifle. This made me say, 'Oh, by the way, did you have any luck?' 'Well,' was the nonchalant reply, 'yes, I did have a bit of luck.' 'What did you get?' 'Oh, two lion and five wild dog!' Curiously enough, these were the two first lions Wolhuter had ever shot, although he had been hunting in the country for so many years, and tends to show how difficult it is to come across these intelligent animals if one is at the same time seeking any other game. The wild dog had been encountered on the way back in two separate packs, from one of which he had bagged three and from the other two. Taking some natives, we walked out about three miles to where the lions had been shot: Wolhuter to superintend the skinning, while I took a photograph of him standing by his trophies. On the way home we again put up more wild dog but were unsuccessful in getting a shot at them.

Some little time before this expedition, the ranger whom I had engaged for the Crocodile River area had left after about two months' service, and I had engaged an old fellow campaigner in the person of Thomas Duke, late of Rimington's Guides. Duke, who was a little over forty years old at that time, had come to South Africa as a small baby, his parents having emigrated from the south of Ireland.

His life had been an interesting one. His father had been a successful farmer in the Eastern Cape up to the time of a native rising in the early eighteen-seventies when his homestead was burnt. Duke himself, then a boy of about twelve, was beaten and otherwise ill-treated, until, during the night when his captors were asleep, he was unbound and released by an old native servant of the family. He then walked and ran in his bare feet and practically naked for about twelve miles till he reached safety. His father, fortunately for himself, happened to be away at the time of the raid. Duke said the natives treated his mother and sisters remarkably well, sending them under safe conduct to the nearest white post. Later he joined the Cape Mounted Police, and in that well-known corps, rose to the rank of sergeant. Indeed, he was so well thought of by his superiors, that he would probably have received further promotion, but that he accepted an attractive offer in the Orange Free State detective service, with which he remained until the outbreak of the South African War, when he joined Rimington's Guides. Attached as intelligence agent to Le Gallais's column, he was responsible for its guidance on the night when General De Wet came nearer to being captured than on any other occasion during the campaign, although during the skirmish following the surprise, the leader, Le Gallais of the 8th Hussars, was killed. For this service Duke had been awarded the Distinguished Conduct Medal.

During the last year of the war I had been in the same column with him under General 'Mike' Rimington, and had become so impressed with his qualities, especially in regard to dealing with natives, that I had determined to secure his services on the first opportunity. He was a perfect linguist in the Xhosa language, which so nearly resembles the other east coast tongues that he quickly became proficient in the local dialect, though his native name always continued to be 'M'Xhosa' throughout the lowveld, until his death more than thirty years later. Most African natives assign their own names to white men of their acquaintance, always representative of the characteristic, physical or otherwise, which most strikes their imagination on first encountering the individual. These nicknames are not intended to be in any way derogatory, and practically every white man living in a native district has his native name. But it sometimes happens in the case of an unpopular person, that while he possesses his ordinary name by which he is commonly addressed, behind his back he may be referred to amongst the natives by some designation quite different and less complimentary. One white man I knew, for instance, while believing himself to be called 'The Great Elephant' (a very complimentary term) was spoken of behind his back as 'Hyena Face'. A man who habitually wears glasses is nearly always named 'M'fastele' (windows); one who was always rather careless as to his dress used to be called 'M'dablahempi' (torn shirt). De Laporte, later for many years a ranger in the game reserve, was known as 'M'Kaose' because he invariably wore leggings. I was soon given the name of 'Skukuza', which apparently implied that I came along and turned everything upside down.

Duke was not long in proving his mettle. Near the Crocodile River had been found in a freshly abandoned native hunting camp, the fires hardly yet cold, the remains of a zebra and of several impala. The matter having been placed in Duke's hands, in due course he produced the culprits with the necessary circumstantial evidence, and they were promptly tried and sentenced. The leader was destined afterwards to become one of our policemen. He was rather a character in his way, and I shall have something to say about him later.

To facilitate communication with the outside world, arrangements had been made for a trolley service on the Selati railway, between Sabi Bridge and Komatipoort. At first this was confined to a mere platform on wheels pushed by half a dozen natives working in relays, but later it was supplemented by a more up-to-date contrivance, which boasted a pumping lever manipulated by men standing on the trolley itself. I called this the 'passen-

*In the early years of the reserve a trolley on the Selati railway
line was used to carry passengers and goods between Sabi
Bridge and Komatipoort – a distance of eighty kilometres.*

ger' and the old one the 'goods' train. To make the former more comfortable
for the traveller, I rigged up on its front part a bench with a back to it like an
ordinary garden seat, and thus travelled in state up and down the line, taking
no more than five hours to do the fifty miles down to Komatipoort, though
twice as long to return. With the goods train the itinerary was a matter of
days, how many depending partly on the weight of the load, and partly on
how eager or otherwise the propelling natives were to finish the journey.

Unfortunately for the entire efficiency of the service, there was one small
fly in the ointment in the person of the general manager of the Selati line. It
appeared that in the construction days ten years previously, the contractors –
Messrs Westwood & Winby – in order to carry out their agreement on the
specified terms, had been compelled to seek the financial aid of one
Toulmain, who had advanced them considerable sums of money. On their
becoming bankrupt and the said Toulmain having meantime died, his estate
laid claim to all the completed items for which his money was held to be
responsible, such as the permanent way, the rails, and the four or five corrugated iron gangers' cottages, which were spread along the line at certain
intervals. The bondholders (who had lost three-quarters of a million sterling)
and the Government also apparently had some kind of claim, the nature of

which was not defined. The other plant – derelict trucks, picks and shovels, wheelbarrows, old tanks, crowbars, and so on – lay about in the veld by the thousand. For years these had formed a supply depot for many a low country store and the outfit for many a deserving prospector. They seemed to have no owner at all, since they had been apparently bought and paid for by the contractors before they were obliged to seek the aid of the financier and should have formed part of their assets in bankruptcy. However, as things were, the items belonged by right of acquisition to anyone who happened to have a handy wagon or one or two natives available to remove the spoil. It was remarkable what a number of useful things still remained, and for a good many years they saved the Government from having to supply a lot of material of the kind to the game reserve administration.

The agent for the estate of Toulmain, who liked to be referred to as 'General Manager Selati Line', was one Jules Diespecker, who with his late brother Rudolph, had been a sub-contractor in the construction days. His headquarters were in Komatipoort, where he maintained as a guarantee of his position, an old engine and tender with driver complete, all of them relics from the same period. These, during the war, had been commandeered and made use of by Steinacker's Horse, and Mr Diespecker himself had held the position of private secretary to the commanding officer of the corps. During the following years, his ancient locomotive appeared on the line only on rare occasions, when it was utilized for bringing official parties up to Sabi Bridge. But the general manager always had it up his sleeve as an asset to make use of in case he wished to descend upon me with a view to seeing if I was in any way misusing railway property.

When it came to his ears that I – in complete innocence of the position, be it said – was using a trolley on the line, he waxed highly indignant, and on the very next occasion on which it appeared in Komatipoort for the purpose of bringing back a consignment of stores, he sent his natives to seize it. My own men of course resisted the attempt and a free fight ensued, with the result that the contending parties were all taken to the police station on a charge of brawling. Meantime I waited vainly for my stores, and after a week or so had passed, I felt impelled to mount my horse and ride in the fifty miles to discover what had happened. The first thing I saw on arrival was my trolley, derelict, off the line; the next my own natives, suffering from a certain loss of morale and complaining that they had eaten no food for three days – which statement, after having studied their general appearance, I took with the proverbial grain of salt. There then came to me the general manager, afire with such a flame of righteous wrath as could only be quelled by several consecutive doses of whisky at the local bar. Things then simmered down, and I was able to establish what is nowadays referred to as a gentleman's agreement, by which (1) on consideration of my undertaking to guard as the apple of my eye the various buildings by personally seeing that the long grass was annually removed from their vicinity; (2) to do no damage by overuse or otherwise to the rails or permanent way; and (3) to instruct my natives to report to him on each and every occasion on which the trolley might arrive in Komatipoort, I would in future be permitted to use the line.

Generally speaking, this arrangement worked well enough, though a little later the general manager conceived the idea that I must – as was the case he said on all other railway lines – cause my trolley to be preceded by someone with a red flag. The omission of this formality was subsequently the cause of an incident rather resembling the one above referred to. It was pointed out to me that if my trolley, not duly preceded by a native walking at least fifty yards in front of it and waving a red flag, should chance to meet the Selati train, the driver of the latter might be forced to back his engine for a considerable distance, when the locomotive might very possibly be precipitated over the Crocodile Bridge into the river below. The prospect of journeying the fifty miles from Sabi Bridge to Komatipoort at the standard rate of three miles per hour was not alluring, but I was able to get out of the difficulty by having the emblem carried on each trolley, and when half a mile out from Komatipoort, displayed prominently – indeed frantically waved – by one of the team walking slowly in advance. Since in the ensuing three years the Selati engine made only four attempts to traverse the line, two of which were unsuccessful – one indeed being, so to say, stillborn – no unfortunate incidents occurred.

At the moment poor Jules Diespecker had other troubles to contend with, even less calculated to bring placidity to his naturally rather mercurial temperament. His official residence in Komatipoort was a wood-and-iron building of considerable size, known as Selati House. This had been occupied for the past two years by Colonel Steinacker as his private quarters, and when martial law ceased and the corps had been disbanded, Mr Diespecker considered it time that it should again become available for himself as general manager of the Selati line. Accordingly, a polite request was sent embodying the idea. But the Colonel was not a man thus easily to be dislodged from a consolidated position, and indeed he deemed so ill-timed and presumptuous a summons altogether unworthy of his notice. A more peremptory demand was met by the scornful refusal which the occasion warranted, and the general manager then applied for an order of ejectment. On hearing of this the Colonel let it be known that if forced to leave he would cut down and remove the wooden supports for the veranda, which by his orders had been repaired or replaced during his tenancy under martial law, and must therefore quite obviously be his private property.

When this latest development was reported to him, the general manager was with a few friends, discussing his grievances in the bar of the Railway Hotel, and leaving his drink unfinished – almost a criminal act in the eyes of any old time lowvelder – rushed off to stay the impending calamity. The course of the events immediately following can but be surmised since they were known only to the two participants, who were about equally matched as to height and weight. When asked about it, the general manager merely shrugged his shoulders and said 'Oh. That Miserable Creature!'

The Colonel, when he emerged from retirement about a week later, was more eloquent, describing how Jules, raised from a lowly position to the honourable post of his own private secretary, had basely bitten the hand that had fed him. But he added with a hint of self congratulation, 'So, I did him like vun dog shake!' Nevertheless, the disappearance of the Colonel for nearly a week, and the fact that when he did again become visible in public, even a pair of dark glasses could not entirely conceal traces of discoloration near one eye, definitely inclined the public to conjecture that the combat had not been entirely a one-sided affair. The duel formed the chief topic of interest for some time to come, among all the men about town, as they gathered at the bar of the Railway Hotel, and many were the regrets expressed that even at the cost of abandoning the 'just one more', they had not followed at once to the scene of action.

It can at least be said for the lowvelders of those days that they were none of them moulded to a pattern: each was a character in his own way. Whether or not this was in any way due to the absence of any levelling feminine influence I am not prepared to say. At any rate there were then and for some time afterwards but two white women resident in that part of the country, and these both of mature years. There was one man for instance, who with no visible means of livelihood, spent practically his entire time in bed, only dragging himself down three times a day to the hotel to eat on each occasion a hearty meal, and yet who, when there was any question of joining a shooting trip, would spring up alert and active, and show himself capable of walking miles on end without visible fatigue. Another – Hotchkiss – designed originally for a bank, had before the war adopted the more congenial pursuit of a professional hunter in connection with the Beira Railway, and now, this avenue closed, purported to earn his living by keeping a trading store, which indeed he had lavishly stocked with every kind of commodity. But alas! the Old Adam proved constantly too strong, and for five days in the week he might be encountered, his shirt waving in strips from his shoulders and covered with perspiration, laboriously following the tracks of some solitary duiker through seas of dense grass and thorns, or plunging about among high mealie stalks in quest of guineafowl, while a more or less intelligent native conducted the business. Indeed, after a year or two it was clearly apparent that, whether owing to lack of capacity or the reverse on the assistant's part, the business was a failure, and a fortunate legacy having permitted of settlement with creditors, poor Hotchkiss – a good fellow in every way – vanished into the wilds of Rhodesia.

Towards the end of January 1903 I made an expedition across the frontier. It seemed a good thing to establish personal contact with our neighbours, the Portuguese officials, so armed with the necessary credentials, one day I trekked over to the neighbouring military post at Nwanedzi to be received by the commandant with the charming hospitality which I have invariably found to characterize the Portuguese as hosts. The station was perched on a spur of the Lebombo, which on the eastern or Portuguese side displays characteristics, in this part at least, differing entirely from those of its western face. In place of masses of rough boulders and stony wastes sparsely clad with scraggy thorn *Acacia*, there were pleasant grassy slopes where the soil was deep and many fine shady trees found root. About a square mile of ground had been completely cleared round a small fort, which mounted a seven-pounder Krupp gun. The garrison consisted of about twenty white and a number of native soldiers, all dressed in khaki; the natives wearing red tarbouches, or fez caps, without tassels, and the white men ordinary slouch hats. The commandant's wife was with him, and in default of any mutual understanding of one another's home languages, we all found indifferently pronounced and expressed French to be a sufficiently adequate conveyor of thought.

There roamed about in the immediate vicinity a considerable amount of livestock of one kind and another – goats, pigs, crested guineafowl and a young tame baboon, while another home pet was a half-grown caracal, or African lynx. This creature, when not chained to a chair in the corner of the room, was generally held on the knees of the lady, in which position its

*Stevenson-Hamilton undertook regular patrols in order to
reconnoitre the game reserve, but transport methods were
cumbersome and crossing flooded rivers by ox-wagon
presented serious hazards.*

ceaseless monotone of menacing growls, varied only by vicious spitting,
did not inspire a stranger with complete confidence, in spite of its mis-
tress's repeated assertions that it would neither scratch nor bite. The little
baboon usually walked about on its hind legs like a human being, which
method I was given to understand was due to the discipline, when it had
offended in any way, of tying its hands behind its back for a time – rather
an interesting illustration of special muscular development artificially
induced.

A series of misfortunes marred the return journey, which was by a different route, the Lebombo being crossed not far south of the Olifants River and
the wagon track used by Steinacker's Horse followed thence south towards
the Sabie. First, the best ox in the span was bitten by a black mamba and was
dead by the time I saw it. Then a batch of native prisoners, caught red-handed in a hunting camp surrounded by the remains of many animals they had
killed, escaped one night. On my return from a fruitless pursuit, I found that
all the oxen had strayed, and the driver, Toothless Jack, was down with a
bad attack of fever. In the end, after a long and unavailing search, I was
obliged to leave the wagon derelict with the invalid to guard it, and to ride
home in light marching order, while the countryside was roused to prosecute
the quest, which resulted in the recovery of the span miraculously intact
about a week later at a point thirty miles north of the Sabie. The first news to
greet me on arrival at home was that some white men had just run two hundred head of cattle from Portuguese territory across the game reserve and had

defied Wolhuter to stop them, thus more than ever emphasizing the crying need for definite regulations and of some executive authority for the staff.

On the conclusion of the above expedition I settled down more or less for the next month at Sabi Bridge, receiving reports and trying to get administration generally into some sort of running order. It was my custom at this time to undertake daily, long solitary bush rides with the idea of becoming thoroughly conversant with the local topography and of learning to find my way readily without native assistance. In the light of further experience it was hardly either a very wise or even a very safe procedure, since in the event of a bad fall with subsequent injury or some other incapacitating accident, it would have been a long time before one could have been tracked and found. Still, undoubtedly one learnt a lot and acquired a large measure of self-confidence in getting about on one's own in trackless bush, which it would have been difficult to attain in any other way.

On one of these rides, I put up a small waterbuck calf out of the form in which it had been lying. After first starting away, it came back, smelt the pony, and then lay down again about a yard from me. Thinking, as I saw no signs of its mother, that she might have been killed by a lion and that the little creature would therefore soon either die of starvation or fall victim to some beast of prey, I undid the riem, or rawhide rope, which, with a head-collar, I always carried over the bridle, and made a noose which the calf allowed me to slip over its ears without any trouble. The moment it felt its neck encircled, however, it rushed off, threw itself down and generally flung itself about to such an extent that I feared it would incur some permanent damage; all the time bleating loudly just like a cow calf. It was amazingly strong for its size, and afraid of strangling it, I had to play it like a fish and let it drag me all round at the end of the riem.

Presently, as if in answer to its loud cries, a waterbuck cow appeared quite close by, but on seeing me at once made off again. The appearance of the presumed mother took away most of my reason for wanting to catch the calf and I was really very glad to see her. I was seven miles from home, and encumbered as I was with an unsteady horse and a double-barrelled rifle weighing twelve pounds, I did not see how in addition I could manipulate a very sturdy and struggling little animal of at least fourteen pounds. Nor could I leave behind either horse, rifle, or calf while I went to obtain assistance, since the spot was in the midst of dense bush and I was not at all sure that I should be able to find it again. So, while the calf was doubling itself up in a knot and kicking with its hind legs, I slipped the noose back again over the ears. It then lay panting for several seconds before finally bolting off. I saw the mother again as I rode away, so no doubt they were happily reunited. In fact a few days later I noticed a waterbuck cow and calf near the same place, and I felt pretty sure they were the same ones.

A few weeks after this I was riding along the banks of the Sabie and stopped at the place where Wolhuter and I had made our camp. Through the reeds I noticed, sticking out of the water, the head of the big croc we had then seen, and after some devious crawling about through very wet vegetation I managed to shoot it. Next day, accompanied by two police 'boys' and a couple of malefactors, I returned equipped with a rope. After much probing with a pole, the carcass was discovered in about ten feet of water at the tail of the stream. No one was very willing to undertake the task of diving in and putting a noose round it, so in the end we cut two long forked poles, and thus, after great labour, contrived to get it out. It turned out to have been a female, measuring just under fourteen feet from snout to tail, and with a girth behind the shoulders of six feet one inch. The teeth were as long as the canines of a lion and much thicker. In the stomach was a mixture of stones, fish scales, bones, and impala horns. This was the largest crocodile I ever shot in the game reserve, and though I have often seen what appeared to be reptiles of enormous size in various African rivers and lakes, I have always felt I would like to run a tape over them, for before I measured the one in question I was certain it was about eighteen feet long.

During my solitary rides I often tried the experiment of throwing the reins on the pony's neck and seeing where the animal would take me. It struck me that there exists a great difference between individual horses as regards natural aptitude for picking up direction. The chestnut, Jantje, besides being an excellent shooting pony, warranted to stand in the same spot for hours without moving, if left with the reins over his head and resting on the ground. He was a very intelligent animal and would always make straight for home wherever we were. The roan, Charlie, on the contrary, was much less reliable and did not seem able always even to follow his own back tracks. One day, for instance, he proceeded with such confidence that I felt sure he must be taking a short cut, and it was only on getting on to some rising ground that I realized he was making straight for the koppies on the Selati line and going at an angle of sixty degrees away from Sabi Bridge. Even after I had taken matters into my own hands, he still kept doing his best to edge off in his old direction, trying to tell me in every way he could that he was right and I was wrong. During all these rides I never once saw a lion, though I encountered wild dog on several occasions, and was able to bag a good many of them.

About the middle of March 1903, I paid belated heed to the advice of all the 'old hands' to the effect that the Sabi must at all costs be avoided during the rainy season, and trekked up to Sanderson's, he having very kindly placed at my disposal his late brother's house at the top of the hill. I was fitly rewarded for my folly, for the situation proved to be so cold and damp that it promptly brought out the dormant malaria in my system and I had a severe attack, which indeed I did not entirely throw off for several months. Sanderson himself was feeling so overcome by the impending advent of a repugnant civilization, that he would have seriously considered packing up, abandoning his farm, and trekking off into the wilds but that, as he sadly remarked, 'There's nae place left for a body tae gang!'

About this time, Gray, the honorary ranger at Lower Sabie, accepted a post under the Witwatersrand Native Labour Association, an organization just formed to recruit Portuguese natives for the Witwatersrand gold mines, and having made his permanent quarters in that territory, I sent Duke to take over his duties. I then acquired the services of Mr C.R. de Laporte, who had been the lieutenant in charge of the intelligence in Rimington's column in the late war. De Laporte, who had been in the country for some years before the latter event, was a great acquisition to the staff. About twenty-eight years of age at that time, he was able, tactful, and keen, a combination of qualities very necessary, as subsequent events proved, for the controlling of the difficult section of the reserve bordering on the Crocodile River, which he now took over from Duke and in which he was destined to remain for more than twelve years.

Game preservation seemed to be for the moment on the up grade. The Government reproclaimed the Pongola Game Reserve, which was a strip of seven farms lying below the Lebombo and forming a narrow wedge of Transvaal territory between Swaziland on the north and Zululand on the south, the Pongola River being the boundary with the latter. It had been a reserve under the old government, and a Hollander named Van Oordt, an ex-naval officer, had been in charge of it. There was also a movement to proclaim as a reserve all the land lying between the Olifants and the Limpopo rivers, which, being entirely government unsurveyed ground, uninhabited by whites and only very sparsely so by natives, seemed to offer an ideal sanctuary. As an addition to the staff, Windham, secretary of the Native Affairs Department, recommended a certain Major Fraser, late of the Bedfordshire

Regiment, who had long experience of Indian shikar and who was now in Scotland. He was accordingly written to and offered the post of a ranger to be stationed for the time being in the new Pongola Game Reserve, which had also been placed under my charge.

CHAPTER FOUR
1903 TO 1904

MAJOR FRASER; AN OFFICIAL VISIT; TROUBLE; WOLHUTER'S ADVENTURE;
EXTENSION OF THE RESERVE; VISITS TO THE SHINGWEDSI AND THE
PONGOLA GAME RESERVES; NATIVE CENSUS; MORE TROUBLE; PERSONAL
MATTERS

JUNE 1903 FOUND HEADQUARTERS back again at Sabi Bridge, from which they were never again to be moved.

Major Fraser, the new ranger, had arrived from Scotland, and pending his departure for the Pongola Game Reserve, spent a few weeks with me. If a little bit on the senior side – to be accurate, forty-eight years old at that time – he was a fine figure of a man. Well over six feet in height and rather more than proportionately broad, with his big red beard he might have been the head stalker on a Highland deer forest – a post which, under other conditions, he could indeed have filled admirably. Through the twenty-five years during which he had soldiered in India, he had never left the country. All the periods of his leave had been spent in shooting trips, and there was little he did not know about that part of the world from a shikar point of view. I have seldom met anyone more observant of facts relating to wildlife, or with a memory more retentive of what he had noticed, and he adapted himself to parallel conditions in Africa with the ease of a duck moving from one pond to another.

He was a beautiful marksman with either rifle or shotgun. With the former, indeed, he had no superior, even among the best of the old hands of those days. On principle, he would never take what he considered too long a shot at any animal and would never willingly use anything but a heavy calibre firearm. He was, in fact, a sportsman in the higher sense of the word, and a born gamekeeper – essentially of the Highland variety.

*Major Affleck Alexander Fraser, warden of the Pongola
Game Reserve and later of the Shingwedsi Game Reserve in
the North-Eastern Transvaal, seen here at his post at
Malunzane in 1911.*

No gillie it must be said, even of the most hardened type, could have excelled him in the absorption of unlimited quantities of Scotch whisky without the slightest visible effect. In fact, I have heard his capabilities in this direction mentioned with awe by lowveld residents of the old school, who rather fancied themselves on the same lines. One story told of him is typical of his capacity.

Some years later, during my absence, he was in charge at Sabi Bridge and had asked two well known 'hard cases' from Komatipoort to spend a week-end with him. They sat up till a late – or rather an early – hour on the block-house veranda, Major Fraser regaling his guests with a succession of anec-dotes relating to Indian shikar. Many opened whisky bottles sporadically decked the table, and by a previous mutual understanding, one or other of the visitors would from time to time, whenever their host's attention seemed momentarily to be diverted, pour another inch or two of neat liquor into his tumbler. If the Major noticed what was taking place, he at any rate affected complete ignorance of anything unusual, and sitting solidly in his chair,

puffing contentedly at his pipe and piling one yarn on another, he methodi-
cally drained each glass to the last drop, until at length the time arrived when
the others discovered the world to be rocking round them and their chairs to
be making curiously unexpected movements. Alive to the necessities of the
case and of his duties as a host, Major Fraser then quietly rose from his seat,
supported each successively to bed, and having tucked him up and put out
the light, went back to his chair to smoke one more pipe and enjoy a night-
cap before turning in himself. Some three hours later at grey dawn, he made
his appearance at their bedsides, fresh and smiling, woke them up by successive douches of cold water and forced both the reluctant and sadly deflated
practical jokers to come out fishing with him. It seemed a matter for regret
that, possessing as he did many latent abilities, Major Fraser always obstinately refused to be anything more than a gamekeeper. Though he wrote an
excellent, well-phrased letter in a good legible hand and, on the few occasions when he happened to be in the mood, showed himself to be proficient
with both pencil and brush, he would never make any notes nor transmit
what he knew, except by way of casual conversation. Thus much of his wide
– and in some ways unique – knowledge of beasts and birds died with him.
The truth was that his contempt for literature generally, which included all
those connected with it in greater or less degree, was whole-hearted and I
doubt whether, since leaving school, he had ever taken the trouble to read
anything in print other than an occasional daily newspaper and of course the
Field, which he absorbed weekly from cover to cover.

During the cold weather of 1903 Sabi Bridge was honoured by a first-
class official visit. Sir Godfrey Lagden, accompanied by Mr Hogge, the
native commissioner for the Eastern Transvaal, and a considerable retinue,
arrived one day in a private coach laboriously drawn by the panting Selati
engine, especially (and with some misgivings) patched up for the trip. Its
triumphant completion of the fifty-mile journey, largely uphill, without
serious mishap, was certainly a feather in the cap of the energetic and zeal-
ous general manager. He, however, did not himself venture on the expedition, rightly feeling that his proper place was at his headquarters, ready to
dispatch on the instant any first-aid, such as a breakdown trolley, that
circumstances might demand.

The rank and file of the visitors arrived apparently satisfied that they were
about to embark on a shooting trip fraught possibly with some peril. One,
indeed, had brought specially for the occasion a new .450 Express cordite
rifle, though he had inadvertently omitted to bring any cartridges for the

weapon. All expected, it seemed, to find a lion crouched under every bush, patiently waiting to test their prowess. I am sure they anticipated for dinner nothing less than elephant trunk, and so their disappointment was proportionately bitter when they found that it was proposed to feed them on the ordinary army ration of bully beef. There was, in fact, nothing else to offer. Then, and for some years afterwards, no shooting for meat was carried out by the staff, and so far as animal food was concerned, we lived on poultry, and things out of tins.

It was, perhaps, a little disconcerting when one had been practising self-denial in the midst of comparative plenty, to find people – and officials connected with game preservation at that – fresh from a hearty beef and mutton diet, crying out for game meat, and to hear one of them exclaim, as an impala ewe, inspired with newly engendered confidence, stood gazing at him within fifty yards distance, 'Oh, what a lovely shot; how I wish I had my gun!' Great surprise and some incredulity was evinced when I confessed I never shot any game and I was told I 'ought to keep my eye in'. Indeed, it was not long before I received what amounted to an order to go and slay a buck for my guests. With assumed cheerfulness I fared forth accordingly. Presently, having returned and made confession that I had been so unfortunate as to miss the only animal seen, a deep gloom settled upon the party, which was maintained until, by a happy inspiration, a member of it, reputed to be a good shot, volunteered to see if he could do better than the discredited warden. I lent my rifle and in due course guided him to within range of a herd of impala, when rather to my relief, the expert made two clean misses and the animals disappeared into the blue. In justice to him, I ought to add that I had stupidly forgotten to tell him that the rifle shot high.

The attitude of these officials merely reflected that of the general public towards game at that time. Wild animals were viewed purely from a utility standpoint and were most admirable when they were dead. 'The only good Injun is a dead Injun.' 'But, my good fellow, what is the use of keeping the things?' has been said to me not once but a hundred times. I remember in either Pretoria or Johannesburg someone envying me for the 'wonderful shooting' I must be having. When I replied that I never shot any game at all and neither did my staff, he stared at me for a moment in speechless astonishment, and then blurted out, 'Why? Can't you hit them, then?' It happened in these early days also that some member of the Legislative Council who was not particularly favourable to game preservation was cavilling at what he called the extravagant salaries paid to our staff. 'Why,' he added, 'I would do it myself without any pay at all, just for the shooting!' In due course my extraordinary attitude became generally known and accepted with a smile and a shrug. A local paper printed a leading article headed 'Major Hamilton's Queer Hobby', and I did not quite know whether to feel hurt or flattered when Sir Godfrey at a later date said to me, 'Hamilton, what a good thing it was I didn't appoint a *sportsman* to your job!' No doubt the term is capable of different interpretations!

The official visit was not, however, entirely free from exciting incident. A lion grunted some miles away in the early morning and the whole party set off armed to the teeth and discussing their programme at the top of their voices, subsequently returning much disappointed at not finding the animal waiting for them just outside the compound. One evening, too, we were having tea on the blockhouse veranda when a single wild dog chased an impala through the compound fence and into the river, within one hundred and fifty yards from where we were sitting. The impala jumped in and swam across, but the pursuer stopped dead at the water's edge, being, in common with the rest of its kin, far too wily to venture into deep water, no matter how great the temptation. It thus differs widely from the unsophisticated domestic dog, which always plunges straight in under similar circumstances and more often than not is seized and pulled down by a crocodile before it has got half-way across.

The entertainment of so comparatively large a party – eight or nine altogether – had rather strained my limited resources; in fact, the situation would have been impossible had I not fortunately secured the services from Komatipoort of a Swahili cook named Ali Sharif. Hailing from the Comoro Islands, he was therefore a fellow countryman of most of the other so-called 'Zanzibar Boys' who, clean-looking and picturesque in their long white robes and red fez caps, usually form the servant class all along the east coast of Africa from Mombasa to Delagoa Bay. My latest acquisition was rather a character in his way and spoke a language which I think he believed to be English. At first, before he married a local wife and so became to some extent one of the people, he was rather a useful intelligence agent in connection with the numberless minor intrigues which are inseparable from native administration. As a cook he did not perhaps reach the highest level, but at least he was an advance on Toothless Jack, who had left me when at Legogote and whose attainments in the culinary line had not extended beyond the stirring of mealie porridge with a stick. Yet the debut of the new chef was very nearly disastrous. On the last evening the main item on the menu was curried bully beef and rice. When the dish was placed before me I thought it did not look quite right and missed the familiar curry smell. So I called out, 'Ali, bring me the packet of curry powder you have been using'. With an indulgent smile he bustled out and back, to lay before me a half-empty packet of Cooper's Sheep Dip, which is a potent concoction of arsenic and sulphur intended for external use only, though one may adminis-ter, with care, a few grains to a horse as a tonic powder. At least my guests had not departed without having had a thrill.

The year 1903 was full of incident. In August occurred an event which, unpleasant at the time and in its immediate consequences, had I believe the ultimate effect of conferring on the administration of the game reserve a reputation for strict dealing without respect of persons, and on myself by implication one of being a thoroughly disagreeable person. This, whether justified or not, proved in later years not wholly a disadvantageous attribute. Indirectly it set the stage for the amazing display of cool courage and resolu-tion which, for a time, made Wolhuter's name more or less world famous.

On return from a short official visit to Pretoria, I learnt on arrival at Komatipoort that several senior officers of the South African Constabulary, accompanied by a white guide and orderlies with two ox wagons, horses and mules – quite a little army in fact – had just left that place for Portuguese ter-ritory. They had come down through the whole length of the reserve from the Olifants River and had stated their intention of re-entering the Transvaal just south of the latter. The newly imported and virulent cattle disease known as east coast fever having broken out in the Portuguese country, it was of course undesirable that any transport oxen should return from the infected region and thus perhaps bring the disease with them. There were, however, as yet no definite regulations on the subject.

Feeling certain that there must, under the circumstances, be some expla-nation, I dispatched Wolhuter to the Olifants River to meet them on their return there. Unfortunately, before he had gone far his horse succumbed to horse-sickness and he had to return for another one. Meantime natives reported that the party had crossed back into the Transvaal and had shot, a little way south of the Olifants River, a giraffe, a zebra, some wildebeest and other game. The area had not actually been named in the *Gazette* as part of the reserve, but the Government had gone so far as to prohibit all shooting of game therein. It was further stated that their cattle had contracted east coast fever and had been dying all along their return route. Though it was now too late to cherish any hope of overtaking the party, Wolhuter made a second start with the object of collecting enough evidence on the spot to establish whether or not the law had actually been broken, casual native reports being often unreliable as to times and precise localities. I recollect very well his sharpening his hunting knife on my whetstone just before he set forth from Sabi Bridge. Later, he had good cause to be thankful that he had done so!

A few weeks only had elapsed, when one evening his police 'boys' appeared leading his horse, which bore several fresh and ugly-looking scars on its quarters. These natives related how, on his way back from the Olifants River, at a point some thirty miles north of Lower Sabie, Wolhuter had been seized and badly mauled by a lion, but had managed to dispatch it with his sheath-knife and was now gone to Barberton Hospital. That was about all any of us knew for the moment, as the 'boys' could give but the barest outline of what had taken place. The full details were gathered much later from Wolhuter's own account of what had happened and after a minute examination by myself of the scene of the occurrence. Meantime the wounded horse and the skin of a large male lion with two obvious knife holes behind the left shoulder, were sufficient confirmation of the general truth of the story.

Sir Alfred Pease, at that time magistrate in Barberton, and myself, sent a jointly signed account of the incident to the *Field*. It aroused considerable interest. Although the popular press was still in its infancy, there were yet plenty of bright young literary aspirants on the look-out for a good 'stunt' even in those days. Various distorted accounts appeared and our modest little letter to the *Field* was embellished out of recognition. One particular romance, gracing a well-known illustrated monthly magazine, irritated Wolhuter himself so much (largely, I think, because he was depicted in the guise of an American cowboy with a revolver and huge Mexican spurs) that he asked me to write to the editor, pointing out the various inaccuracies. I wrote, adding that I had Wolhuter's own authority for doing so. The answer was a short and sharp rebuke of our presumption. Merely about two lines, but to the point. 'We consider our South African correspondent to be at least as well informed about the matter as Mr Wolhuter states himself to be.' A worthy addition to the 'Without Comment' file!

Wolhuter having thus become a casualty, I sent De Laporte, then temporarily stationed at Lower Sabie, to the Olifants River. He also had recently lost his horse from the usual cause, and so proceeded on foot which, if slightly slower, appeared at that time to be a safer and surer method of reaching one's objective than riding. He spent a considerable time there examining native witnesses, and in the end made out a case concerning the

*Cecil Richard de Laporte, who joined the Sabi reserve in
1903. He did not command a particular section but was
moved around the game reserve as circumstances demanded.*

killing of a giraffe and several other animals in the protected zone, which
seemed strong enough to act upon. The giraffe had apparently been ridden
down and shot at a point near the Bangu Spruit, far inside the Transvaal.

I did not for a moment credit that the animals had been deliberately and
knowingly killed in defiance of the law; but I believed, and I still think
rightly, that the officers, knowing nothing whatever of the country or the
conditions, simply took all their white guide told them at face value as to
localities. Therefore, when he assured them they were in Portuguese territory, they believed him, reflecting perhaps that if there did happen to be any
mistake about it, their position would be sufficient to silence all criticism.
For my part, I felt very strongly that a great deal more than was patent on the
surface depended on my pushing such a case to the utmost of my ability.
Already there was too much talk about 'pampered officials hanging together';
'one law for the ruler and another for the ruled', and so on. The public
expectation was that whereas I would at once prosecute any ordinary individual who was guilty of poaching in the reserve, I would be more than likely
to turn a blind eye to the doings of anyone in authority. I thought that if I let

this case drop, I should never be able to establish a reputation for equal dealing without respect of persons. Moreover, the incident had already attained considerable publicity and aroused some speculation in the lowveld. There was the general feeling – justified or not – that some of the new officials behaved as though they belonged to a superior caste and were above the law. On the other hand, I had no delusions as to what I was up against. To prosecute criminally – with no sure hope of conviction – the two senior police officers of the colony was surely inviting trouble. It required, therefore, a certain hardening of heart to place the necessary evidence in the hands of the public prosecutor and urge that the case should be strongly pressed.

As I had anticipated, every possible obstacle, legal and other, was put in my way. Lunching one day with Lord Milner, Sir Arthur Lawley, the Lieutenant-Governor (to whom I sat next at table), asked me if I was sure my information about the case was correct. Colonel Lambton, who was Military Secretary at that time, told me he had heard the prosecution was being pushed vindictively. However, I carried on, and ultimately, after nearly nine months' delay, the case came into court.

The defence had managed to arrange that the trial should be held at Pietersburg, which was the headquarters of one of the officers, although the alleged offence had been committed in another district. I began to feel less confident of the result, since the magistrate, Major Bolton, had impressed on me quite early in the day, and before anything had been settled as to place of trial, that the whole thing must be a 'frame-up' and that the officers were being unjustly accused. It was, therefore, a tribute to British sense of justice as well as to the strength of the evidence as given by De Laporte and the native witnesses, that one of the accused was found guilty of having shot a wildebeest and fined £5. As the giraffe was killed close by, I could never quite make out exactly how the magistrate managed to convince himself that its death *might* have happened across the frontier.

The stock of the game reserve rose locally as a result of the case, but, as was to be expected, the aftermath proved less heartening so far as I myself was concerned.

While we were busy with the above, the proclamation of the addition to the Sabi reserve and that of the Shingwedsi area, as well as promulgation of the longed-for and quite indispensable regulations drafted by myself, had become accomplished facts. I at once started to explore the – to me – unknown Shingwedsi country. I left in September, riding my best shooting pony, Jantje, with six donkeys and four police 'boys', crossed the Olifants and Letaba rivers – the former by no means a light undertaking at that time – and plunged into the unknown. De Laporte was instructed to meet me with the wagon and supplies in a month's time somewhere south of the Olifants River. I found a vast, sparsely inhabited country, well watered, and possessing plenty of excellent pasture, but almost entirely denuded of its *raison d'être* as a reserve – game.

About fifteen miles north of the Letaba River and close to the Lebombo mountains, at the kraal of a small chief named Makhuba (which held rather a sinister reputation as the site of the disappearance and supposed murder of a white trader some years before), I encountered one of the last, if not the very last, of the old-fashioned hunting parties that ever came to the eastern lowveld. It consisted of four typical Boer hunters with their families, two large buck wagons and oxen, a number of obviously excellent shooting ponies and some useful looking rough dogs. They told me that they had passed through the Shingwedzi poort into Portuguese territory and had been shooting along that river east of the Lebombo, re-entering the Transvaal again by the Letaba gorge. They had, they said, shot three elephants and ten giraffe as well as other game during their trip, and found the country east of the Lebombo was still full of game, though there was so little on our side, they added, that it was not worthwhile stopping to hunt. They were, of course, ignorant of the newly proclaimed game reserve, and when I told them, professed themselves amused at the idea, since 'there was nothing left to preserve'. However, they were very obliging about it and said they were moving off to Pietersburg next day, and in fact did so – rather to my relief. I discovered later that on their way home they had accounted for a wildebeest, a waterbuck, a reedbuck and a roan antelope!

The kraal natives were surly and disobliging, especially when they understood my mission, and would tell me nothing of the country. From their hang-dog look I judged them capable of murdering any number of traders, but no doubt I was prejudiced. Afterwards we had considerable trouble with them, and a few years later I had the kraal moved out of the reserve.

Pushing on north, I found at a place called Malunzane, a fairly new white-washed hut built by a departed labour recruiter, and thought the site might be suitable for a ranger at a later date. I then went on to the Shingwedzi River and travelled along it as far as I could. It proved to be an attractive river. A dry sand-bed in winter, relieved by occasional long deep pools, its banks were clad with masses of dwarf fan and feather palms, lending to the scene a tropical appearance absent from the southern bushveld. Here and there towered a lofty borassus palm, and everywhere was the mopane with its scented double leaf, which north of the Letaba, forms two-thirds of the tree life.

During the two hundred miles or so which we covered on the outward and home journeys, after having crossed the last-named river, we saw at different times nine kudu, five waterbuck, three tsessebe, and perhaps half a dozen duiker. We also noticed the old tracks of two giraffe – the local natives said the last ones remaining – and one day the 'boys' caught a fleeting glimpse of a lion. All along the Shingwedzi we found native hunting camps, simple affairs, consisting of a few upright sticks roughly thatched with reeds or grass, a grass bed, frameworks of poles for drying meat, and ashes of fires. The natives we came across were of a rather poor type, and unlike those in the south, carried bows and arrows – the former strongly made and about five feet long, the bow strings of twisted rawhide, the arrows usually barbed and plumed with nondescript feathers.

In its general character and the appearance of its inhabitants, it was the wildest bit of Africa I had seen south of the Zambezi, and it would have been perfect had there only been present a little more wildlife. But the native hunting camps told their own tale, and the flats north and south, only lightly clad with stunted mopane, had for years been the favourite hunting-ground of the mounted Boers. Until quite recently elephant and eland had been there but the last of the latter was said to have been killed during the war, and of three elephants which had ventured in from Portuguese territory during that period, one had been shot and the other two had recrossed the Lebombo. In this remote part of the Transvaal there had been, between human beings at least, complete peace, and parties of hunters evading the commandos had carried on pretty much as usual, safe from any interference from their own party or its opponents.

I was loath to turn back, but all luxuries such as tea, coffee, flour, etc. were finished before we had marched more than two days up the Shingwedzi. We had to rely for necessities – that is to say mealie meal for ourselves and grain for the horse – on the uncertain and exiguous supply to be obtained from an occasional impoverished native kraal, helped out with fish from the pools. The 'boys' and myself did well enough but I was concerned about the pony, as the grass, where not all burned off, was dry and poor at this time of year. There was therefore great rejoicing when, a day's march south of the Olifants River, De Laporte appeared with the wagon loaded up with supplies, including even camp equipment.

At the conclusion of this trip, the Sotho youth, John, gave notice. He said that accustomed as he was to civilized surroundings, Sabi Bridge appeared to him to be the back of beyond, and when I dragged him to outlandish places such as the Shingwedsi, where the people appeared to him to be hardly human, he felt he had adventured enough. Accordingly, he shook the dust of the wilds from his feet and departed by train from Komatipoort. His future, no doubt, would be spent living in a single-roomed, but *real* house built from old kerosene tins, outside of which he would cook his daily food over a fire made from dried cow dung, while he gazed over some miles of treeless grass veld to the little group of exotic gum trees, marking, on the distant horizon, the site of the mission station at which, in his best clothes, he would attend service on Sundays – in fact, civilization. Not for him the pathless jungle, the reed-fringed rivers with the wild call of the fish-eagle ringing down the long reaches, and the still, warm nights, their silence punctuated by the throb of the lion's roar.

Very likely he was right, and no doubt the majority of civilized white people cherish very similar notions; though their idea of what constitutes the acme of luxurious ease may differ in degree, the underlying idea is the same. Whether he is the artificially nurtured product of what some say is a decadent civilization, or the barbarian with his foot only just on the first rung of the ladder which the other has already climbed, each average human individual is very like another in demanding for himself the highest degree of comfort and safety which lies within the orbit of his own experience. Everybody to his or her taste; no doubt it is only congenital idiots who deliberately and unnecessarily seek hardship and discomfort. The kerosene-tin house and the cow dung fire probably represented to John his goal of ease and happiness; anything more complicated would have bored him. Born in other spheres of life his conception of the perfect existence might have been the lounge of a New York hotel-de-luxe, or again an armchair in the bar parlour of the Pig and Whistle. Even the native of the wilds hates leaving the comfort of his mud hut and seldom does so except under press of necessity. Primitive savage man no doubt felt the same about his cave. So I am driven to the unwilling conclusion that those of us who deliberately invite the austerities of life, must, in some way or another, be mentally deficient.

A visit to the Pongola Game Reserve where Major Fraser had been installed, completed the year's travels. It was a little over two hundred miles' ride by way of Swaziland, and it took me about a week to cover on Pompey – the grey horse which I had purchased from Colenbrander. The journey included the crossing, both going and returning, of the Usutu River in flood, which was carried out successfully by swimming the horse along-side the large flat-bottomed ferry boat.

I found Major Fraser installed in the somewhat dilapidated stone fortress of the late game ranger Van Oordt. The latter had wielded considerable local authority, and to add to the impressiveness of his appearance had, it was said, been accustomed to wear naval uniform on such important official occasions as the trial of tax defaulters and game poachers. For these, when convicted, a large stone cell under the 'castle' had been reserved, now – *sic transit gloria mundi* [7] – occupied by Major Fraser's donkey-pack gear. The site was excellent, the house perched on the edge of the Lebombo, which here falls away almost sheer for a thousand feet to the plain below. The game reserve itself, lying that distance beneath and thus completely over-looked, was a strip less than five miles wide and about twenty long, stretch-ing away to the Drakensberg foothills in the west. North of it was Swaziland, while south and east lay Zululand, with the magistracy and town-ship of Ingwavuma within an hour's ride. The little oasis of three or four acres at the top of the hill was therefore, except on one side (and that the uninhabited one), quite cut off from the country to which it belonged, and practically surrounded by 'foreign' territory.

The geographical position suited Major Fraser's companion on the island very well. This was one Moses 'Zinyawo' or 'Moses of the Feet', a native missionary who had built a small wattle-and-daub chapel and a few living-huts close by. Moses apparently found the female rather than the male ear willingly receptive of his teaching. At all events, on Major Fraser's arrival he discovered the reverend gentleman installed in Van Oordt's house, and the whole of the small space around, forming Transvaal territory, a camping ground for a large collection of ladies, all young, from the adjoining Zulu and Swazi villages – among them not a single man, so far as could be dis-covered. Major Fraser took possession of the house but found life generally, especially the hours designed by nature for sleep, rendered rather trying by the almost unceasing flood of melody which flowed day and night from the worshippers, the deep tones of Moses and the music of his mouth-organ a background to the shrill trebles of the ladies.

Major Fraser said that almost as soon as he arrived he began to receive official letters from the magistrates and native commissioners of the adjoin-ing countries. They complained that they were receiving daily petitions from the relatives of the ladies praying that the latter should be made to return to their homes. But since no Transvaal authority had hitherto been available in this remote corner of the colony, and since the ladies themselves appeared unwilling to leave the stimulating atmosphere created by the mission for the humdrum drudgery of their own homes, and as of course it was illegal for the police of one colony to cross into the territory of another – this was long before Union – matters were at a deadlock. Moses, in fact, had been triumphant all along the line, and he and his congregation, secure in their refuge, could smile at the efforts of infuriated relatives and helpless officials. Acting under the game reserve regulations, Major Fraser was in a position to give orders to quit to all 'foreigners' and the surroundings soon became more peaceful, but constant complaints from the relations of the ladies continued to arrive about the teacher. I am sure most of them were entirely unjustified and that his actions had been dictated by nothing but pure proselytizing zeal. At the same time there was no denying that he was a fine figure of a man in his clerical outfit and white choker, while one glance was enough to show that his surname was a fitting one. One felt that his tremendous bellowing voice must have inspired just the right feeling of enthusiasm among his devotees.

Moses, who was a Transvaal subject, proved a harder nut to crack than his congregation had been. His mission, too far away to have any idea of the state of affairs, backed him up, and it took a great deal of official correspondence before we were able to make the ranger's residence and garden available for him only. In fact the eviction of the Reverend Moses antedated only by a little time the departure of Major Fraser himself. It did not take long to realize that this narrow strip of country, though crossed by animals travelling from the Swaziland game reserve on one side to that of Zululand on the other, itself held very little game permanently. In fact a few kudu and one small herd of impala was about the entire stock. With the great Shingwedsi reserve of some four thousand square miles crying out for a resident white officer, it was obviously a waste of time and money to keep a man to look after this tiny strip of country. Accordingly, with Major Fraser, I interviewed the magistrate of Ingwavuma and made a private arrangement under which, although officially he had no right to perform any duties in Transvaal territory, he agreed unofficially to keep an eye on the two native police whom I decided to leave in charge and to pay them the monthly wages which I agreed to remit to him on their account. This arrangement worked well enough for some years, until in fact, the Pongola reserve was deproclaimed in 1921. Major Fraser meantime packed up and proceeded early in the following winter to the Shingwedsi, where he took up his quarters at

Malunzane, remaining the 'father' of that reserve for the next sixteen years.

Early in 1904 we held the first native census of the Transvaal. It was rather ingeniously carried out. Each head of a kraal was given a long string and a big bag containing beads of various colours and sizes. On the day of the census he had to put on the string a big black bead for every married man and a big blue bead for every married woman present, and so on down the scale, with beads of lesser size relative to the importance of the individuals, until one arrived at a little yellow bead for a male and a little red one for a female baby. In theory it was excellent but exactly how in practice it worked out is another matter. The native is intensely suspicious of any innovation that he does not fully understand, and is convinced that somehow and in some way it is connected with taking his cattle, taxing him or limiting the number of his wives. So one never will know how many medium blue beads each representing an unmarried woman were not put on the string when, in accordance with the wish of the Government, they ought to have been so

Tim Healy was initially appointed as a junior police corporal to assist Stevenson-Hamilton in executing his functions as justice of the peace. In 1908 he became a game ranger, responsible for the Nwanedzi – now Satara – area.

placed. I remember how greatly the natural conditions at Tshokwane and Salitje at the time of this census-taking contrasted with those obtaining in later years. The grass everywhere grew four feet or more high and there were visible none of the great herds of game which afterwards ate and trampled it down. Not once did we hear even a distant lion's roar. Yet in the future these areas were to hold more game – and also more lion – to the square mile, than any other portion of the reserve. I had by now assumed the full judicial functions of a justice of the peace, and that the dignity of the office might be fitly maintained, was provided with a public prosecutor and clerk of the court, the two posts united in the person of a very junior corporal of the South African Constabulary. After several misfits – one of them, during the reaction following on a week's too free living, threw himself into the Crocodile River and was drowned – the authorities sent me G.R. Healy, rather apologetically, as they did not seem sure 'if he would do'.

Healy was then about twenty-one years of age. He had come to South Africa as a second-lieutenant in an Irish militia regiment after some time spent as a medical student in Dublin. The war over, he had resigned his commission to stay in the country, and having experienced various vicissitudes, had finally enlisted in the South African Constabulary. He was a tall, loose-limbed, angular youth, with a head small for his body, fair hair and large innocent blue eyes. These, coupled with a simple expression, were apt to give strangers a mistaken idea of his character and thus tempt the rash to try to get the better of him – to their subsequent regret. Later he was to become not the least efficient of the old guard of rangers.

The very first day of his arrival provided a little excitement. I had just got back one evening from a trek, and the wagon, a long way behind, did not arrive on the other side of the Sabie River until the following morning. Meantime, during the night, the river had come down in partial flood and some rather urgently required belongings were marooned on the opposite bank with four hundred feet of rapidly running brown water intervening. Stimulated by Pompey's successful breasting of the Usutu River a few months before, I conceived the idea of riding him over bareback. So, with a halter to guide him, and clad only in a shirt, I got on his bare back and rode into the stream. All went well until we were half-way across and struck the main current. Then, in spite of all efforts, downstream went his head, and in a moment away we were racing on top of the flood, straight for Delagoa Bay, occasionally submerged, amid a medley of branches, logs and other bank debris which also were being borne along. After a quarter of a mile or so of swift career, during which Pompey kept his head well up, continued to swim and deftly avoided several half-hidden rocks, while I – with no time to be frightened – clung tenaciously to the mane, a kindly eddy bore us near in to the right bank. There Healy, surrounded by a crowd of 'boys' with whom he had raced along the bank keeping pace with us, was waiting. When fairly near I flung myself clear, caught hold of the end of a proffered pole and so was dragged ashore, while Pompey made good his own landing about thirty yards further down. It was a practical lesson in the power of a flooded river, and Pompey and I were no doubt lucky to have got off so easily.

During June and July, Major Fraser and I undertook an extensive exploration of the Shingwedsi reserve, where he was by now established at Malunzane. We traversed the country right up to the Limpopo River; indeed, through following too far an old hunting road from Shikundu Kop, we found ourselves on the bank of the big river in Portuguese territory, some ten miles below its junction with the Pafuri, and had to follow it up to the military post near that place, where the commandant expressed a desire to see our shooting licences! All through our journey, but especially along the Shingwedsi and its larger tributaries, the Mphongolo and Phugwane, we discovered a great many native hunting camps, where we often found firearms and invariably bows and arrows, wire snares and gin traps, catching also several unwary individuals in the act of hunting game. Since, however, we felt that the new order of things had scarcely yet had time to sink into the native mind, we contented ourselves with confiscating skins and weapons, burning the camps and making offenders caught in the act accompany us on our march, to be released a few days later. From first to last we saw very little game and that wild in the extreme, while the northern areas in the neighbourhood of the Pafuri River seemed to be completely denuded of all larger wildlife.

In fact, for long after this the area northwards from the Shingwedsi was beyond any possibility of adequate control. Major Fraser had a staff of but ten native police, and all he could do was to stop poaching as much as possible in the southern two thousand square miles, leaving the equally-sized northern part more or less to its own devices. It was no doubt fortunate that in those days the lowveld was still so much shunned by white men, though at that time, and for a good many years afterwards, the region about the Limpopo-Pafuri junction was the haunt of a number of what may euphemistically be termed 'frontiersmen', containing among them some elements of the former bandits of the southern portion of the Portuguese frontier. These made a hand-to-mouth living by illicit labour-recruiting, poaching elephant in Portuguese country and no doubt selling firearms and ammunition to natives. In fact, this little corner continued to be the no-man's-land of the Transvaal right up to some time after the First World War. So hopeless did its position as a game reserve appear to be, that I was several times in the course of years seriously – though unofficially – sounded as to whether it would not be better to deproclaim all country lying north of the Shingwedzi River, since it held practically no game and we had not the means to administer it. But to all such friendly suggestions I turned a deaf ear. The country was not at present required for any kind of development. It seemed to me that even a nominal protection was better than none at all, that perhaps some day in the dim future better times might come and it would be possible to translate the theory of protection into practice.

In 1904, the southern game reserve extended from the Crocodile River to the Olifants River, and from the Lebombo mountains in the east to the foothills of the Drakensberg in the west: this was known as the Sabi Game Reserve. North of the Olifants River as far as the Letaba River, was a strip of country twenty miles wide, which being a proclaimed mining area, I was unable to get included in the reserve. Therefore it interposed, as a bit of alien soil, between the Sabi Game Reserve and the Shingwedsi Game Reserve, which began north of the Letaba River and extended to the Pafuri River. This little strip of foreign territory proved a thorn in our side for many years. I succeeded after a while in having all shooting forbidden within it, but it was outside my jurisdiction, and legal enactments did not do much to prevent all and sundry from coming down in the winter months and, under one pretext or another, killing any game they desired. Although in 1923 I was successful in getting the eastern part included in the game reserve, it was not until the boundaries of the Kruger National Park were proclaimed in 1926 that the whole of it was finally brought under our administration. However, in 1904 the reserves comprised nearly fourteen thousand square miles of country, quite enough for our then staff of five white men (including myself) and fifty native rangers to look after.

South of the Sabie River protection was adequate. Three of the four rangers and thirty natives looked after this, the old Sabi reserve. Between it and the Olifants I had stationed a dozen natives in various isolated posts at important points, who periodically reported to myself at headquarters. At present no white officer was available and I and the rangers from south of the Sabie River took it in turns to patrol the country. North of the Letaba, as mentioned above, was a white man with ten natives, who kept a fair guard over all the area between it and Shingwedzi River. Unless previously equipped with a special permit, no one was allowed to enter the game reserves and even then no firearms might be carried. Heavy penalties were prescribed for infraction of regulations. Of course, in those days things were simpler than at the present time in many ways. Although our means of transport were slow according to present ideas, being confined to horseback and pack animals for ordinary work, yet we had less to contend with. Not only were motor cars practically unknown, but at that time the white population was too busy getting the country straight after the war to have much time for shooting relaxation. In addition, the reputation of the lowveld generally as being a white man's grave (except for a few months in the year) was still firmly maintained. For their part, the natives, though mostly confirmed and natural hunters, were less sophisticated than they later became.

Immediately after my return from the long tour round the Shingwedsi country, I began to realize for the first time that certain inimical forces were

Each year, around June, Stevenson-Hamilton set out to explore and patrol the far-flung parts of the game reserves. Pack donkeys and an ox-wagon were loaded with two months' supplies and the party consisted of the warden, several African police and servants.

107

at work. During the two years I had held the post the clouds had slowly been gathering. Considerable disappointment existed among some of the lowveld people in that they had not been given entry privileges, as they put it 'to assist the officials to destroy the carnivora'. Many were annoyed not only that all hunting had been so rigorously stopped, but that even prospecting and trading were no longer permissible. There were some who considered that they had claims greater than my own to the post of warden. I had come as a stranger to the lowveld, and it was pointed out that I could not be expected to have the ability and knowledge to deal with the natives and still less with the lions and other carnivora, which, unless dealt with drastically by someone qualified to do so, would within three years exterminate all the herbivorous animals. Seen from outside, a grass fire in the game reserve would call forth the instant remark: 'Ah, the usual thing; natives hunting game, and no one stopping them!' One, formerly a storekeeper in the neighbourhood, who besides having made annual hunting trips into the area during earlier years, did not lack a certain facility with his pen, had indeed come to regard himself as my early successor – so far may the constant expression of a desire convert, in the mind, mere aspiration into accomplished fact. Nor was my name popular at police headquarters. *Espirit de corps* had been injured by the successful prosecution of the deputy commissioner (largely through my efforts) and it was not to be expected that any opportunity of, so to say, 'crying quits' would be missed.

Taking one thing with another therefore, it was not very surprising that I shortly began to find myself in difficulties. During my absence at Shingwedsi, strict regulations had been promulgated with a view to hindering the spread of east coast fever, and no cattle were allowed to be moved without a permit signed by a veterinary officer. I had innocently started off with my ox wagon before the regulations came out, to find them in force on my return. To make things worse, by previous arrangement with Sanderson, in my absence a cow had been driven over to his bull, and on arrival unfortunately ran into the local vet, who at once ordered her slaughter and reported the matter to the police. I was able to evade the penalties of the law, but for some considerable time afterwards Sabi Bridge was subject to surprise visits from troopers of the constabulary sent down to see if they could not haply find me committing some offence against one or other of the many new laws and regulations, which it would be possible to turn to account.

Local papers also bristled with anonymous letters signed 'Indignant' or 'Law-abiding Citizen', asking how it was that such a person as myself could be permitted to hold a government appointment. There were scathing remarks about 'pampered officials' and enquiries concerning what the police were doing (they were really quite eager and active). What really was most troublesome was that I was no longer in a position to use the government ox-wagon, a form of transport indispensable to my work. Although east coast fever had not appeared in or near the reserve and the cattle at Sabi Bridge had no contact with any other, either when at home or when travelling, yet in their ignorance of local conditions and amid the general prevailing panic over the disease, the authorities – to be on the safe side – considered it best to prohibit all movements of cattle throughout the country. Trekking had to be confined within the limits of the farm on which the animals were located. This last inhibition gave me an idea. Having travelled to Pretoria and done the round of such government offices as were concerned, I eventually succeeded in getting the whole Sabi Game Reserve officially regarded as one farm; whereby, and in happy possession of the necessary written authority, I was able to carry out my inspection tours for the next ten years without the impending fear of arrest. In the ultimate event, thanks to our own very strict regulations, which, under heavy penalties, denied entrance to all human beings and domestic animals, the Sabi and Shingwedsi game reserves were almost the only areas in the Transvaal in the days of the disease's widespread virulence that escaped any visitation by east coast fever.

Just when things seemed at last to be quietening down, I received an urgent cable from the War Office ordering me to return at once and report myself in London, since my period of secondment had expired and I was required to rejoin my regiment. I was torn this way and that: on the one hand lay a reasonable prospect of commanding a crack cavalry regiment within possibly three years; on the other was the Call of Africa. I could not bear the thought of abandoning the little child I had tended from babyhood just as it had begun to toddle, or, to employ another metaphor, I felt I would resemble a captain deserting his ship while it was threading its way amid dangerous shoals. I temporised by obtaining six months' leave from the Native Affairs Department and departed for England to ascertain how I might react to a military atmosphere. I think what really decided me in the end, were letters from various friends in South Africa, accompanied by press cuttings, which showed that all sorts of strings were being pulled to get me deposed in favour of someone else, and that a kind of defamatory campaign was in progress. I began to develop a certain hitherto unsuspected strain of obstinacy. If I were to resign under such conditions, a wrong interpretation would be placed on my action, and moreover I simply could not bear the idea of anyone else handling, and perhaps killing, my nursling. So, not without regret, I severed my active connection with military service and returned to the Transvaal.

CHAPTER FIVE
1905 TO 1909

CRITICS; FRASER AT SABI BRIDGE; A CHANGE OF DEPARTMENTS;
TAKEOVER OF THE BORDER CUSTOMS POLICE AND SELATI RAILWAY;
FRICTION OVER NATIVE AFFAIRS: BIRTH OF THE 'GREAT IDEA'; QUEST
FOR BURIED TREASURE; FIRST WHITE RIVER SETTLEMENT; A VISIT TO
INHAMBANE; FIRST TRANSVAAL ELECTIONS; CONCERNING THE STAFF;
SELATI RAILWAY RECONSTRUCTION; THE COMING OF UNION

IN JUNE 1905 I FOUND myself once more back at the Sabi Game Reserve.
My return seemed to dispel the agitation, though disappointed would-be
wardens and persons with axes to grind from time to time continued to voice
in the press their disagreement with the policy followed in the management
of the reserve. These plaints usually struck the same note. 'Why have all the
lions, wild dogs and crocodiles not been killed? The game will soon be non-
existent.' Critics – since the institution of the Kruger National Park, friendly
and would-be helpful critics – have followed the same line to the present
day, and I have no doubt that in twenty years' time, supposing the national
park to be yet in existence, the newspapers of the country will still publish
similar warnings from anxious amateur experts.

Major Fraser had been officiating at Sabi Bridge. His *métier* was not
administration; he shone more lustrously in situations demanding robust
physical qualities. In fact, as he said himself, he 'did not come here to be a
damned clerk' – a statement which appeared to be only too well justified
when it came to gathering up the broken threads. However, no really serious
harm had been done: Pretoria was mollified; the ruffled feelings of neighbouring officials – including those of the general manager of the Selati railway – were gradually soothed. The latter, in the person of Jules Diespecker,
to my regret – for we were good friends in reality – died in the following

year, and after a short interval I was installed, in my official capacity under the Government, as his unpaid successor, with the duty of burning firebreaks each year around the various wood-and-iron buildings along the railway line. My appointment, of course, included the asset of free and unrestricted use of the railway for my trolleys, and it was a proud moment when I first rumbled into Komatipoort with none to question my right, the 'boys' chanting a triumphant chorus.

The game reserves had now changed departments and we were taken under the aegis of the Colonial Secretary, corresponding to what later became the Department of the Interior. Sir Godfrey Lagden, who had been overseas at the time the alteration took place, was rather hurt about it as he had looked on the reserve as his adopted child. However, apart from sentiment, the change undoubtedly made for greater efficiency. The administration of the general game laws of the country had, since the peace, been under the Colonial Secretary. Hitherto it had been necessary for the Native Affairs Department to send every little bit of reserve legislation to him for approval before it could take effect and hence had arisen much of the delay in getting our regulations promulgated.

The Colonial Secretary was at that time Mr Patrick Duncan, later to be a prominent cabinet minister of the Union Government, and his assistant was Mr Moor, a warrior from Ceylon of great efficiency, but one whom it was well for his clerks to approach with circumspection during the earlier hours of office work each morning. His attitude to myself and my work was always one of amused tolerance and he was never tired of telling me it was 'doomed' and that I ought to seek other employment.

In 1906, Mr Furley, the Border Customs Officer at Komatipoort, died rather suddenly. After the dispersal of Steinacker's Horse at the end of 1902, the Customs Department took over their frontier posts as far as the Olifants River, and Mr Furley, with a personnel of ten native customs guards, was placed in charge. Furley was an old lowveld resident, a relic from the railway construction days, whose name appears more than once in the late Sir Percy Fitzpatrick's books, *Jock of the Bushveld* and *The Outspan*. Any species of dual control, especially when it is a matter of dealing with tribal natives, can seldom be satisfactory. By friendly personal relations with Furley it had been possible to get along, so far, without any friction, other than that which inevitably sometimes occurs between police 'boys' of two organizations operating in the same area. But it seemed to me that this relatively satisfactory state of things might not continue with a stranger in the post; that there might even arise a state of mutual semi-hostility which would be bad for both sides. We should expect the customs police to observe our regulations, which might sometimes incommode them; while on their side they might submit reports of uncalled for interference against us to their new officer.

Nor did I want an official unconnected with game preservation to have the right to travel about in the reserve armed, at his own sweet will, vested with authority, and no doubt accompanied by other similar officials or friends. Definitely it would not do. Fortunately I happened to be in Komatipoort at the time, and going straight to Pretoria I sought a private interview with the Director of Customs and offered to save his Department £500 a year, the amount of the salary involved, by undertaking the work gratis, provided I got the approval of my own department for doing so. He fell in with the idea at once, and so did Mr Moor. Within the next few weeks I took over ten excellent native police, sixteen good lowveld transport donkeys with an attendant, and a couple of salted horses. Moreover, I now drew 2 000 lbs of mealie meal per month as rations for the new native police. By the new arrangement the respective duties of the game reserve and customs police were interchangeable; that is, while the latter acted in all ways as native rangers, the former became responsible, when stationed at border posts, for carrying out such customs work as the prevention of opium and firearms smuggling. Since we had suffered from a serious shortage both of transport and of native police, this reinforcement, coupled with the dispersal of all apprehension of future disagreement between the departments, was most welcome. Some of these native police after more than thirty years' service, are still working in the Kruger National Park.

In furtherance of the policy of eliminating dual control, I had got the white and native rangers duly sworn in as police, invested, within the boundaries of the reserve, with the full powers of white and native constables respectively. It was arranged that the South African Police (or South African Constabulary as they were then called) should have no patrolling duties within our boundaries and should operate, in case of any serious crime, only through the medium of the corporal stationed at Sabi Bridge as clerk of the court and public prosecutor, who was under my practical control. By arrangement with the land companies I had acquired full control over all natives living on their farms within the game reserve. There remained only the Native Affairs Department. Our native residents had to pay their taxes to the native commissioners of the different magisterial districts in which the reserve was situated, and these officials were, nominally at least, the executive authorities responsible for native administration. After the first year or two I was able to save them the trouble of making tax collecting expeditions to the reserve, either by collecting on their behalf, or by sending the natives to their stations to pay there; but neither was a very satisfactory method.

Natives are adepts at playing off one master against another where divided authority holds place, and a great deal of my time was spent in cultivating friendly relations with my official neighbours (the nearest some days' journey distant, as things then were) and in arranging a *modus vivendi* with each. Even so, misunderstandings and mutual recriminations were all too frequent. A gang of natives would, for instance, be arrested while poaching, and such of them as succeeded in escaping, would then make straight for their appointed native commissioner, carrying a piteous tale of how they had been sitting harmlessly in their villages, when the brutal emissaries of 'Skukuza' had suddenly pounced upon them, beaten them, maltreated their women, and pilfered their goods. There being no telegraphic or other rapid means of communication between the two offices, often the first thing that brought the matter to my notice would be a warrant for the arrest of several of my own police on a serious charge. Occasionally, indeed, the arrest would be summarily effected at some remote point by the orders of a native commissioner, and the native rangers lodged in gaol before I knew anything about it, or had any opportunity of stating the other side.

Thus it was only by personal and friendly contact, whenever the opportunity occurred, that I was able to arrange (more or less) that when such reports were made, my office should be advised before action was taken, and much of course depended upon the disposition of the official who happened to be concerned. At that period the native commissioners had their own native police lent them from the constabulary, and acting entirely under their orders. An absurd position; but it was a good many years before I could get it altered.

It was shortly after my return to the Sabi Game Reserve in 1905 that inspiration came to me; that I suddenly saw myself as guardian of a trust, and my charge as a little maiden with a possibly important future before her. I remember I was sitting one day in Hannemann's Hotel at Komatipoort when a gentleman, who was one of the old-timers and, though a good personal friend of mine, not particularly favourable to game preservation, remarked, 'When is this reserve of yours going to be thrown open for shooting?' I said I did not know, but I hoped never. 'What!' he exclaimed. 'Do you mean to tell me that the Government is going to spend thousands of pounds every year just to keep game? What is the use of it anyhow? And even if the Government does so, you mark me, the public won't stand it! Some day this lowveld will be opened up, and then where will you be?'

Although I had heard a good deal of the same kind of thing before, somehow on this particular occasion it set me thinking deeply. After all, what goal were we striving for? In common with everyone else in the country who had devoted any thought at all to it, I had hazily accepted the idea that some day – I hoped a long way ahead – parts at least of the reserve, when fully stocked, would be hired out for some kind of controlled shooting. In those days to be shot eventually was the sole end for which wild animals were supposed to exist. On the other hand, it did seem a waste of time and money if all the labour and care of the last three years, not to speak of the £15 000 or so which already had been spent, was ultimately merely to provide hides and biltong for a section of the local public, with the result that in two or three years we should be back where we had been at the beginning, and, if any game at all was to survive, with all the work to do over again. I knew that most people frankly thought the whole thing childish and a waste of government money which might be more profitably employed.

What then exactly was I working for, beyond the mere enjoyment of the life itself and the interest inseparable from all development? While in London I had been a good deal in touch with wildlife preservation matters which were then beginning to arouse interest in certain circles, mainly through the efforts of Mr E.N. Buxton, who had shortly before founded the Society for the Preservation of the Fauna of the Empire. I had incidentally heard a good deal about the American national parks and of their success as a public attraction. Would it conceivably be possible to wean the South African public from its present attitude towards the wild animals of its own country, which was that of regarding them either as a convenient source of exploitation or as an incubus hindering the progress of civilization? It seemed pretty hopeless. The lowveld was wild, dangerous, unhealthy; there were not many scenic attractions; few people had any interest in wild animals unless they were dead. There were no roads either in, or leading to, the reserves, and fortunately so, since they would only have provided easy access for shooting parties. There was no money for development, nor likely to be. In fact, at the commencement of each financial year I gave a sigh of relief when I found our small grant of £5 000 still on the estimates, a sum which barely sufficed to pay salaries and wages with nothing over to construct dwellings for the staff, or to carry out the hundred-and-one improvements I had in mind. Government, in fact, beyond paying the monthly wage bill left us in the main to shift for ourselves. But for the debris of the abandoned railway, and the various remains of old buildings scattered about, the former owners of which had disappeared, we should have been very hard put to it. The former provided picks, shovels, axes and wheelbarrows, besides quantities of nondescript scrap metal, the latter mainly more or less serviceable sheets of corrugated iron. Yet government was more sympathetic on the whole than the public.

Obviously one could just carry on and hope; but at least I had now a definite goal to work for, which was much to the good. I sent for and read all the literature available concerning the American national parks, especially the Yellowstone, and was astonished at the vast amount of money which the United States government thought it worth while to spend on it, and at the public enthusiasm displayed. The American public must surely be very different from ours! The main object at present must be to use every effort to increase our depleted fauna, hoping that some day it might be recognized as a definite asset; as something more admirable alive than dead. Long years – more than twenty in fact – were to pass before the goal then visualized was attained, and many set-backs, disappointments, and dangers to the reserves were to intervene. But the then incredible thing did actually come to pass, and I shall always think of that day in Hannemann's Hotel as a red-letter one, on which first faintly dawned the Idea which later found its culmination in the creation of the Kruger National Park, and of Hannemann himself as *deus ex machina*.

An outstanding feature of those early years was the 'Great Buried Treasure Quest', better known as the 'Hunt for the Kruger Millions'. It provided the staff with a good deal of quiet amusement, which in some degree compensated for the trouble it caused us.

Rumour had it that in the year 1900 the republican government treasure, amounting in value to approximately two millions in bar gold and specie, had been buried for safety at some point within the Sabi Game Reserve. Varying accounts of the manner of its disposal were current: two men in a Cape cart had transported and hidden it at dead of night; a commando had brought it along in an ox wagon; local natives had been employed to dig the necessary hole, had then been shot and their bodies thrown on top of the treasure to ensure their silence! The site was said to be marked by a piece of wood nailed on a tree; by a cairn of stones; by some peculiar marks made on the ground; or, there were no marks but an old native woman knew the secret. At the beginning of the quest no one could be found who had actually been present, but plenty of people possessed a friend who 'knew someone who had taken part'. At a later date, as will be seen, more personal knowledge was claimed.

Few paused to calculate the amount of transport required to carry so huge a load of gold, though allowing 6 000 lbs to a full-sized buck wagon, it would have required quite a fleet even of those ponderous vehicles to convey it. Knowing from experience how little can be done by white men in the wilder parts of Africa without the ubiquitous, and in his own sphere omniscient, native learning all about it practically at once, I had my doubts almost from the beginning. However, wondering if there might be at least some kind of foundation for a rumour which was then so widely credited, I used sometimes to broach the subject to those of our local inhabitants who lived near one or other of the selected sites. This always aroused amusement: 'Skukuza, you can't really think that white men could bury anything, even a small thing, in the bush and we not know all about it. Of course we should know, and the moment they had gone away, we should have dug to see what they had put there. It is foolishness. Why, we always followed their spoor

Stevenson-Hamilton's thatched office at Sabi Bridge in 1906.
The lack of a flag pole did not deter the warden from flying
the Union Jack.

117

and searched the smallest camp as soon as it had been abandoned to see if anything had been left behind.' The locality of the hidden treasure varied even more widely than the method of its disposal.

The first on the scene was Captain De Bertodano, who had been a member of the British headquarters intelligence staff. He arrived in the middle of 1903, accompanied by several ex-officers and burghers of the republican forces, who presumably knew something of the country and no doubt had some notion of where the treasure – supposing there to be any – was most likely to have been interred. The object of the expedition was supposed to be a close secret and they wrapped all their movements in mystery, but of course it was not long before everybody in the lowveld knew all about it. As this was the first any of us had heard concerning buried treasure, the staff were as much thrilled as everybody else, and continued to be so, until the close enquiries we soon set on foot convinced us of the futility of the search. This party hung about the Lebombo for several months, being well provided with government transport and stores. In fact, it was the first and last of the treasure-hunting expeditions which had practical official backing and so may be regarded as the most important of all those quests.

This was the beginning. Very soon the whisper 'Buried Treasure' began to penetrate to all parts of South Africa. Through the winters of 1904, 1905 and 1906 we were inundated with parties of treasure-seekers, who, spurred on by unquenchable optimism, dug and searched frantically in the most widely separated places. 'Why,' asked the natives more than once, 'do these white men come and try to cultivate such barren pieces of land and at the wrong time of year?' A great many more parties would have arrived than actually did so, but for our regulations, which fortunately prohibited all entry to the game reserve except by special permit and forbade the carrying of firearms under any circumstances. This last restriction eliminated all would-be biltong hunters and confined the applicants to the bolder spirits among the genuine treasure seekers, those who were prepared to brave – unarmed – lion and other dangers in the pursuit of wealth. One party consisted of 'Scientific Mystics', and their plan of campaign was to sit down in camp at a central spot and await a message from someone in Johannesburg, who at the right moment was to notify them where to look.

There was a period when the Crocodile River was the strongest magnet. Thence, in 1904, came our greatest thrill. One of the parties, digging along the river bank, struck a lead of old telegraph wire, which, followed along by trenching, ended within a distance of fifty feet at an iron safe. The treasure at last! The safe was in good order and locked. The South African Constabulary corporal on duty with the party (the Government still half believed the story and claimed the lion's share of any find) telegraphed to Pretoria, and by the next train a contingent of armed men arrived to guard the gold while in transit to the strongroom of a bank. Only then, before the eyes of a crowd of eager spectators, was the safe forced – and found to contain some bundles of consignment notes connected with the railway construction twenty years before! This rather shook the confidence of the Government and for a long time afterwards the practice of providing police escorts ceased.

However, if the seekers themselves went unrewarded, at least it is an ill wind that blows good to no one. A new profession arose, that of 'Treasure Guide'. It was exclusive in numbers and confined to not more than half a dozen lowveld 'old hands'. The usual procedure was to haunt some place of public resort – such as a bar – where mysterious hints could be dropped into likely ears. When a fish seemed likely to bite, the guide would explain that he himself was the only man now left alive who could point out exactly where so much wealth lay buried; all others who might say they knew the place were frauds; it was quite simple, merely a matter of going there and digging. He would, of course, have gone himself without telling anyone, but unfortunately he had no money to get him there and was therefore forced to take someone into his confidence. So it was generally arranged that the stranger, always of course a man of some means, should either by himself, or in combination with some friends who were let into the secret, fit out the necessary expedition. The guide for his part received, in addition to a promised share of the treasure, a fixed remuneration for the period spent on the search, and of course free living.

At first these expeditions would seek various spots as the fancy of the guide might suggest, but latterly a fixed itinerary seems to have been adopted, and each guide had his favourite locality – the most successful of the band usually taking his party to the neighbourhood of a solitary koppie just north of the Sand River and about twenty miles from Sabi Bridge. On arrival, several days would be spent searching for the direction board, which the guide said he had himself nailed to a tree when the treasure was buried. Eventually he would admit that in course of years it must have been burnt or otherwise destroyed. However, the treasure was certainly somewhere within half a mile, or at most a mile and so digging operations would commence. These would last until the party became discouraged or the food gave out, when they would trek back to civilization, either disillusioned, or to make preparations for a fresh effort. Sometimes, before the industry was put on a proper footing, two guides – each the one and only holder of the essential knowledge – would lead their respective parties to the same place at the same time, when they would have to find some kind of mutual explanation, such as that they had not met since the war, and each thought the other dead. Of course the longer the search lasted the better for the guide. One day I came across Mr X, a well-known guide, bringing down what I knew to be his third party that same winter. I said, 'Well, here you are again!' 'For God's sake, major,' he replied, looking nervously round, 'not a word. I am a poor man and have a large family to support.'

I am sure most of these treasure guides really believed that there was money hidden somewhere, and that if only they could get the public to persevere long enough something would eventually be discovered. When General Smuts became Colonial Secretary in 1907 and I brought up the matter, he said at once that if any treasure had been buried he would have known all about it; that the whole thing was nonsense, and that he would stop all permits for the purpose to the game reserve. Thereafter we had a rest for a few years. After Union, when the game reserves fell under the control of the Transvaal Provincial Council, permits to seek treasure were again granted; but the 'kick' had gone out of the movement. Some of the old guides were dead, others had abandoned their profession in despair and entered other fields of activity. The palmy days were gone when treasure-guiding provided not only a pleasant holiday in the wilds, but even a livelihood to a small and deserving body of men. The public was no longer enthusiastic. Yet from time to time there came reminders that the old hope still burned in some breasts.

Shortly after the conclusion of the South African War, a scheme was devised for settling a number of discharged soldiers on the land. One of the sites chosen was the White River area, lying among the hills to the west of the Sabi Game Reserve. It is fine, open, healthy country, about three thousand feet above sea level, in what is known as middle-veld. Prior to the war it had consisted of unallotted government land, occupied by a sprinkling of Boer *bywoners*, or squatters without any titles to the land they occupied, who had subsisted mainly by transport riding and hunting in the neighbouring lowveld. The land was what is known as sourveld, which was probably why it had not been taken up by more well-to-do people. A benevolent government proceeded to construct an irrigation canal, and built the beginning of a township (later to form the nucleus of the present flourishing settlement) consisting of a store, hotel and manager's house. My friend Mr Tom Lawrence of Hilltop Farm was installed in the latter – at a generous salary, as he admitted himself. The settlers were then distributed in the immediate neighbourhood, each with a little plot of ground and a wood-and-iron cottage, which, together with all necessary farm tools, ploughs, wagons and oxen, were supplied free by the Government.

Nor did generosity stop there. Realizing that they would take some time to adjust themselves to what were, to them, novel conditions, each drew a small weekly allowance from public funds. The idea was market-gardening and mealies. The budding colonists were mostly ex-privates of the regular army, practically all from London or other big English cities, and although it is possible that some of them may have seen a ploughed field in their own country, it is reasonable to suppose that these were the exceptions. The result was such as might have been expected. Mr Lawrence did his best. A weekly market for the sale of produce was held every Saturday at the new hotel and was attended by all the settlers, since even if they had produced nothing in the course of the week, at least they had the important duty of drawing their government allowance. The equally pleasant one of spending this cash consumed Saturday, in some cases also Sunday night, but in the course of Monday or Tuesday most of them had managed to get back to their plots to await impatiently the coming of the next blissful weekend.

After a couple of years of this Arcadian existence, there came a rude shock. Government suddenly bethought itself that its settlers must by this time be well established and making good profits, so the allowance was stopped. An indignation meeting was held: 'How can we live if we have no money?' Mr Lawrence wearily hinted that he had done his best to show them how to make money for themselves. It was not a popular suggestion. Still, there were some assets: a ready local market for farm implements and tools at give-away prices. But one cannot live indefinitely on capital, and when finally the iron roofs of their houses had also gone, the military settlers gradually disappeared, some indeed, like the Arabs, 'stealing silently away in the night'. In the end, Mr Lawrence wound up the affairs of the settlement and returned to his own farm. Wolhuter bought the manager's house and his mother and sisters went to live there. The *bywoners* watered their trek oxen at the irrigation canal, and White River sank back for many years to its former placid serenity.

At the end of 1905 I went on a mission to the Inhambane district of Portuguese East Africa to endeavour to obtain some eland, animals which were believed to be extinct in the game reserve. It was an interesting trip in a delightful country, where everything seemed to grow and flourish of itself; the excellent roads were even lined for miles with pineapples growing three feet apart. As usual, the Portuguese proved themselves delightful hosts; indeed, their hospitality was at times almost embarrassing.

Deeply impressed on my memory is a visit to the commandant of a place called Muena. He was ample in person. Indeed, I should have been sorry even to guess at his waist measurement. In manner, he was heartiness and joviality personified. His house stood in the middle of a grove of closely planted shade trees, and extending from it like the spokes of a wheel, of which it formed the hub, were four paths. The ends of these paths were connected by a circular road – the tyre of the wheel. The whole circumference would be about four hundred yards. At the point where each 'spoke' joined the 'tyre' a canework bench stood under a big tree, each bench effectually concealed from the next by the dense covert. Around the circumference of the 'wheel' the commandant was used to take his daily constitutional and, arriving successively at the end of each path, he would sit down on the bench and clap his hands. Instantly would come speeding down the path from the house two native servants, one bearing a small round table, the other a bottle of light port wine and the necessary glasses. The table set down in front of him, he would drink a glass of wine, smoke a few cigarettes and rest awhile before pursuing his leisurely way to repeat the ritual at the next point a hundred yards on, and so forth till the circuit was complete and he had got through the best part of a bottle of port.

On the occasion of my visit we faithfully went through the function, and then adjourned to the 1 o'clock meal which the Portuguese call breakfast. This lasted about two hours and consisted of at least nine courses, mostly of the same goat, served in various guises. Already slightly dizzy from the port, I found that I was expected to face an assortment of liquors, beginning with red *collares* and ending with liqueurs – beer and port coming in at odd times between. This task accomplished, I hopefully anticipated a rest. But no! The meal and its concomitants seemed to have endowed my host with fresh vigour and turning to me with a happy smile, he asked if, like many Englishmen, I was fond of game shooting. 'Ah, I thought so. I also love the sport.' 'Where do you generally hunt, Commandant?' I asked naively, not picturing this Falstaffian figure toiling through the bush. 'Why, where do you think, but just here. See, you are puzzled. I will show you, but first let us get the rifle.'

From amid a heap of odds and ends in one corner of the room he proceeded to select an ancient and neglected-looking kind of rook rifle, remarking, as with many fat chuckles he picked it out, 'Ah, here he is – my old friend – but first it is necessary we have a little practice, and then we will go and shoot the game.' So having proceeded out of doors, we took turns for what seemed a long time in shooting at a mark, without any more conspicuous success than might have been anticipated under the circumstances. Bullets, in fact, flew everywhere but in the right direction.

At last my host pronounced us sufficiently practised for more serious business. Notwithstanding that all I wanted from heaven or earth at that moment was to throw myself on the ground and fall fast asleep, I was yet intensely curious and so displayed, I hope, the requisite eagerness. After we had gone a little way through the wood, we suddenly came to an enclosure of perhaps fifty yards square, shut in by wire netting twelve feet high. Within, amid long grass and small bushes, were running about a great many guineafowl, francolin, bustard, and other ground birds, all with their wings clipped to prevent them from flying over the wire; also various hares, duiker and steenbok. 'Ha!' cried the commandant, his eyes glowing in anticipation. 'Now you shall see how game should be killed. You English go out in the forest and make yourselves hot and tired, and perhaps after all shoot nothing. But, as for me, I just stay at home and drink my *vinho*, while my servants bring here all the live game I require. So when I have the desire to hunt, there is no labour.' With these words he handed me the weapon. 'Now make a good shot. Let us have an international competition!' I made the best excuse I could think of, saying I would much like first to see how he did it. Nothing loath, he took back the rifle, advanced slowly to the wire, pushed the barrel through the mesh, and, after a long aim, slew, at a distance of three yards or less, an unfortunate duiker, which apparently was approaching to be fed.

Gratified at my congratulations on the excellence of his marksmanship, he now insisted on my taking my turn. Knowing if I refused he would be likely to take offence, I promptly complied by immolating a francolin, reflecting that it was, after all, no worse a deed than killing a domestic bird for the pot; also I picked out one which was to me a new species. Honour satisfied, we left the deer park, and repaired to the private natural history museum, where he showed me his trophies, rather obviously self set-up. Thence we passed on, by way of a splendid vegetable garden, to orchards where peaches, mangoes, pineapples and bananas grew in profusion – the soil amazingly fertile and tropical insect pests apparently largely absent. A huge dinner on the same lines as the luncheon completed the day, and thereafter, having bidden farewell to my kind host, I rode, much to my benefit, all through the night under brilliant moonlight, to the next station. Here the commandant kept a young eland, so tame that it ran after, and licked the hands of, the passers-by. A small native boy habitually rode about on it, and the commandant announced his intention of doing the same when it was capable of bearing his weight – a time, one felt justified in concluding, very much in the future.

In the event, I was able to transfer this same young bull and a female calf to the reserve, where, in domesticity at Sabi Bridge, they multiplied eventually into a herd of ten. These animals were just as easy to deal with and to handle as domestic cattle, and I had dreams of putting them to the same uses. The drawback was that the neighbourhood not being country natural to their species, they had to be fed artificially during the winter months, and this duty having been neglected while I was absent during the course of the Great War, I found on my return that all except one had died. In the meantime, however, eland had trickled back to the northern areas of the reserve from Portuguese East Africa and by 1920 had become well established. The loss of the domestic herd was therefore of less account than it otherwise would have been.

Early in 1907 we held our first Transvaal general election since the war. Sabi Bridge had been constituted a sub-district of Barberton. There were two voters on the roll, Healy and myself. We both held official positions in connection with the election. On Healy, as the police corporal in charge, devolved the duties of guarding the ballot box throughout the day, and afterwards of conveying it safely to Barberton, where the votes were to be counted. I was in chief official control during the course of the election. I cannot now recollect the exact nature of my own responsibilities, but I know that the instructions concerning them formed a thick and heavy pile of printed and typed foolscap.

At 7 a.m. on the fateful morning, Healy, in full uniform, brown belts, revolver holster, and leggings polished until they shone like mirrors, appeared at the door of the mud hut which was at once the Court House and my office as Special Justice of the Peace. Behind him stood two native policeman, one bearing a large black japanned tin ballot box, the other staggering under the weight of vast sealed packages containing voting papers.

The box was placed on the table and Healy duly mounted guard. I had intended to record my vote, consistent with my dignity, at a later hour of the day. Man proposes but God disposes. Within an hour, having run foul of a spitting cobra, I was in bed with my eyes bandaged and taking no further interest in the proceedings. Healy therefore, having presumably himself recorded the solitary vote cast in our sub-district, duly departed on the following morning for Komatipoort, the precious ballot box with him on the trolley, and, I think, a rifle in his hand in addition to the revolver at his belt – the orders to the police were very strict on the subject.

However, misfortunes were not yet at an end. During the period since the line had been last used, a large ant-heap had sprung up across the rails. Running downhill at considerable speed, the trolley struck this fair in the middle and was hurled down an embankment – which unfortunately existed at the spot – together with Healy, the natives, and the ballot box, which last burst open in the fall. Luckily no one was hurt but the delay was so considerable that he lost the train at Komatipoort and kept everyone waiting in Barberton, since the counting of the votes could not commence till the tally of ballot boxes was complete.

At this election, Mr R.K. Loveday, who had been the member for the district in the old Volksraad, was again elected by a large majority. During the course of his election campaign he visited Komatipoort, where the local butcher and one of the storekeepers were insistent that the price of their votes must be his promise to see that the game reserve was abolished. The butcher's motive was a not unnatural one, and I think the other petitioner had recently made an unsuccessful application for an open road to and from the reserve to be made past his store. Anyhow, Mr Loveday, having been largely responsible for the original proclamation of the reserve in 1898, was hardly the best man to approach with a request of this nature.

I had for a long time been trying to get another ranger appointed. It was not possible to maintain less than three of these officers south of the Sabie River; we were there too close to settled country, with the multiplicity of disputes entailed thereby. In the far-off Shingwedsi, which it was beyond hope at present to supervise adequately, and where, besides, game was still scarce, one man was for the time sufficient. But the four thousand square miles of country between the Sabie and Olifants rivers containing all the private land and the majority of the native population, cried out for the personal attention of a special officer. I was anxious to get Healy, the policeman at Sabi Bridge, appointed. He was about to take his discharge and seemed to be eminently suitable for the work. With some difficulty I got Pretoria's approval in principle for the installation of an additional ranger but the appointment did not immediately function. Moor, the assistant Colonial Secretary, had wanted to put in his own man, to whom I objected, because however suitable he might be in other respects, I did not think that with only one leg he would be of much use as a ranger, and so the matter fell through for the time being.

After the Transvaal received Responsible Government, General Smuts became the head of my department, and very soon he began to display a keen interest in the reserves and in everything connected with game preservation generally. I began again to agitate about the new ranger but it was not a propitious moment. In 1906 an Indian Treasury official had been sent to effect economies in the Transvaal civil service, which was undoubtedly at that time overstaffed and overpaid. He was known as the 'Retrencher General' among the younger civil servants. Accordingly, it looked as though not only would I fail to get another ranger, but that I might even have my present staff reduced. General Smuts was friendly, but quite firm on the necessity of retrenchment. I felt it would be really a misfortune to lose Healy, who knew the country and the natives, had passed through his noviatiate in malaria and was temperamentally suited for ranger's work. Eventually, with the help of Mr Gorges, who now sat in Moor's chair, I worked out a plan under which, by reducing my own salary, curtailing all the then very liberal transport and climatic allowances of myself and the staff, and temporarily retrenching some of the native police, it was possible not only to effect the necessary economies, but to allow of the appointment of a new ranger. Healy was therefore duly gazetted early in 1908. It became practicable in due course again to raise the numbers of the native staff to the level of efficiency, and I myself was able to boast at a later date that I held a probably unique position in having concluded twenty-five years of government service on a lesser salary than that with which I had started!

The years from 1905 to 1909 showed a record of steady progress. The lowveld was still largely *terra incognita* to the citizens of the Transvaal, let alone of South Africa, and now that the annual winter grazing and hunting expeditions of the farmers thereto were at an end, excepting for our treasure seekers practically no white men visited the country. Our resident population, moreover, was still confined to the railway and other officials, who, with the nondescript 'old-timers', composed the inhabitants of Komatipoort; a few farmers along the south bank of the Crocodile River, plus a handful of

Some Africans resident in the game reserves were frequently
recruited as police, their duty being to patrol as trackers and
also to report on and prevent poaching.

storekeepers and land company agents scattered sparsely below the
Drakensberg on the western edge of the reserve. The lowveld still maintained its sinister reputation for being a death-trap in summer.

By this time, the natives within the reserve had ceased to cause us any
anxiety. They recognized that they remained tenants conditionally only on
their observing the regulations and assisting the staff. They had settled down
to the new conditions; the younger men enlisted in the police and were sent
to posts sufficiently far removed from their respective friends and relatives.
In those days there still existed strong mutual mistrust between people
belonging to different clans of the Tsonga, to say nothing of the feeling
between all members of that tribe and the Swazi. It was therefore not difficult to place native policemen in localities where they would not be likely to
shield unduly the inhabitants.

Native police were provided with suitable and becoming uniforms and

there quickly grew up a strong feeling of *esprit de corps*, which later resulted in excellent individual work. The African native, properly treated and
given some sort of discipline, usually makes an admirable policeman or soldier. His tradition teaches him loyalty to whomever may be his chief for the
time being, and among the Shangane the memory of the strict regimental
system of the Zulu still lingered. The majority of our reserve native police
were loyal, trustworthy, courageous and hardy; all possessed some knowledge of bushlore, were well acquainted with the country, and were largely
immune from fever. They knew that they were paid to see that the game was
not poached, and whatever their secret thoughts may have been as to the sanity of such a policy, their actions were not in the least affected thereby; the
man who killed a buck was a criminal!

The first of our fatal casualties occurred in 1905, when a policeman called
Mehlwana was murdered by native Portuguese poachers whom he was no
doubt trying to arrest. This crime occurred in a lonely part of the Lebombo
hills, a mile or so on our side of the frontier, and from that time onwards all
patrols in that area consisted of at least two men. Later we had to arm our
people on duty there with rifles for self protection. As soon as the game
began to increase on the Transvaal side of the border, inroads from the
Portuguese country began and increased through the years, necessitating
always more patrolling and in larger parties, until at last the conditions for a
time amounted almost to those of guerilla warfare.

Notwithstanding the still considerable native poaching on the borders, the
game had responded in a really surprising way to the first chance it had ever
been given. Giraffe became quite numerous; wildebeest spread westwards
from a narrow strip under the Lebombo and began to reappear even at
Pretoriuskop, whence they had vanished for many years. All this encouraging success was largely due to the efficiency and zeal of the section rangers.
Wolhuter, with his life-long knowledge of the natives, of the wild animals,
and of the country, was in a class by himself. Duke, an old Cape Mounted
Policeman, and for a time a detective in the C.I.D., possessed an almost
uncanny knowledge of the native mind. When some animal had been illegal-
ly killed and no traces of the offenders were discernible, Duke was like a
bloodhound on the trail. Following devious ways, it was seldom he failed
ultimately to land the right men in court.

As in the higher spheres of espionage, so in our lowly one, women were
found often to be the most useful agents. De Laporte, though less of a native
linguist than the two first named, was yet able to command excellent service,

and in no section was better work done than in his. He was at his best in dealing with Europeans. A ready tongue and a pretty wit, combined with the requisite firmness and tact, made him at once popular and successful in dealing with our sometimes difficult white neighbours. Fraser, left to himself in his remote fastness, was solid and reliable, while, though he never attempted to utter a word in any language other than Anglo-Saxon, it was remarkable how deft his own 'boys' were to catch his meaning and to carry out his orders. In knowledge of wildlife as derived from practical observation, there were few who could equal him.

Healy was much the youngest of the staff, only about twenty-five years old when he left the South African Constabulary to become a ranger. He had more than a full share of the energy of youth. With only fourteen native police he controlled – and controlled admirably – an area of about four thousand square miles of wild country, through which the only means of progression was on horse-back, the belongings loaded on pack donkeys, the average pace three miles an hour and the usual day's march not over twenty miles. Yet we were able, at a pinch, to move faster than anyone else could in those days before mechanical transport invaded the lowveld.

Healy made a great impression on the natives and had a lot of influence with them. They never quite knew what he would do next. He was essentially Irish. He used to have a favourite greyhound bitch which he called Mary. One day while accompanying him she died from heat apoplexy at a point close to the track, about four miles from Sabi Bridge. Healy had a cairn of stones built at the spot, and the spruit nearby is universally now known as Inja-ka-Methephe, or 'Healy's Dog', a name likely to puzzle future generations. The same evening he had the remains brought into camp, and having collected all the natives, held a wake, whereat everyone had to mourn at the top of his voice during a considerable part of the night. The tombstone was a fine block of granite, on which were neatly carved the words, 'Erected by G.R. Healy in loving memory of Mary, aged three years', followed by the date. In recent times I have often heard tourists, after looking at the stone, remark how wrong it is to bring young children to live in the lowveld!

At one time he studied mesmerism and practised it successfully, up to a point, on his cook, but could not bring him round again when he thought it time to do so. His other followers gazed in horror-stricken silence; it was clearly witchcraft, and Healy acquired the reputation of one whom it was well not to offend. He himself was rather alarmed at his success, and thenceforth eschewed hypnotic science. For all his impetuosity he was cool in

129

emergencies and certainly owed his life to his having had the presence of mind to stand perfectly silent and rigid when, with an empty rifle in his hand, he found himself charged by a wounded lioness, which, awed by his perfect immobility, swerved from him almost at the last moment. He was resourceful, keen, full of initiative and never depressed, even after the most violent attacks of malarial fever, that most dispiriting of ailments.

Those were the men who composed the old staff of the game reserve, by whom the delicate infant was nourished towards maturity, to whose unnoticed and forgotten efforts the modern tourist owes what he sees today.

Early in the year 1909 I received an official intimation that the Selati railway was to be abandoned finally and the rails to be pulled up. A working gang might shortly be expected to come and carry out the task. I was on the point of starting for northern Zululand to ascertain how the Pongola reserve, where we still kept two native police under the unofficial control of the magistrate at Ingwavuma, was progressing. On my return a month later, I found

Around the time of Union in 1910, funds from the Transvaal's coffers were allocated to upgrade the accommodation of the warden and his game rangers. The new warden's office of 1909 was mosquito-proof and shaded by a wide veranda.

a number of railway men at Sabi Bridge, but learnt to my astonishment that during my absence there had been a change of policy and that instead of destruction, construction was in the air. Indeed, the line was to be remade and carried on to Pietersburg at once; Sabi Bridge was to be a bridge in fact, and not only in name; the permanent way was to cut through my block-house dining-room; the temporary working deviation through first my living hut and secondly my kitchen garden.

The reason for all these activities was that union was in the air. A conference was shortly to assemble at Cape Town to discuss details. The Transvaal was the only province which was not only not groaning under a burden of debt, but actually rejoicing in a budget surplus of £2 000 000. How to employ this for local benefit ere the greedy hands of the rest of South Africa could seize it? The first item was the Union government buildings, an extensive scheme designed to consume the greater part of the money, and next came the Selati railway, which might link up the northern Transvaal and later Rhodesia with the sea at Delagoa Bay by a route shorter than that to the Cape. Surely there might yet remain a few unallotted crumbs! I went to Pretoria, and there pointed out energetically that, up to date, we (the staff) had all been living for many years in a malignant climate, sheltered from the elements by nothing better than roughly thatched huts, native-made and unscreened either from mosquitoes or from any other kind of noxious insects and reptiles. There had always existed a deep-seated belief that the game reserve was only a temporary affair; that sooner or later it would be thrown open for shooting, and the staff thus no longer required. Under these circumstances – and rather to my surprise – the plea was favourably considered. Instructions were issued that mosquito-proof wood-and-iron houses were to be put up for all members of the staff living south of the Olifants River. (Fraser was not only beyond reach, but himself strongly protested against being 'forced to live in a damned birdcage'.) The necessary tenders were called for and so 'poor Cinderella' – as the Sabi Game Reserve was by then figuring in my thoughts – had the privilege of sharing to the extent of some £3 000 in the surplus wealth of the Transvaal!

The coming of the Union of South Africa seemed to hold out a possibility of bringing a step nearer realization my dream of a national park. If only the game reserves could be placed under some department of the main government of South Africa, they might be less susceptible to local – and usually antagonistic – influences, than were they to remain purely Transvaal belongings. They might even come to be regarded as national assets by the public!

Unfortunately, General Smuts had already left for Cape Town when I reached Pretoria, so the suggestion that the game reserves might find higher status had to be conveyed by proxy, which is seldom quite the same thing as urging a case personally. Probably it was a forlorn hope, doomed in any case to be overlooked amid the stress of weightier matters.

CHAPTER SIX
1910 TO 1914

THE APPROACH OF CIVILIZATION; CONSTRUCTION AND OPENING OF THE
SELATI RAILWAY; NEW AMENITIES; WINTER GRAZING; GAME FARM SCHEME;
AN ANNUAL ROUTINE; PROPOSED EXPLOITATIONS; THE WORLD WAR

MANY CHANGES OCCURRED DURING the year 1910. The game reserves, together with the general wildlife preservation of the province, were placed under the Transvaal administration, of which Mr Johann Rissik (Johannesburg's godfather) was the head. Nationalization remained still no more than a pleasant dream.

But what alteration in our local surroundings! Industrialism was at our very doors. It seemed as though the old peaceful aloofness of the lowveld was permanently shattered. With a railway cutting through its very middle, it was no longer a land apart, mysterious and unknown to all but its own few selected. Yet the state of affairs then deplored was, in after years, to be looked back upon with regretful longing as one of blissful tranquillity compared with the conditions which time in its fullness subsequently brought to us.

An iron railway bridge of nine spans now traversed the Sabie River; its supports high stone piers, whose incomplete foundations had once found use only as pedestals for the over-mature eggs which, from my seat in the over-looking blockhouse veranda, I had made my daily targets for rifle practice.

The well-known firm of Pauling & Co. were the contractors for the railway construction. The main camp of their employees from 1909 until 1912 was at Newington, an uninhabited government farm about twenty-five miles north from Sabi Bridge. A little town grew up – station buildings and workshops, canteen and store, a hospital with a resident doctor and sisters, the houses all of wood-and-iron protected against insect invasion by mosquito-

*In 1912 the Selati railway line between Sabi Bridge and
Komatipoort was extended as far as Tzaneen. It passed
through the Sabi Game Reserve and a major bridge crossed
the Sabie River near the warden's headquarters.*

proof wire gauze. Strict discipline was enforced. No liquor could be
obtained save at the company's own canteen, which was open only from
after work on Saturday until Sunday night. It was all very different from the
first construction twenty years earlier, and those of the old-timers still living
who had been patient supporters for many years of the bar of the hotel at
Komatipoort, suffered sad disillusionment in their belief that once the line
went ahead the good old days would come back. In fact, the very event to
which all had looked forward with so much happy anticipation, proved their
nadir. There were no pleasant sub-contractorships offering and few, if any,
obtained even a working job, as Pauling & Co. brought their own employees
with them. As its habitués faded away, Komatipoort gradually shed its old
individuality; it had to change with the changing times. Ichabod, in fact!

In the light of previous railway construction experiences in Africa, including that of the Selati railway itself, when the game had as a matter of course
always provided free meat and thus cheapened working expenses, there was
some cause to be anxious. Although no animals might legally be killed and
we had full power to enforce the law, yet, amid so large a crowd of invaders,

many of whom had served on other constructions under the old-fashioned go-as-you-please conditions, there were certain to be some ready to break through what they might consider unjust restrictions. I need not have worried. It was only necessary to explain how matters stood to the chief, Mr Jimmie Butler, for drastic orders to be issued to all subordinates; the penalty indeed for interference with game being instant dismissal, over and above the attaching legal penalties. In fact, from the first to last, the relations of the staff of the Sabi Game Reserve with that of the contractors were of the happiest. During some of this period, when the warden was absent on a 'busman's holiday' in East Africa, De Laporte had officiated most capably in his place. Apart from Duke (who was a grass-widower), De Laporte was at that time the only married member of our staff. He and his wife had been popular with all, and his tact, combined with a certain humorous firmness of which he was master, had kept the machinery running smoothly during a difficult time.

In 1912 the railway was completed as far as Tzaneen, about a hundred miles north of Sabi Bridge, and Pauling's contract came to an end. The total cost had been approximately £200 000 for over one hundred and fifty miles of line, as against £1 000 000 lost in 1893 over the original abortive construction of seventy-five miles. Though there had been naturally a good deal of malarial fever among the employees, the excellent arrangements made had reduced serious results to a minimum, and against the many deaths which accompanied the first construction, Pauling & Co. had hardly lost a man.

On November 7 the opening ceremony took place at Tzaneen, the then terminus of the railway. There were present many leading lights, local and other, the 'other' including Mr Hull and Sir Thomas Price, respectively Minister and General Manager of the Union railways, Mr Johann Rissik, the Transvaal Administrator, and a representative of the Governor of Mozambique. The temperature in the shade was 111° Fahrenheit; yet, although the ice for the champagne had either been forgotten or was insufficient for the large and thirsty company, the proceedings were conducted with the utmost enthusiasm, and the speeches conveyed a cheerful optimism regarding the future of the line, an optimism shown later to have been scarcely justified. It was a relief to learn that no one, on the journey through it, appeared to have been impressed by the pastoral or agricultural possibilities of the Sabi Game Reserve. Fortunately we were just at the end of a long period of drought and the country looked its very worst.

The line was now taken over by the South African Railways and Sabi Bridge found itself served by one train a week each way, the hour on both occasions being about 2 a.m. For some inscrutable official reason, the siding and water tank for the engine had been placed on the other side of the river amid uninhabited bush; while our side – the inhabited one – was not a scheduled stopping place. Thus, for some years we were dependent for the delivery of supplies and the taking up and setting down of passengers on the good nature of the guard of the train. If he did not happen to be in an amiable mood he could, for instance, 'deliver' fifty bags of mealie meal in the bush a mile away across the Sabie, whence our only means of getting possession of it – unless the river was very low at the time – would be to bribe the ganger to bring it over on his trolley, an act on his part liable to get him into serious trouble if found out. Of course, as soon as the railway construction began, I had been obliged to hand over both my trusty trolleys, and now, with only one connection a week with Komatipoort (and that involving sitting up at the siding until 2 a.m. over a campfire) I felt that the coming of civilization had altered my lot for the worse.

The railway had also been responsible for the death of my faithful cook and body servant, Ali Sharif, a Swahili who had been with me since 1903 and had accompanied me in all my travels to different parts of Africa since that date. His wife and child resided at a village across the Sabie River, and hearing that the child was sick, he essayed one night when his work was over to walk the three miles to visit it. He was crossing the railway bridge over the river, which he considered a safe proceeding since only one train per week ran, but unfortunately for him, two employees of Pauling & Co. were returning – it being Sunday night – from a jollification in Komatipoort, and, travelling at a great pace on their motor trolley, cut him down and killed him. (Encumbered by his long white robe, he had been unable to get out of the way.) One of our police 'boys', Jase, who was with him, escaped by swinging himself on to a girder of the bridge.

The houses for the staff were duly completed: five of them. They were made of corrugated iron, wood-lined, mosquito-proofed, and stood on concrete piers. We were well housed at last! I may say here that I have never seen any reason to alter my opinion that, for out-of-the-way places in hot countries, there is nothing to beat the double-roofed wood-and-iron house. It may be hot in the day, but its roof and walls quickly cool at night. Raised well from the ground, it is immune from snakes, scorpions and other unpleasant uninvited visitors. There is always a draught of air under it, and if you feel discontented with the site, you can take your house to pieces and set it up again complete, anywhere you like. Nowadays in South Africa things are rapidly levelling up to European conditions even in the lowveld. It is fashionable to decry this old-fashioned type and to erect what is called a permanent dwelling, perhaps of concrete, which retains the heat in summer and the cold in winter longer than any other known substance. Such a building, if given a thatched roof in addition, is probably, on a hot night after a hot day, the best substitute for a Turkish bath that could well be devised. Yet the Government's motive at that time in supplying us with wood-and-iron houses was probably less their habitable fitness than that if and when the reserve was abolished, they could be easily removed and disposed of elsewhere!

The building of Healy's house at Nwanedzi (later known as Satara), by two young German contractors, had been a long and arduous proceeding. It was fifty-five miles from the nearest point on the new Selati railway at Sabi Bridge, with no connecting road or track, and every bit of the material employed had to be conveyed in the warden's light wagon drawn by six oxen. It was one of the loneliest houses in South Africa – a tiny speck of white in the wilderness – the nearest white man's habitation being the other solitary house now at Sabi Bridge.

Following the industrial lead given us, we began to better communications all over the Sabi reserve. Rough wagon tracks were improved, and along them, about twenty miles apart, were built small standing camps, consisting of a couple of living huts for a white man, similar quarters for accompanying natives, a rough stable and a thorn zeriba to accommodate draught or pack animals. This system facilitated travelling, especially during the wet season when it obviated the necessity of carrying tents about. I made a great advance in my own mobility by the adoption of a Canadian buckboard drawn by a couple of ponies. I could thus carry all I required for several days in the way of bedding, supplies for myself and a native servant and forage for the ponies. The average rate of travel in the bush was more than doubled. A buckboard is an unsurpassed vehicle for getting about rough country. Its construction is so elastic that the front axle and wheels can be turned almost at right angles to the rest of it, without risk of locking; its body is so light, yet strong, that it hardly ever gets held up either in heavy ground or in rocks. In fact, I found it could penetrate almost anywhere except into the densest bush. On a fairly decent bit of road Whisky and Soda, the first two animals I broke to harness, could proceed comfortably at a hard gallop without the fear of a capsize, and indeed, we always took the steeper dongas or ravines

137

*Stevenson-Hamilton considered a Canadian buckboard –
large, light, strong and easily manoeuvred – an unsurpassed
vehicle for getting about in rough country.*

at this pace. Once, having missed the track, we suddenly came to the edge of a sand river having a precipitous drop of about five feet into the bed. There was no chance to pull up, so both the ponies jumped for it, the buckboard sailing happily behind and landing comfortably on all four wheels in the soft sand below, with no untoward result except that I was shot forward, and found myself bestriding Soda, the off-side pony, while the native rolled in the sand alongside.

Soda cherished a deeply rooted fear of lion, though so far as was known he had never had an adventure with one. His uncanny instinct for winding or sensing the presence of these animals even at a considerable distance made him, at night in camp, as useful as a dog. Sometimes, while jogging along slowly in the buckboard, without any preliminary warning he would dash forward at full speed, dragging his companion along with him, to be pulled up only after considerable trouble, snorting and panting. Very fortunately, on the only occasion when, while in harness, he really was in some danger, he did not seemingly appreciate that a lion was quite close to him. I was driving back from Tshokwane one afternoon and the ponies were just breasting the steep pull out from a sandy spruit. As we came level with a bush about three yards from the right of the track at the top of the rise, I caught a glimpse of something yellow disappearing behind it. Fifty yards on I pulled up, and taking the rifle walked back. Sure enough, behind the bush and quite close to the road, were the fresh pad marks of a lioness, and the flattened grass where her body had pressed to the ground. She had no doubt either winded or heard the ponies, and had been lying in wait for them. Only at the last moment had she become aware of the buckboard, no doubt to her a sinister-looking apparition, with two human beings, moreover, sitting on the top of it. In those days lion in the reserve were less accustomed to passing traffic than was the case later, and this one had not stood upon the order of her going; her tracks, followed for several hundred yards, betrayed her extreme haste. Had she felt compelled to act contrariwise, without doubt we should have been badly down on points, at the best a mauled pony and a smashed buckboard.

Healy was the only ranger who, at that period, realized the advantages of driving over riding, but his choice, a two-wheeled American sulky drawn by my old shooting pony Jantje, was a less dependable conveyance than the buckboard. It necessitated his sitting perched between two large wheels, with his face slightly below the level of his steed's quarters, and many were the adventures and hairbreadth escapes from complete catastrophe which they together passed through. Indeed, Healy's more or less unharmed survival was due largely to the methodical habits of Jantje, who knew that when anything unusual occurred, the first rule was to stand quite still, pending adjustment. This excellent habit had once undoubtedly saved his own life, when a black mamba, rushing unexpectedly across the path, paused directly underneath his belly, waving its head wickedly at me as I stood near by, unable under the circumstances to use my shotgun.

There now remained but one impediment to the smooth working of the administrative machinery – lack of full control over the native residents. On the company farms, by agreement with the absentee owners, the warden collected for them the ground rights and held their authority in regard to tenancy rights. But every native in the reserve had to pay his annual poll tax to the native commissioner of his magisterial district, and all those living on Crown lands were, for administrative purposes, nominally under the same official, who might live a hundred or more miles away and be personally unknown to them. The authority of the warden was limited to infractions of the law. For many years this system had resembled a simmering stew, with occasional bubbles reaching the surface.

In 1910, to continue the metaphor, the pot boiled over. Soon after Healy became the ranger north of the Sabie River, he discovered that a certain headman whose kraal lay in the centre of the best game country, was and doubtless always had been, systematically encouraging poaching, not only on the part of his own people, but also on that of members of his clan living in Portuguese territory. Mnyamane had a certain sinister reputation as *umthakathi* and evidence sufficient to justify a prosecution could not be obtained. De Laporte, who was at the time acting-warden, decided to have the kraal moved to near the western border, where game being then scarce less damage could be done. Mnyamane refused to budge and complained to the native commissioner. The latter told him to remain where he was and at the same time wrote officially, asking the warden by what authority he was interfering with the distribution of the natives in his district.

The news very soon got round that 'the Government was taking sides against Skukuza and the reserve' and immediately there was a great outbreak of game-killing, culminating in the arrest of our native sergeant by the commissioner's police on what proved to be a totally unfounded charge of assault. This provided the required concrete grievance which haply might be used towards remedying an intolerable situation. Immediately on my return from leave, I took the matter up with the departments concerned as strongly as possible, asking how it was expected the staff could carry on its duties of wildlife preservation in the face of this kind of official hostility. Luckily the Native Affairs Department proved amenable to argument, and to prevent further friction, appointed the warden *ex officio* native commissioner for the game reserves. This at once cleared the air and never afterwards was there any trouble of the kind.

The warden's new duties, which were of course financially unrewarded, included the collection of taxes from, and the general administration of, all told, about five thousand natives. Office work was more than doubled, and without the services of a special clerk, meant not only keeping registers up to date, but having to write out every native pass and tax receipt with one's own hands. Nevertheless, the change was entirely satisfactory, and not least welcomed by the natives themselves, who, accustomed in the past days to the undivided authority of a single chief, dislike nothing more than being responsible to two masters at the same time. Moreover, they greatly prefer a personally known ruler, to whom they can come for settlement of their disputes, to an authority living at a distance who must inevitably be a stranger to them.

It was in 1912 that the first clouds appeared on the horizon, presage of the storm which later was nearly to wreck the game reserves.

The first agreement with the land companies had been for five years and this had been extended for another similar period, which expired in 1912. The Transvaal was growing more prosperous. It might be possible to find purchasers for the uninhabited farms in the Sabi Game Reserve and some companies were tired of the arrangement with government. In short, as represented by the secretary of the Landowners' Association, they were not disposed to renew the agreement. I had many discussions with Captain Madge, the land manager of the company owning the most property, and personally sympathetic to the national park idea. We thought something might be made of the situation, provided the Union government could be induced to take over the company farms now included in the reserve. At a meeting between him, the Administrator and myself, the same system of farm exchange was discussed which took shape years later, that is to say, roughly, the bisection by a north and south line of the part of the reserve between the Sabie and Olifants rivers which contained all the private property, followed by a mutual bartering of farms, to result in all east of the line becoming the property of the Government, and all west of it that of the land companies. However, no definite agreement was arrived at.

One day when I happened to be in Pretoria, Mr Rissik sent for me. He sat with a map of the Sabi reserve spread out before him, and I knew at once from his expression as he looked at me through his spectacles, that something untoward was afoot. His first words, couched in rather apologetic terms, confirmed my fears. It appeared that recently pressure had been put upon him by certain farmers with a view to allowing them to resume the old winter grazing in the lowveld, which had been such a feature before the South African War and had been so fatal to the game. At present the applications were only for sheep grazing – the movements of cattle fortunately being restricted by the east coast fever regulations – and to enter a restricted area, namely, the country lying in the south-west of the reserve, extending from our western boundary to, and including, Pretoriuskop, a tract about forty miles long by ten wide.

Of course anyone could see it was only the thin end of the wedge, but since evidently the Administrator had already committed himself to some sort of undertaking, it was useless raising objections. The only course was to make the best bargain possible. I insisted that if this permission were given it should be on a proper basis; that the ground be divided into areas and a fee charged; while it must be clearly impressed on all that no shooting was to be allowed, and that the regulations would be strictly enforced. I thought it just possible that we might by these palliatives be able to stave off the worst for some years, when perhaps the situation might in some unexpected way take a favourable turn. Otherwise it surely meant the beginning of the end for the

Sabi reserve. What with the landowners reasserting their rights to the private land, and the Boer winter graziers occupying the government land, I could not see much room for game preservation in the future! For the time being, only this strip in the south-west corner between the Sabie and Olifants rivers, was in question. It had been added in 1903 and was not part of the original reserve of 1898, but it was a splendid game country, especially for sable and kudu, and Wolhuter had taken great trouble in nursing it. The numerous bushman paintings which the caves below Legogote mountain contained, showed that in the distant past it had been the favourite dwelling place for these hunters. The game, limited to small buck and bushpig in 1902, by 1912 embraced most of the larger kinds of antelope, and we naturally felt apprehensive concerning the undoing of our work.

Things evolved much as might have been expected. In the first year all went well. About a dozen lots were taken up at £5 for the season, from May to September, and nine thousand sheep baa-ed their way down to the Sabi reserve, the farmers for the most part sending employees to look after them. Firearms had to be allowed for the protection of the sheep from carnivora, though by stationing an extra ranger in the area, it was at first hoped that it might be possible to keep all destruction of predatory animals in the hands of the staff. Very soon – and not unnaturally – complaints arose about the restrictions, nor was the grazing all that had been anticipated. Many sheep died or were killed by carnivorous animals. In 1914, the fee having been raised to £10, no graziers came. In fact, it was not until 1917, when it was reduced to the original figure and the restrictions about shooting and grass burning greatly relaxed, that the farmers thought it worthwhile again to take advantage of the concession. Thenceforward, until the Pretoriuskop portion of the grazing area became a part of the Kruger National Park and the rest a native reserve, some four or five only were accustomed to send their sheep down each year, the demand therefore proving less urgent than had been represented. One of the lessees was, however, the former part owner of Pretoriuskop, and, having exchanged it for a good government farm elsewhere, he was now able to use his former land for winter grazing at the modest figure of £5. It was not surprising, therefore, that he was anxious to become a permanent tenant, with the full rights attaching thereto, and did his best to get Pretoriuskop excised from the reserve.

Matters remained in a state of uncertainty during the earlier years of the Great War, but always the agitation against the size of the Sabi reserve was increasing. Some of our neighbours, who had hitherto lacked much support for their criticisms, began to have allies. Ultimately a commission was appointed by the Administrator to enquire into and report upon the advisability of altering the boundaries of the Sabi and Shingwedsi game reserves and on matters generally affecting them. Of the proceedings and findings of that commission, more later.

With the opening up of the country by a railway in 1912, public attention had become at last focused on the game reserves with respect to their potential value for settlement and pastoral purposes. The movement of the land companies and the demand for winter grazing, were signs of the times. The South African Railways were anxious to make the new Selati line justify itself and felt it would be of considerable assistance to goods traffic were the land on both sides occupied by human beings rather than by wild animals. I wondered if anything could possibly be done to transform the reserves into a financial asset. Up to now they had cost a small sum annually and had brought no visible return to the country. I speculated if it would, for instance, be possible to make money by capturing and selling wild animals to the zoos of the world.

At that time high prices were to be obtained; in fact, a giraffe landed in England safely was worth £1 000 and a hippo about £600. The plan I conceived was to establish in the Sabi reserve a 'game camp' under a special staff, to which young animals would be brought immediately after capture, and there hand-reared until old enough to pick up their own food. They would then be transferred to a government farm, in the lowveld but outside the danger zone of the larger carnivora and close to the railway, where they would be kept in paddocks and sold to the buyers for the various zoos and dealers of the world who were constantly visiting Africa. Good advertisement was essential, not only in South Africa, but all over the world.

I still think there were considerable possibilities attached to the scheme. We should have had a large and varied selection of animals on the spot, all weaned, and therefore past the dangerous stage for young captive creatures. The buyers would have been spared the long and expensive journeys into the interior of Africa whence most of their acquisitions came, followed by the anxiety of getting them safely to the coast or railhead. Our prices would have been reasonable, since our running expenses, after the first capital expenditure was over, would not have been large. As we became better known I have no doubt we should have had annually increasing orders from Europe and America, and would have been from the beginning the main source of supply for all South African zoos.

We required for the initial capturing and weaning, only one special ranger extra to the establishment, and to begin with, about twenty 'boys'. Some were to be specially trained for looking after the young animals, while the remainder, in collaboration with the native police and residents, would be used during the calving and lambing season and for seeking in likely spots newly born antelope left alone – according to custom – by their mothers while away grazing. Such easily-tamed animals as impala would be, as sometimes in the past, caught in nets and transferred at once by rail to the game farm. The latter would have required a rather more elaborate staff consisting of several white men of the type of zoo-keepers. The whole would have been under the general supervision of the warden. There would have been required a good deal of capital outlay on fencing, but not necessarily on buildings, and a small herd of cows was essential for feeding the young animals. Some of the Crocodile River farmers had not long before applied to be allowed to enter the game reserve to look for wild ostrich eggs, pointing out of how great an asset they were being deprived through our 'dog in the manger' policy. It was thought therefore that the hatching and breeding of young ostriches might also form a part of the scheme.

Meantime to test things practically, a small beginning had been made by the catching and rearing of a few young animals at Sabi Bridge. Having a few private cows, I was able to feed them and to discover exactly how far and in what manner cow's milk required dilution, as well as what grasses and herbs were most nourishing to each species after weaning. At one time there were in captivity several waterbuck, a kudu, two sable, a wildebeest and a number of smaller buck, all past the bottle stage. Two 'boys' had become quite expert in the handling of baby animals.

However, the idea in its fullness never had a chance. The plan of the attached farm was treated with derision, and to get any money for such an item was out of the question. The only terms on which the Administrator would allow the experiment to be tried was that all the animals caught should be sent gratis to Pretoria Zoological Gardens. There such as might be required for show could be kept and any remaining surplus sold, the accruing sum, less a good stiff percentage, to be credited to the reserves. I had to accept this emasculated plan as better than nothing, and by doing so at least I gained the services of an extra ranger, ten more native police, three milch cows, purchased in Pretoria, and enough fencing to enclose a small camp into paddocks. The new ranger was one Siewert, a nephew of Hannemann of Komatipoort. He was a German by birth but an American by naturalization, and a good man in the veld and with animals. For about a year or more we collected young antelope and sent them to Pretoria. The result was disappointing. Although all weaned and in good health when dispatched, no surplus ones seemed to survive, and we never made a single penny from any sale on our behalf. When it was quite certain that nothing was destined to come of the scheme, I suggested that we should stop sending any more animals, since doing so was apparently merely a waste of life, and the official to whom I put this at once exclaimed, with a bright smile, 'Thank God, you have at last shaken off your mad idea'. However, nothing was said about reducing the staff again, and so we were that much to the good, as well as by the supply of wire, which was used for fencing in the new ranger's quarters.

The ostrich-breeding scheme also came to nought. We obtained a couple of ostrich-incubators, collected a lot of eggs and hatched out a number of young birds. We then found that the farmers did not really want them at all, and as no one else appeared to do so either, we turned them loose into the veld. Of course, as regards capture of young antelope we were at a certain disadvantage with the professional game catchers, who usually ride down the young animals on horseback or shoot the mothers. By our plan there would have been nothing of that kind, for the young would have been merely picked up as and when found. This process would no doubt have taken more time than the usual one. On the other hand, by our knowledge of the country, of the habits of the animals, and by living permanently on the spot, we should have largely made up for other disadvantages, while of course there would have been the minimum loss of life and our young animals would have been quite tame from the beginning.

There is, or was, an appalling amount of cruelty and waste of life connected with the business of catching animals for zoological gardens. Apart from that consideration, even were I allowed to carry it out according to my own plans, I would not now care to attempt any such scheme. Zoo animals, especially the antelope, seldom look natural, and convey little idea either to the public of how they appear in a wild state, or to students of what their true habits are. With the adoption of the national park concept everywhere, the people of a country can be given the opportunity of viewing their existing indigenous wild animals under natural conditions, while, in my opinion, exotic creatures are best studied in a museum. The confined wild animal is usually a mere travesty, physically and mentally, of itself as nature intended it to be.

Constantly on the move as we all were, travelling and camping in every

145

part of the reserves through the greater part of each year, we had unrivalled opportunities of studying the ways of beasts and birds, while for their part the animals, no longer oppressed by the necessity of fleeing from man whenever seen, gradually gained confidence, and though they never quite threw off their suspicions of the human being, at least they treated him more as a potential than as a certain enemy. Thus, having never been shot at, they had no idea of the range of firearms, and considered a safe distance about that which they would accord to a lion – say a hundred yards. Within that distance they would stare, snort, prance about, and after a time dash off; beyond it, certainly at two hundred yards, they paid practically no attention to one. Exceptions were the larger carnivora, which at that time we hunted strenuously. Indeed the most wary of all animals, at least by day, was the lion; while wild dog, instead of betraying their curiosity by jumping up and down and barking at the human intruder, as had been their custom in the early days, now made off at best speed, in silence, and with hardly a backward glance.

For my part, I gradually fell into a more or less regular annual routine. About mid-May the rain was practically over for the season, and it became possible to camp with a reasonable likelihood of keeping dry. Since, however, there was still plenty of water remaining in the veld, this was the most suitable time of year in which to explore, with the aid of pack donkeys, the drier portions of the reserve between the Sabie and the Crocodile Rivers. About June I would start on my annual inspection tour of the northern Shingwedsi, Letaba, or round the northern part of the Sabi reserve along the Olifants River. For such a trek the ox wagon, as well as the pack donkeys, and perhaps a couple of horses would be taken, with as much as two months' supplies of food and horse fodder. Arrangements would be made for mails to follow by runner to agreed places. It was a delightfully free and easy method of getting about and offered the widest opportunities of seeing the country. Accompanied by a couple of police 'boys' one rode on ahead, followed at some little distance by the donkeys running free in front of their attendants, the little bells, hung by straps to their necks, pleasantly tinkling. With the wagon came more police and domestic servants leading the dogs, lest these should feel tempted to give chase to some of the many animals visible all around them.

When the distance travelled seemed sufficient, and a pleasant shady spot was reached, with water at hand, one could decide to stay there for the rest of the day and the night, or as long as might appear desirable, and so would dismount, off-saddle and sit down under an inviting tree to await the cara-

van. After a time the donkeys would come trotting in; shortly afterwards the
ear would catch faintly the pistol-like cracks of the wagon whip, and, ever
drawing nearer, the raucous shouts of the driver, 'Tom', or 'Ntutu', or
'Seventeen' as the case might be. 'Ah, Witpens! Ah, Steenbok! Ah, Bles,
jou skelm, trek.' Then as the brake was turned, and the lumbering vehicle
came to a creaking halt ... 'Ah-h-h-h na-o-o' and a long whistle. At once the
casting loose of the philosophic oxen, to be driven with the donkeys to water
and presently to be left, adequately guarded, to their own devices. The
horses and donkeys roll luxuriously in the dust, and from the recesses of the
wagon appear camp-table, chair, bottle, glasses, all the things tending to mitigate the asperities of life. The cook quickly has a fire under way, the kettle
boils anon and tea is ready. If it be intended to spend the night in this place,
there is a general scattering to carry out well-accustomed duties. Some gather firewood, others set about with axes and bill-hooks, the making of the
essential zeriba, tents are pitched, water fetched, and oneself may take a solitary stroll round to explore the environs, returning at sundown to see the animals tethered, fed and all snug for the night, before settling down to one's
own excellent dinner by the campfire, eaten amid the slowly swelling sounds
of the night: the call of the little Scops owl, the throbbing of the crickets, the
yelp of the jackal, perhaps the distant rumble of a lion bestirring himself
from his daily slumber.

On one of the above-mentioned evening strolls, I followed the course of a
small dry spruit further than I intended, and the sun was almost setting when
I crossed its bed intending to return by the other bank. Unfortunately for me,
I followed a tributary by mistake, and it led me diagonally away from,
instead of towards camp. It became dark about the time I realized what had
happened, and there being no moon, it would have been foolish to try to
retrace steps under the circumstances. A few shots were fired, but proved
unavailing, the distance too great for them to be heard. So, on the whole I
judged the wisest, if not the most dignified course, was to seek shelter
among the branches of some tree. I soon found an umtoma (*Diospyros
mespiliformis*) with a fairly wide fork about ten feet from the ground, and
promptly climbed thereto, expecting, since the weather was quite warm, to
sleep not too uncomfortably till morning.

I don't know if any reader has ever tried to spend a night thus, if so he
will doubtless realize that after about three hours of it, I did not care if all the
lion in Africa were assembled close by. I disengaged my cramped limbs,
descended to the foot of the tree, lay down on my face to keep warm, and

was awakened only by the sun shining brightly on me. Finding the way in daylight was simple, and in less than an hour I was having breakfast at my camp-table, the search party coming along on my spoor in the course of the morning.

Often the wagon would be established as a base, usually at one or other of the permanent rest camps erected along the main routes, whence a trek of a few weeks into more difficult country would be undertaken with half a dozen pack donkeys, which with loads of 80 to 100 lb. each, could ramble along at a steady three miles an hour for twenty miles a day. As pack saddles, plain wooden crutches set on unpadded wooden panels, the whole weighing only a few pounds, were employed; the saddle was placed over a dressed sheepskin, folded in front, to keep it from slipping forward. The loads were packed in large leather saddle-bags calculated to hold 50 lb. each and joined by a wide leather thong to which each was firmly riveted, so that when full they could be lifted as one, and laid over the saddle, a piece of wood running fore and aft between the crutches, to keep the weight off the back. By following this method the donkeys were rarely troubled by sore withers, while a well padded and softened strip-leather girth eliminated fear of galls, though I always made a practice of halting at least once an hour to examine and adjust loads.

Donkeys and oxen find their own food in the veld, and travelling with

After some years of regular patrols, Stevenson-Hamilton
refined the art of loading pack donkeys so that the maximum
load could be carried by each animal without undue strain on
its withers.

their aid was more satisfactory than using native carriers, some of whom always have to carry food for the gang. Of course, today the advent of the motor lorry and its general use for camping purposes has largely eliminated animal transport, and with it all the pleasant interludes and the leisurely progress which formed the greatest charm of bush travel. With a lorry there is usually a definite purpose to be achieved, or a prearranged place to be reached. With pack donkeys there was a delightful irresponsibility, one just wandered as the spirit moved, to be stopped neither by the rockiest hills nor the densest thorn jungle. The main drawback in a lion country was, no doubt, the constant anxiety about the animals. It was always necessary to travel with dogs as camp-guards, and though one got used to it in time, their salvoes of furious barking within a few yards, as they carried out their duties at dead of night, were not always conducive to easy slumber.

After returning from the annual tour, perhaps about the middle of August, I generally established myself at a permanent camp for about three months, surrounded by all the domestic animals, because grazing at Sabi Bridge ceased to exist after July. From 1910 onwards I made a regular practice of going to Tshokwane, which was a camp in the hook of the Nwaswitsonto River, some twenty-five miles north from Sabi Bridge. It provided excellent grazing and water, was a good central point for minor expeditions, an easy day's ride from my headquarters, and held more game and lion to the square mile than any other part of the reserve. In 1902 a large number of native kraals stood in the vicinity, but a series of drought years had gradually pushed them westward to the better watered country outside the reserve, and by 1910 only old Tshokwane himself, with his family, remained. He was a man of between seventy and eighty years of age and a mine of local history, for although his own memory did not carry back so far, his father had told him of the days when Soshangane, or Manukosi, with his followers, had swept through from Zululand towards the Limpopo, and how the impis of Shaka, following on vengeance bent, had become so famine-stricken while passing through the purposely denuded country, that they were reduced to gnawing the leather of their shields and sandals. He also pointed out the grave of a former headman who had been killed by the Swazi in a general massacre, within his own memory, about fifty years before. After Tshokwane's death, about 1915, his family moved away, and the place was left entirely to the wild animals.

Having eventually built a commodious camp at this place, I usually stayed on until the rains in November made it possible to take the animals back to Sabi Bridge. The summer months from December to the end of April were devoted to the arrears of office work, to visiting rangers at their different stations and, so far as weather allowed, to hunting carnivora in the neighbourhood of my station. It was a good and full year; there never was a moment when time hung heavy, and it was all one's own, to do with as one would, without any outside interference. This last was perhaps the greatest charm, apart from the life itself and the nature of the work. It is impossible to imagine anyone having a freer hand than I had during all these years with regard to matters within the reserve; I could make or mar it as I pleased, and alas, nobody was likely either to praise or blame me whatever happened! It is better to crow alone on a little midden, than to form a mere unit of the chorus on a bigger one. Only when I thought about the future, did doubt and despondency creep in; so I thought about it as little as possible, and talked at great length about national parks – when I could get anyone to listen to me.

The year 1914 is no doubt deeply imprinted on the minds of all those old enough to remember that portentous year. South Africa, always highly strung and liable to brainstorms, must have felt intuitively some presage of coming events, and expressed her feelings through a general strike in Johannesburg, which extended to the railways of the Transvaal.

My first intimation of anything wrong was the cessation of the weekly train, which put us at Sabi Bridge in an awkward position, partly because the monthly native food supply from government was overdue. The telephone to Komatipoort, long dumb to our queries, ultimately apprised us of the position. My friend Timberman, the ganger, said he dare not take me down the line on his trolley, and two days later he and the ganger on the next section of line arrived at Sabi Bridge almost scared out of their wits. From a passing native lad they had heard that the white men at the railhead had killed all the police, and were marching armed down the line, destroying everything, and that all the natives were running away! My own feelings at the moment were expressed in the entry in my journal: 'Before the railway came here I was independent and had my own transport. I am forced to use the beastly thing and now it stops working. Confound all railways, telegraphs, telephones, and so called progress. We were better off and happier without any of this modern paraphernalia and I lived here quite comfortably for ten years without it!'

I am far from citing the above as my reasoned opinion even at that date, but it gives an idea of how one felt at the moment, and there is no doubt that although people would today find it difficult – at least at first – to live without the many conveniences that science has provided, these are by no means essential to happiness, nor even to comfort. Quite possibly such a sentiment is a token of atavism, and should have no place in the mind of a twentieth-century human being of Western origin. But to me, at least, after having endured a spell of civilization it was always a joy and a relief to get back to the wilds where all one's food was grown more or less on the premises, and for local movement one was dependent on no source other than one's own transport. I think Wolhuter, who was invariably extremely self-contained in these respects, at one time never had to buy anything except tea. He produced all else himself, including sugar and coffee, and he grew his own wheat for bread.

Eventually, through the good offices of the Permanent Way Inspector, who, I gathered, did not come within the scope of the trades union, I was able to travel to Komatipoort on his own pump trolley. As we trundled towards the familiar siding the whole line, up and down, was revealed blocked with derelict rolling stock, while strolling about in rather aimless fashion, were many men armed with rifles and equipped with bandoliers full of ball cartridges. The situation tuned a personal note when one of them, perceiving me, held me up at rifle point and demanded to know who I was and where I was going. It was natural to assume that the strikers had captured Komatipoort and that I was witnessing the first stage of a revolution of some kind. However, my suspicious captor led me to his commandant, one Kritzinger, a clerk in the magistrate's office at Lydenburg, and from him I gathered that they were not strikers, but, on the contrary, a government force of burghers sent to guard the line from sabotage. It also transpired that a train was just starting for Lourenço Marques. I took advantage of this and the strike ending a few days later, I was able to return and arrange for the necessary supplies to be sent up.

During this strike the Government, in country districts, employed the local commandos for line protection, under the orders of the police. A story was current concerning such a party on duty on a lonely section of the line somewhere west of Kaapmuiden. The local police officer, in the course of his inspection rounds visited the post late one night, and found the old burgher in charge – a veteran of the Boer War – obviously much worried. 'Commandant,' he said, 'I do not know what I must do; have we to shoot at all the trains, or only at the goods trains?' The good man was in fancy back again in his guerilla days, when every train was a potential magazine of creature comforts, as well as a natural enemy.

After the strike had collapsed, things quickly returned to normal at Komatipoort, where Mr Brand, the stationmaster, held a considerable moral influence. The engine driver of the Selati train, whose pay was £35 per month plus allowances for extra time, had apparently been the leader there, and had been arrested under martial law for calling out 'Scab!' but his incarceration must have been short, for he was driving his engine quite cheerily the following week.

Two unexpected visitors arrived at Sabi Bridge in the early part of the year. One was Colonel Woolls-Sampson,who told me that he was forming a syndicate to take up all the company land in the game reserve near Sand River for citrus growing. 'You may take it from me, you will see this place, within five years, one of the busiest spots in South Africa!' Another was a mysterious person who turned up with a permit to inspect ground for farming on the north bank of the Sabie. As the guide I lent him informed me that he spent his whole time turning over stones along the dry watercourses, I felt that 'farming' was not the true explanation, and taxed him with it. 'Major Hamilton,' he said looking very serious, 'do you remember a Mr Smith (we will call him Smith, as I forget the name) coming here two years ago next June?' I said I did not remember, and was pretty sure no one of that name, or any one else in fact, had been here then. 'Well,' he said, 'you are mistaken, and, Major Hamilton' – fixing me steadily with a rheumy eye – 'that man made the most wonderful discovery that has ever been made in South Africa; this place is going to make history.' After that he went away and I never saw nor heard of him again. The man of whom he spoke had never been in the reserve and I can only suppose someone had been pulling his leg.

Where gold, diamonds and buried treasure are in the picture, there is no limit to human credulity. This kind of thing showed, however, how fast we were losing our remoteness and how many dangers were menacing the reserve now that civilization was beginning to encroach in the lowveld. Had I not already realized this, it would have been forced on my notice by a letter I received about this time from General Smuts's office, written on his initiative, inviting my ideas regarding the future policy for the Sabi Game Reserve in view of the various present complications and the hostility which it seemed to have excited in certain quarters. Of course I replied that it was essential to make it a national concern, to take it away from the province and to expropriate all privately owned land lying within it. (This was what was done, though twelve years later!) It was a good opportunity for sowing some seed in the right place.

Another visitor was Lieutenant-Commander Bridgeman, R.N., who had just completed a shooting trip in Portuguese East Africa. It was exceedingly interesting to hear at first hand of the overtime work the British navy were doing; he said, among other things, they could not keep on long at the present high pressure. Bridgeman lost his life early in the war while scouting the mouth of an East African river in a seaplane – the story of how he and a companion wandered for days foodless, through swamps and jungles, after the loss of their machine, forms an epic of gallantry and endurance.

Having opened in an exciting manner, 1914 seemed to have settled down to a normal procession of hum-drum months, just like any other year. In July I started on a donkey trek to inspect the north-western boundary of the Sabi reserve where the Klaserie joins the Olifants River. I passed through Rolle on the railway, where Healy had established a camp for himself, alternative to Nwanetzi. He had married at Cape Town earlier in the year, an Irish girl of nineteen from County Meath, and he said Rudyard Kipling had made a speech at the wedding breakfast. Mrs Healy was a great horsewoman, and on this visit I found her busy schooling, over a fence erected at the back of the house, a huge and not very amenable steed which Healy had recently purchased. The idea was to enter it for the jumping competition at the Johannesburg show the following year.

But it was not to be. On my way back from the Olifants River a few weeks later, on July 30 to be exact, I camped near the line, on the farm Acornhoek, where there is today the beginning of a township. There was then only a small corrugated iron native store belonging to Mr P.W. Willis, who was, however, away on a shooting expedition at the time. The store was in charge of an old Irishman called O'Donnell, who, as I rode in, met me waving a newspaper and crying excitedly, 'They are all at it'. I asked, 'Who are at it?' thinking that there must be a renewal of the strike in Johannesburg. 'Why,' he said, 'all of them, of course – the Russians and the Austrians and the whole crowd of them.' I asked who was fighting who, no rumour of a crisis having appeared in the press when I had started north. O'Donnell was not quite sure of the details, so we went through the several days' old paper which had just come in the train, and arrived more or less at an appreciation of the situation as it had been about July 27.

It would be interesting if one could know the various ways in which news of the outbreak of war first reached humble people living in remote parts of the world. Of course, at that time the happenings had not got beyond the ultimatum stage, in spite of O'Donnell's prophetic instinct; but even then it

153

seemed fairly clear that Armageddon was coming. I did not get back to Sabi Bridge until August 3, and getting on the telephone, found Mr Brand, the stationmaster at Komatipoort, almost bursting with excitement. It seemed he had been made censor of telegrams and according to him declarations of war were going off like crackers. I still went on with my preparations for moving as usual to Tshokwane in the second week of August, and did not know about the British Empire having joined in until the 7th. On the 9th, which was the first available chance of going down, the train was several hours late, consequent upon the engine-driver stopping to discuss the situation at length with all and sundry at each siding he passed.

In Komatipoort a Captain Pfapf, a Hollander, was now in charge of the censorship but only one telegram had come since his arrival two days before. The local war news was that an unfortunate German had been arrested on the train as a spy – probably someone trying to escape internment. On getting back to Sabi Bridge I learned that in my absence, Saddler, the sergeant of mounted rifles stationed there as my assistant in court work, had been called out to join the forces; his house was a desolate waste of papers, straw and empty boxes, and he just departing. It was the first practical indication in the Sabi reserve of the world catastrophe. Shortly afterwards I was able to pack up and get away myself. The news of a war quickly got round among the natives, and just before I left, the head 'boy' at Sabi Bridge – old Jafuta – asked me in surprise why I was going to campaign without the ox wagon, the rifle, and the horses. 'How can you carry your *mpahla* (belongings) if you do not take the wagon?' He also expressed some surprise at a war against Germans. 'Germans,' he said, 'are all storekeepers like Mfuzngwenye (Siewert) used to be before he came here. They do not go on commando.' (I wonder what the great General Staff would have thought about this!)

On departure I handed over to De Laporte, who agreed to stay as 'long as his conscience would allow him to do so'. Siewert, the junior ranger, was a German by birth, but as he was an American by adoption and, moreover, a man whose main wish in life was to be right out in the veld and as far from another human being as possible, I saw no reason why he should not carry on with his job as usual. Unfortunately, at a later date, some of the local patriots, whose devotion to the British Empire found expression in words rather than in deeds, got up a petition for his removal, which I am sorry to say was acceded to, on the pretext of reduction of staff.

At Komatipoort, my old friend Mr Hannemann came to say goodbye at the station. He was a thoroughly patriotic German and had always held the courage of his opinions. Now, tears in his eyes, he said with genuine feeling, 'Oh, Major, I wish I had never lived to see this happen.' Poor man! He did not survive to see the end. Cold-shouldered by the local patriots, many of whom he had befriended in the past, his depression aggravated an ailment which he had long suffered from, and he died in 1916. Tragic was the fate of the whole family. The daughter took poison and died; kindly Mrs Hannemann was confined in a mental home, and Siewert, after his discharge from government service, took to drink and eventually shot himself. Hannemann had for many years been the leading citizen of Komatipoort – veldkornet before the South African War – but when I visited his supposed grave years afterwards, there was nothing whatever to identify it by, and I had to take the information given me on trust.

CHAPTER SEVEN
1915 TO 1922

THE RESERVE AND THE WAR; GAME RESERVES COMMISSION; FRESH
APPOINTMENTS; MAJOR FRASER AS WARDEN; THE PRETORIA MEETING;
MAJOR GREATHEAD'S EXPEDITION; RAILWAY TOURS; LOWVELD
DEVELOPMENT; DEATH OF LLOYD; ILLNESS OF LEDEBOER; FURTHER
BURIED TREASURE QUESTS

LIKE MOST OTHER PLACES, however isolated and unimportant, the Sabi
Game Reserve was not unaffected by the World War. To save expense
the native police were cut down by over fifty per cent. Of the white staff, Healy
departed overseas before the end of 1914, obtained a commission in the King's
African Rifles and was killed in one of the earlier engagements of 1916. R.I.P.
He was a cheery soul, never to be depressed by illness or adversity, and not the
least efficient of the 'old guard' of rangers whose work so largely helped to
make the Kruger National Park ultimately possible. De Laporte, whose wife
had gone to France as a nurse early in 1915, stayed as he had promised, 'so
long as his conscience permitted', but by the end of 1916 he found that breaking point had been reached. So he enlisted in the South African contingent,
and proceeding with it to France, became an officer after a few months, went
through the fighting of 1917 to 1918 with the famous 9th Division and was
severely wounded on the day before the armistice. The working staff was
therefore reduced to Wolhuter, Fraser and Duke. The first-named, still suffering from the effects of his mauling by a lion years before, had been rejected on
medical grounds; the two latter were considerably past military age. Fraser
took over the wardenship from De Laporte at the beginning of 1917, and a
man named Streeter, an old lowvelder, was temporarily appointed to the
Shingwedsi reserve in his place. Several of our native employees went overseas with the South African Labour Corps and some lost their lives.

One of the few lowveld residents – outside the staff of the game reserve – who offered his services was Mr P.W. Willis of Acornhoek; an ill-rewarded display of initiative, for, in the course of the South West African campaign, he stopped a bullet, and through faulty attention, unluckily lost one leg. A sad blow indeed to so keen a sportsman, and though he later attempted to do some hunting and even shot several lion, he was soon obliged to give up the rifle entirely in favour of the camera, eventually to become one of the best known photographers of wildlife in South Africa.

All through 1915 there had been a growing agitation from various quarters against the Sabi reserve in its present form, and following on a motion in the Transvaal Provincial Council by Mr S.H. Coetzee, requesting the Administrator to 'urge the Union Government to reduce the area of the Sabi Game Reserve', a commission was appointed under date June 13, 1916. The duties of this commission were to inquire into and report upon the advisability of altering the boundaries of the Sabi and Shingwedsi game reserves and on matters generally affecting the said game reserves. After several changes, the personnel was constituted as follows: Messrs J.F. Ludorf (Chairman), S.H. Coetzee, H. de Waal, A. Grant, G. Hartog, F.A.W. Lucas, C. Wade; with Mr C.H. Sheard, of the Administrator's office, as secretary. The published Report notes:

> Before proceeding to take evidence, it was decided with a view of obtaining first-hand knowledge of the conditions obtaining therein, that the commission should as a preliminary visit the Sabi Game Reserve. A visit was accordingly arranged, first under the guidance of Ranger H.C. Wolhuter in that portion of the reserve known as Pretoriuskop, or 'buffer area' west of the Nsikazi River, and later under that of the acting-warden, C.R. de Laporte, in the area near the western boundary (Klaserie River) and also at Sabi Bridge, the headquarters of the warden. It was impossible to visit the Shingwedsi reserve, without unduly delaying the report.

The above itinerary was completed during the dry season of 1916, apparently to the satisfaction of the commission, the members of which were given all facilities for a full understanding of our methods of administration, of what had been accomplished, and of the general contemporary situation. It was the first time any one of them had set foot in the Sabi Game Reserve, or in fact in any game reserve, and some, whose only previous experiences with wild animals had been those of the hunter, may have felt themselves chafed by the regulations. But few can sojourn long within the unspoilt wilderness of a game sanctuary, surrounded on all sides by its confiding animals, without absorbing its atmosphere; the Spirit of the Wild is quick to assert her supremacy, and no man of any sensibility can resist her. At any rate, every member of the commission not already converted, soon became a confirmed game protectionist.

Yet it is difficult entirely to suppress the Old Adam, and a certain restlessness became evident towards the end of the tour, when the party, under De Laporte's guidance, finally arrived on the north-west border of the reserve. Might not an animal be shot outside the boundary? The less initiated were eager to win their spurs as big game hunters. Accordingly one day an expedition was duly organized; such small solace surely being due to man's primitive instincts. Alas! After much tramping in the heat, great expenditure of energy and elaborate stalking, the animal which at last, it was said, fell to their rifles proved to be a stray cow from a neighbouring kraal, so the day ended disappointingly with the payment of compensation to the owner of the defunct animal.

As indicated, the commission was unable to reach the Shingwedsi reserve, where Major Fraser, apprised of its probable arrival, had apparently misinterpreted its duties, for he wrote to De Laporte: 'If the census lads are coming here it would be well to warn them to bring horses, and salted ones at that. I will divide the party into pairs, and each pair can take a block of 1 000 square miles and count (?) the game.'

Some of the members might have found the Shingwedsi rather trying at that period under the conditions arranged for them by its ranger.

The commission sat at intervals through 1917 and 1918 and heard from many sources a large amount of evidence bearing on the reserves. Towards the end of 1918 it issued its report.

Whether the members originally came to curse or not, they had certainly remained to bless. The report was extraordinarily favourable to the reserves and the ideals embodied in them, besides doing full justice to the efforts of the staff, 'working,' as the report pointed out, 'under very considerable difficulties'. The only thorn in the rose was the confirmation of the winter grazing for sheep farmers over the portions west of the Nsikazi River and about half the Pretoriuskop area – one felt here that *l'appétit vient en mangeant*[s] – and that it was only a matter of time before the rest of this fine bit of country would be practically cut out of the Sabi reserve. However, as a set-off to this, occurred the following momentous pronouncement which was the first official pointer given in the direction of the long desired goal:

> In the course of our investigations we were not a little struck by the uselessness of having these magnificent reserves merely for the *preservation* of the fauna – in an area practically unknown and, by the effect of a somewhat stringent policy, made to a great extent inaccessible to the bulk of the people – a policy which it will be increasingly difficult to maintain as applied to so large an area ... for these and other reasons we recommend that the policy of the (provincial) administration should be directed toward the creation of the area ultimately as a great national park where the natural and prehistoric conditions of our country can be preserved for all time.

It was clear that the seed assiduously sown for so many years was at last beginning to germinate, and in the quarters that really mattered. From the date of the issue of this report the stage was definitely set for the creation of a national park.

The report proceeded to recommend that there should be no curtailment of the boundaries of either sanctuary, though it provided that 'Government should have the power to open portions of the Sabi reserve experimentally for winter grazing'. In conclusion, the report recommended that the depleted staff be not only brought back to pre-war strength, but that two additional rangers should be appointed.

In 1919 three new rangers were appointed: De Jager, Coetser and Lloyd. A new station was made in the extreme north of the Shingwedsi near the Pafuri River and Coetser was placed there. He called it 'Punda Maria', a name which has adhered to it and has puzzled tourists unceasingly. The origin of it was that Coetser, while in East Africa with the forces, had come across the Swahili term for zebra – *punda miliya* or striped donkey – but apparently not getting it quite right, thought the last word was 'Maria', his wife's name. Hence the title – not very flattering to Mrs Coetser. The strength of the native police was also brought back to normal, and so far as possible the gaps made in the personnel by the events of 1914 were filled up.

De Laporte returned from active service about the middle of 1919, only just in time to adjust the internal machinery before it had gone too far out of gear for repair. Major Fraser had been brought down from Shingwedsi

*In 1919 Johannes Jacobus Coetser, seen here with one of the
African police, was placed in charge of the newly opened
northern station – which he called Punda Maria – near the
Pafuri River.*

in 1917 to assume the role of acting-warden, Wolhuter being then unwilling to take the responsibility of the post. The two-and-a-half years during which he officiated at Sabi Bridge – much against the grain it must be admitted – might be looked on as a comic interlude, were it not for the serious setback which his reign inflicted on the reserve, from which it took some years to recover.

He at once took up his quarters in the warden's house, sharing it with his pack of twenty-five large dogs, their easiest and ordinary means of entry and exit being through the gaps they tore in the wire-gauze mosquito-proof netting, which formerly screened the veranda. A lover of the simple life, he disdained the amenities of garden and orchard, even to having their contents, including fruit trees, pulled up and thrown into the void.

The office work he considered undignified, and since, by the end of a year no official letters had been answered and no pay account kept, it was arranged that the services of the police non-commissioned officer, of which the station had been deprived in 1914, should be restored and that he should undertake all the clerical work. It is said that he found the office so congested with cobwebs that a path had to be cleared by a labour gang before he could get inside! Relations inevitably soon became strained with the Major, office work lapsed once more and on his return, De Laporte found the cobwebs again holding the field.

During this period Wolhuter had occasion to pay a visit to Sabi Bridge, and riding into the compound one forenoon was surprised to find no visible sign of life. Usually some dozen or more natives – police 'boys' and others – were to be found engaged in various routine tasks about the place. But this day complete silence reigned; only a few fowls wandered aimlessly about and a donkey stood unattended under the shade of a tree. Presently, after he had shouted long and loud, from behind a bush just outside the fence a head protruded cautiously, then from behind adjoining bushes, another and another, until finally the whole native staff made its appearance, displaying, however, every sign of being ready at any moment again to take cover.

Enquiries elicited the information that the Major had been angry, had come out into the compound with a shotgun and had chased them all out of camp, threatening the extreme penalty did any venture to return. Having handed over his horse and reassured the more nervous, Wolhuter made for the house, where, surrounded by his dogs, he found Fraser asleep on his bed.

It may be here the occasion to interpolate that one of this remarkable man's peculiarities was that of turning day into night. He would rise early, go out to fish or with his dogs to hunt warthog – animals he persisted quite sincerely in regarding as 'vermin' – and after a late breakfast would retire to bed for the rest of the day. Getting up for dinner at 6 p.m. he afterwards would sit up for the greater part of the night mending fishing tackle, cleaning his rifles, carpentering, darning his socks, or reading the *Field*, retiring for an hour or two of further slumber in the early morning hours. On the present occasion he explained that the noise of the boys working and talking in the compound had disturbed his daily sleep to such an extent that he felt the only way was to drive them out until reveille time in the evening.

Either on the same or on another occasion Wolhuter was staying the night at Sabi Bridge. Fraser put him in the spare room and lent him a bed, two blankets and a pillow. In the early hours of the morning, being winter, it became very cold, so thinking he would try and borrow an extra blanket, he made his way along the veranda to Fraser's own apartment. It was still quite dark and by the light of a candle he could make out, at the farther side of the room, what looked like a great dark pile of something, from which emanated a variety of grunts and snores. Approaching closer, the pile disintegrated, and revealed itself as consisting of the twenty-five large dogs, which were sleeping around and on their master, who, fully dressed, was extended on his back on the bare floor, snoring quite happily. He explained that having no other bedclothes than those he had lent to Wolhuter, he had spent thus such part of the night as he devoted to slumber, adding that it was not an unusual practice with him, even when the ordinary amenities were available, as the dogs kept him much warmer than any blankets ever could do.

Fraser also, unfortunately, managed to fall out with the magistrate of the district, who, having arranged after due notice to inspect the court books, on arrival found himself condemned to sleep on the bare floor of the court house. For some reason Fraser refused even to see him. The rather natural result was that, subsequently, practically every legal sentence which Fraser imposed was quashed on one ground or another.

This calls to mind another characteristic story told of him when he was still in the Shingwedsi reserve, where he also held judicial powers. In the course of his annual pilgrimage to Pietersburg, he one day walked into the magistrate's office there and dumped down on the table before that official a small bag full of golden sovereigns, which, he explained, represented the proceeds of various court fines inflicted by him during the past twelve months. 'But,' asked the astonished magistrate, 'have you no receipts, papers or particulars regarding these fines which you say you have collected? I cannot possibly accept the money in this way.' There was an awful pause; the big red beard began to bristle, the magistrate felt himself wilting under the steady stare from the fierce grey eyes, in which a dangerous light was slowly gathering. 'Papers! Receipts! If you don't think, sir, my word is good enough, you had better tell me so! I don't care a curse what you do with the money; I have not even counted it; you can do that yourself and make out your own damned receipts.' With which words the speaker stalked out of the office and was seen no more. How eventually they managed to allocate the money history does not relate.

In 1918, east coast fever had appeared among native cattle in the White River area bordering the reserve on the south-west. In order to prevent its spreading into the latter, Fraser, acting on Wolhuter's advice, ordered all cattle near the border on the reserve side to be moved back some distance. Unfortunately, on assuming control at Sabi Bridge, one of the first steps he took was to resign the native commissionership obtained for the warden, *ex officio*, with so much trouble. 'If they think I am going to fash myself with that tomfoolery they are making a big mistake.' Very naturally the natives refused to obey his orders and appealed to the native commissioner of the district, who, supporting them, wrote an acid official letter, enquiring by what right the warden presumed to interfere with the natives? The net result was that for the first and last time east coast fever appeared in the Sabi reserve, a portion of which remained under quarantine for the next three years, and incidentally all the cattle of the natives who had objected to moving, died.

Things in fact had come to such a pass that when De Laporte returned, not only was the warden on the eve of being deprived of judicial authority, but an official from the administrator's department was about to be sent down to take over the internal administration of the reserve.

De Laporte spent some difficult months in straightening matters out. No roster of employees having been kept for some years, it was difficult to ascertain who had been paid or even engaged, and who not. Natives kept turning up demanding so many months of arrear pay, with nothing to prove that they had ever been on the staff. Monthly estimates and pay-sheets, when rendered, had been mainly guess-work. There began to arrive reams of correspondence from Pretoria demanding to know the reason for this and that; how such and such a sum had been disposed of, and so on. In fact, the torrent of official eloquence, perforce pent up for a considerable time, now had full play.

We nearly lost our customs police because Fraser had professed ignorance that any such existed. He, himself, now safely back in the wilds of the Shingwedsi, took refuge in complete silence; the many frenzied appeals for information on various points were regarded by him as too childish even to merit reply. He had many good, even admirable, qualities, but the running of any concern which involved clerical work, even of the simplest description, was not one of them. If there were any question of a native not having been paid, and difficulties arose in regard to drawing the money, he would pay out of his own pocket rather than write an official letter, and I am sure a large proportion of his salary was expended in this manner, or in supplying rations to people who ought to have drawn them from government sources. Having no dependants and few personal expenses, he found pleasure in such acts; at least he found them preferable to the tedium of making out the returns which would otherwise have been necessary. He was one of the most honest and generous, if one of the most difficult, of men, and as a character, in some respects unique.

During the war years the reserves had unavoidably retrograded. With the staff reduced by over 50 per cent, native poaching had everywhere become prevalent; organized parties had been spending weeks, even months, camped far inside the boundaries, snaring and almost openly pursuing game with dogs. The morale of the native staff had deteriorated sadly and some of the police on picket duty overlooked – perhaps even encouraged – poaching. Game, great and small, in areas distant from the stations of the few remaining rangers, had appreciably decreased and was far wilder in 1920 than it had been in 1914. Due to the unchecked multiplication of carnivorous animals and the systematic destruction of other game, the fine balance between the two was again in danger of being upset, to the serious detriment of the latter. Further, it was soon obvious to one returned after an absence of years, that an atmosphere differing from the pre-war one existed, *vis à vis* game preservation in general and the game reserves in particular. Of course, some time before the war, in fact ever since the railway had broken in upon us, the lowveld had been changing, and even in our backwater we could feel the growing-pains.

The old free and easy days had already gone: those days when a party of prospectors would subscribe to buy amongst them a horse which had the fascinating habit of drinking beer out of a bucket; or, designing to convey on a mule-trolley a defunct comrade to the place of interment, would so well drown grief before and during the journey, as to arrive at their destination without the central figure; nor would a man, obliged to drink water, longer deem himself reduced thereby to the status of 'a common ox' as I once heard remarked. We were becoming civilized even then. Now, land had everywhere appreciated in value. There was, in fact, a land boom, and for the first time there began to arise a demand for the opening up of the low-country fever belt. A succession of unusually dry seasons with consequent diminution of malaria, further encouraged the advent of white settlers. The native problem was insistent; the Bantu of the low- and middle-velds, existing still more or less under their old tribal systems, had increased greatly in numbers. There were no native reserves nor native locations of any kind in the low country of the Barberton and Lydenburg district, and many of the native squatters, on land lying just outside the reserve and newly acquired by whites, began to press on over its boundaries and were increasingly difficult to keep out. Government began to see the necessity of providing some purely native area. The companies owning the great bulk of the private land within the Sabi reserve became insistent upon its excision therefrom, realizing that its continued inclusion was likely to be detrimental to such schemes of development and disposal as they may have had under consideration. The national park scheme was still occasionally mooted among supporters of wildlife preservation, but, even among the most sympathetic, the difficulties and expense of buying out the private owners appeared too great to allow of it being considered a practical proposition.

The years 1921 and 1922 were black ones in the history of the Sabi reserve. From all sides dark and menacing clouds were gathering. A coal syndicate, backed by powerful political influence, had secured a concession along the Selati railway for some miles north of the Crocodile bridge; beacons were erected and prospecting for the most likely spots to sink shafts was begun. The railway administration, casting about for means to make the Selati railway less of a white elephant in the future, felt that the land lying on either side of it, in its passage through the reserve, might be put to better paying use than its present one of a mere refuge for wild animals. It strongly advocated the deproclamation of a strip on each side of the line and its parcelling out into allotments for timber cutting and, where practicable, farming. The winter graziers, having secured full rights in the buffer area near Pretoriuskop, were agitating to be allowed to penetrate deeper into the reserve. A scheme was on foot for working gold on the Pafuri River. The farmers living south of the Crocodile River were loudly voicing their grievances that the 'unrivalled farming land' lying just north of it in the reserve, was barred to settlement. Heavy infiltration of natives into the Sabi country, with the connivance of our officials, was asserted. 'Why are natives being given advantages denied to white men?'

Most dangerous of all, the principal land company concerned was busy agitating in the press and on the platform for its rights, and making great capital out of the numbers of lion which were being bred and harboured as a menace to farming. As a leading official in the Administrator's department said to me at this time, 'No doubt you will hang on year after year, and every year your reserve will be whittled away slice by slice, until one morning you will wake up and find the last bit has disappeared'. It was, as things were shaping, a prophecy only too likely to be justified, and that before many more years had passed. The reserves existed by virtue of a simple proclamation in the *Gazette* and by another simple proclamation they could be abolished, as it were, by a stroke of the pen. There was yet little or no public interest; enemies were more clamorous than allies. While the leading newspapers were friendly and willing to give a 'leg up' when approached, some minor journals were clearly out to advance special interests. One of these, long since defunct, in the course of a scathing article remarked: 'How long must we endure the slings and arrows of outrageous fortune? This so-called game reserve is merely a refuge for dangerous wild animals, a focus of disease, and should be swept away.' A letter in the press pointed out that in the twenty years which had passed, the land might have held hundreds of happy, smiling homesteads instead of only lion and disease!

Poor Cinderella!

So, with the attitude of the Government, hitherto mildly benevolent, gradually veering to the left in deference to what appeared to be public opinion, the situation seemed to me threatening indeed. I discussed the situation with Charter, at that time chief clerk in the Administrator's department, who advised calling together to a conference representatives of all sections, departmental and other, desiring for various reasons to cut up the reserves, in order to learn how much each required. 'At least,' he said, 'we shall know the worst, and you may be able to save something out of the

Harry Wolhuter and a group of friends camping out in the
Sabi Game Reserve near Pretoriuskop.

wreck for a few years to come – sufficient, perhaps, to last your time out.'

Accordingly, at the beginning of 1923 the meeting duly took place at the Old Government Buildings, Pretoria, the historical setting for so many other momentous matters, and I felt rather as I suppose a shepherd must when a pack of wolves threatens his ewe lamb. One after another the delegates got up and stated their requirements, and as each concluded the poor reserve figuratively got smaller and smaller: railway interests, coal, gold, sheep grazing, cattle ranching, cotton and orange farming; each claimed its bit. Then, at last, as one suggesting the merciful *coup de grace* for a suffering animal, Sommerville, the Secretary for Lands (afterwards one of our staunchest supporters, but at that time a leader of the wolf pack), rose to his feet and said: 'My department wants the whole Sabi Game Reserve abolished!' 'Well,' remarked Van Velden, the Provincial Secretary, in an aside to me, 'there are no half-measures about that, anyway.' He then told the delegates that we would think over their requirements, and let them know later what we had decided to do.

The meeting over, I did a little discreet lobbying, and, in accordance with the accepted rules of strategy, made first for the principal adversaries. Sommerville arranged for me to see Colonel Deneys Reitz, who had recently become Minister of Lands, that I might lay the case for the retention of the Sabi reserve, or some of it, directly before him. This conference had threatened to mark the nadir of all hopes and to put at nought all that had been striven for over the previous twenty years. And yet, curiously, the entry of the national park idea into the region of practical politics, dates from this meeting. Up until that time it had only been a pious aspiration, its one official recommendation forgotten in the dusty files of the Game Reserve Commission of five years before.

In 1922 the Transvaal Consolidated Land Company, which had by then bought out most of the other landowners in the Sabi Game Reserve, dispatched their land manager, Major Percy Greathead, on a mission to spy out the land. He arrived with a considerable retinue and several wagons, apparently, from his manner, in the expectation of a hostile reception from myself. So naturally I went out of my way to be as civil as possible and as hospitable as it lay in my power to be, though I could not grant him permission to shoot, which was what he wanted most. The caravan travelled over a good many of the farms and spent about a month in the reserve. Greathead expressed himself as appalled by the lion menace. I lent him a dog to guard his camp, but unfortunately, early in the course of the expedition, it was shot by one of the party in mistake for a lion or a baboon, I forget which. Mr Hartog, a member of the Game Reserves Commission, accompanied the explorers, and no doubt his tact and friendly disposition to both sides helped towards preserving the outward peace which happily prevailed.

Soon after the departure of the above party, it was announced that the company intended definitely to assert its rights, to the extent of establishing a cattle ranch in the middle of the Sabi reserve and as close as possible to the warden's headquarters. This plan was duly carried out, and, before the end of 1922 some eight hundred 'scrub' cattle were placed on the farm Toulon, four miles from Sabi Bridge, as being the nearest piece of private land to it, and consequently the closest point to which they could be brought. Luckily for me a piece of government-owned land acted as a buffer, or they would have been at my door. I think the underlying notion was that by making things as unpleasant as possible for myself, I in my turn would exert pressure on government to buy out the company. If so, it showed very small appreciation of the true situation and a very exaggerated notion of my official position and influence. To one with knowledge of the situation as it then stood, it seemed ridiculous to suppose that government would be prepared to pay a penny piece to save the Sabi reserve, and fairly obvious that the ultimate answer to the resolute action of private owners in asserting their rights, would be: 'All right, for Heaven's sake take your land and do anything you like with it, only don't bother us. We will simply deproclaim the Sabi Game Reserve and then everybody will be happy'. That was, I am convinced, the feeling at the time, and if the reserve was to survive, the most delicate handling of the situation was wanted.

The new manager of the ranch was a certain Mr A.J. Crosby, with whom I quickly made friends, and it became a weekly practice for me to drive over every Sunday to lunch with him and his charming wife at the improvised home which he had erected near the Sand River. Accordingly, by the time the company took the next step in its programme and instructed its manager to begin shooting the game as a test of rights, Crosby was a firm friend of the reserve. He told me what he had been instructed to do, and I advised him to get on with the good work. Thereupon, with great deliberation, he proceeded to dispatch a lone bull wildebeest and then duly reported his action at my office.

A summons was taken out, and the case tried at some magistrate's court, where the defence was that the wildebeest had been eating grass, and that grass was 'a plant within the meaning of the Act'. (The game law allows owners of property to kill wild animals found in the act of destroying plants or crops). The magistrate said he did not think grass was a 'crop' and gave it against the company, who appealed to the High Court, at which stage the learned judge pointed out with truth that were such an appeal upheld, it would mean the complete breakdown of all the game laws. Fortunately it took a long time – many months in fact – before this case, having passed through every possible stage of appeal, was finally decided against the company, and before the next line of attack had matured, the necessity for any further offensive had ceased.

In the same year, 1923, the South African railway authorities conceived the idea of running a service of fortnightly tourist trains to points of interest in the Transvaal during the cold weather. This service, which became known as the 'Round-in-Nine' because it took nine days to complete the tour, was a model of efficiency, cheapness, and comfort for the passengers. All the most interesting places and those containing the finest scenery, were embraced. Citrus orchards at Nelspruit and mountain passes at Pilgrim's Rest were inspected, finishing up with sea bathing and a dance at Lourenço Marques. When the programme of the service was shown to me I was a little disappointed, though perhaps hardly surprised, to discover that these tourist trains were scheduled to pass through the reserve by night on every occasion, and of course without stopping. I called on the system manager, whom I knew, and mooted the idea of allowing each train to make a halt while passing through, or at least to make the journey in daylight. 'But why?' he asked me, with a surprised air. 'Well,' I said, 'perhaps some of the people might like to look at the game.' He looked at me steadily for a moment or two, as one does at a person of whose complete sanity one is not quite sure, then he leaned back in his chair and burst into a hearty laugh. When he had recovered a little, he gasped out, 'What! Look at your old wildebeests! What on earth do you suppose anyone wants to see *them* for? But look here' – suddenly struck by an idea – 'I'll make a bargain with you. If you will allow us to stop and have a little shooting – I promise we won't bring more than a single rifle on the train – I am sure that would amuse the passengers. We could put an expert shot on board, and some of them might like to have a go themselves. Anyhow, if you will agree to that I think I could arrange for an hour's halt.' Well, well! Twenty years' work of building and no more helpful suggestion at the end than one to allow neophytes to practise with lethal weapons on semi-tame animals. But that was still the public attitude towards game even so recently as 1923.

However, I did not allow myself to be unduly discouraged, and ultimately it was settled that the train, without rifle and expert hunter, should stay the night at the siding opposite Sabi Bridge, where we would arrange a camp-fire for the passengers, and next morning, very early, proceed to Newington (at that time within the sanctuary) to remain there for an hour in daylight. I don't think anyone was more surprised than the railway authorities when they discovered at the conclusion of the first tour that the short halt in the game reserve was, to the majority of the passengers – mainly townspeople from Johannesburg – by far the most interesting and exciting part of the whole trip. Later, it was agreed that more time in the reserve should be spent by the tourist train, and it was further arranged that a ranger should travel on it and at each halt take the passengers for a little walk in the bush. The camp-fires, too, became a great attraction; the people sat round the huge blaze, alternately singing choruses and shivering with delight at the idea of being watched, from the dark bush close at hand, by the hungry eyes of beasts of prey, though I am sure every wild beast within earshot had long fled head-long from the clamour.

One of the stewards on the train, having possessed himself of a lion-skin, would sometimes envelop himself in it and would come crawling stealthily into the ring of firelight, to be greeted with shrieks from the more timid of

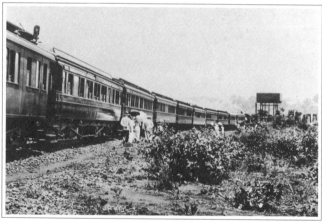

Tourist trains travelling on the Selati line included a stop at the reserve. The success of these brief visits did much to attract support for the later campaign to create the Kruger National Park.

the ladies, while the bolder of the men would assume protective attitudes. To add to the realism, our South African Police sergeant at Sabi Bridge could give a very passable imitation of a lion's roar through a long glass tube, and while his confederate was advancing, would, from a place of concealment, provide the necessary vocal accompaniment. The tourists loved thrills, and De Laporte, our humorist, always did his best to gratify them. Asked if there was any danger from snakes, he assured them that in his experience mambas had boarded the train on only two occasions! A couple of lion, he added, might always be noticed waiting for the train at a certain mile-post, ready to race it to the next one.

The interest betrayed by the public in the animals and the remarks I over-heard when mixing with the passengers, made me at last confident that, could only our national park scheme mature, it would become popular and therefore an asset to the country. It was beyond measure encouraging to feel that the South African public, despite tradition, might be content to look at animals without wanting to kill them. Directly the South African railway administration realized that the Sabi reserve held potential publicity value, it at once became, in the person of Sir William Hoy, the general manager, a whole-hearted supporter of its development into a national park.

Meantime, though threatened by many external enemies, the internal conditions of the reserves were quickly improving. Poaching had again been suppressed and the efforts of the staff were now directed mainly to the reduction of the larger carnivora, a form of activity which further served our interests by helping to mitigate one of the sources of complaint against us. We were now perceptibly closer to the outside world. White River had made a fresh start some years before this time as an orange-growing community and was prospering. The land, citrus, cattle and cotton booms had come and gone, each attended by the mean of success which even a cursory knowledge of lowveld conditions might have predicted. Such wealth, in fact, as had been acquired lay in experience only. All the newcomers were not obviously destined for even ultimate success as agriculturists. One ingenious person told De Laporte how he had read in a popular magazine of an infallible remedy for blight on orange trees. 'And I took good care,' he added, 'that no one else can get hold of the secret, for I have burnt the magazine!'

There had been further changes in the staff. Fraser and Duke had been retired for reason of age. The former, having secured from government a small piece of land near the western boundary of the Shingwedsi reserve, built a mud hut for himself and spent there the remaining seven years of his life very happily and contentedly, surrounded by his pack of dogs. Duke, following his particular bent, was allowed to run a small native store at Sabi Bridge, where, in the process of selling coloured beads and cloth unremuneratively, he established a sort of intelligence agency and gathered up all the gossip of the countryside.

Of the new rangers, Lloyd, stationed at Satara – Healy's old post – was so energetic that he quite forgot he was fifty-six and not twenty-six years old. He would ride forth alone on his patrols, and being a light weight and well mounted, often covered in all weathers immense distances during a day, sometimes sleeping out without food and in his wet clothes, which consisted merely of a pair of lion-skin breeches, self-made, a very inadequate shirt, and a smasher hat. It was hardly to be expected that, acting thus, poor Lloyd would last long in the lowveld climate. It appeared that having arrived at home one hot day, after a long ride, soaked with perspiration, he sat on the veranda till he cooled, and not surprisingly contracted pneumonia. At that time Satara was entirely isolated and a sick man had little chance. His wife, a mere girl, did her best for him, but with no advice, no medicines, and little conception of what ailed her husband, who till the end apparently would not admit that he was really ill, there was little she could do.

I had just returned to Sabi Bridge from camp after an absence of some weeks and was sleeping contentedly in a bed, when, at about 3 a.m., I was aroused by a native messenger bearing a short note from Mrs Lloyd to say her husband had died the night before, and adding that she was quite alone at Satara with her three small children and one native. The messenger had run and walked fifty-five miles in twenty-four hours, which, through lion country, and part of the time in the dark, was a commendable performance. I left before daylight with the buckboard and got through in the day, though Brandy appeared to be developing towards the end of the journey, his periodical recurrence of horse-sickness – symptoms common to most salted or immunized horses, which, of course, necessitated the last part of the journey being done at a slow walk. On arrival at Satara, I found that Mrs Lloyd, with the help of the solitary native police 'boy' who remained, had already buried her husband under a tree near the house. It must be difficult for people accustomed only to civilized surroundings to realize the position of women living far away in the African bush without neighbours, before the days of motor cars, and how they had to be prepared to face any kind of unexpected and sudden emergency.

We in the Sabi reserve, were, in respect of communications, still a relic of the past; and anything more pathetic than the situation of this young woman, absolutely isolated as she was in the savage wilderness with her three small children, and her husband lying dead in the house, it is difficult to conceive. But she rose to the occasion, and throughout maintained an attitude of level-headedness and composure which filled me with admiration.

My wagon did not arrive for a further two days, the interval spent in packing up all the household effects, which, with the help of Lloyd's donkey wagon, it was to transport to the railway. On the fourth day the caravan got away: two wagons, poultry distributed on top of the household effects, led horses, dogs and loose donkeys. I followed with the buckboard the following morning, having remained behind to settle up various official matters. The weather during the last week had been exceedingly hot, the shade temperature never below one hundred degrees; but on the day I left Satara it blew up hard from the south, and in the afternoon a tremendous thunderstorm burst on us, with rain which continued all night. The caravan had meantime arrived at Tshokwane camp where I joined it and noticed that Mrs Lloyd's three bare-footed little boys continued each to wear the same single cotton garment, while playing about in the rain, as they had done when it was one hundred degrees in the shade. Clearly, in their contempt for external conditions they were true sons of their father.

Tshokwane – named after Chief Chokwane, who provided Stevenson-Hamilton with valuable oral history concerning the people of the area – was made a ranger's post in 1909.

The night closed in so dark that one could not see one's hand held a foot in front of the face, and a light rain assiduously fell. Accompanying the party was a donkey mare with her young foal, and fearful of injury to the latter if put in the kraal with the others, I conceived the idea of tying the mare up under a grass shelter in the middle of the camp. I did this, I admit, with certain misgivings, as evidenced by my asking my head 'boy' if he thought it was safe. He looked at me with surprise. 'Why would it not be safe?' 'Well,' I said, 'a lion might come'. He laughed. 'In all the years we have camped here has a lion ever once come to the camp? Don't they always keep as far away as they can, and besides, have we not plenty of dogs?' The shelter under which the mare was tied was about fifteen feet from the door of the rondavel in which I was sleeping, the cattle and donkey kraals were beyond, and midway between the native quarters and the European huts. There were six dogs in camp, but all except two were suffering from badly burnt feet, the result of the march over nearly red-hot ground on the previous day.

Naturally a light sleeper, about 1.30 a.m. I was awakened by the sound of the donkey stamping about. Suddenly, as I lay listening, came a loud resonant snort, and while I groped for my electric torch, a violent commotion erupted outside. As I sprang out of bed, over went the table with everything on it. But finding the torch somehow among the debris I rushed out to find the donkey gone, though I could hear her galloping away somewhere out in the darkness. Then there was a slight thud, like a fall, and afterwards silence. I surmised what had happened and shouted to the 'boys' to bring lights as the lion had 'got the donkey'. Up to this moment the camp had been buried in the profoundest silence; not a dog had barked, not a native stirred; not a sound came even from the horses, cattle and donkeys kraaled close by. Two or three 'boys' having now arrived with a hurricane oil-lamp, I handed one the electric torch, of which the battery was unluckily almost on its last legs, and, rifle in hand, ventured into the outer darkness.

A rumbling growl from ahead before we had gone many steps, solved any doubts I might have had, and convinced my disbelieving followers. We went back to camp to get the acetylene lamp lighted and found everyone had turned out, though of the dogs only Lloyd's little mongrel Irish terrier, Bles, joined us and barked. The lamp blew out in the wind, and, in trying to relight it, some ash got into the burner, so I had to return to my hut, find a needle, and laboriously pick out the obstruction. This completed, we once more took the field. The lion were still there, with Bles, somewhere out in the darkness, barking at them. By getting one of the natives to hold the acetylene lamp high, one could at intervals see the reflection of the light from the marauders' eyes when they looked our way. They were moving points of flickering flame and were absolutely all that could be seen of their owners.

Having sent everyone back to camp, except the native with the light and my head 'boy', I advanced five or six paces to where a lot of reeds and poles, piled round the base of a tree, formed a kind of bell-tent. As I reached this construction, a bewildered black face poked itself out, and it appeared that the herd-boys, who had made this their sleeping place, had only just wakened up. I gave the head a tap and it disappeared, after which, and having called in the dog, I began to take shots at the eyes whenever I could see them. But the first two bullets must have gone high; anyhow the lion took no notice, but just went on eating. However, the next shot evoked a loud roar, followed by sounds of threshing about, and then some grunts or groans, from which we gathered that one of the animals, certainly, was hit. No more eyes were visible, and it was pretty clear the other lion had decamped. Not feeling inclined to push on and clear up the situation, especially with the rather poor illumination at our disposal, it only remained to go back to bed and patiently await daylight. The lion continued to grunt at intervals through the rest of the night, while Bles divided his time between barking at it and fighting in camp with another dog.

At earliest streak of dawn, I took my rifle and went out alone, which, with a wounded lion in question, is usually considerably safer than being accompanied by other people. At first it was too dark to see anything, so I got behind a forked tree and waited, while Bles kept running in and out barking. As it got lighter, I saw something on the ground which I took to be the dead donkey. But as the dog approached it, it reared up on end facing the latter. Upon this I fired and down it went again, a second shot causing it to lie motionless. On going up, I found, lying dead, an old lion with a small light-coloured mane. It had been recently injured fighting, which had no doubt prevented it from catching game. The shot in the dark had paralysed the hindquarters, so actually it would, had we but known, have been quite safe to approach at that time. Its mate had returned after the camp had quieted down, dragged off the remains of the donkey to the reeds of the river-bed a few hundred yards distant, and there finished everything except the head. The shots at dawn had probably frightened this one off, and, though we spoored it for some hours, we could not come up with it.

The foal was found standing rather pathetically outside the camp, the lion having somehow missed it. By the tracks, the marauders had followed the footpath from the river-bed straight to where the donkey was tied. The latter, having broken her riem, had rushed blindly off and dived underneath the body of my buckboard which was standing close by, moving it a few paces. The first lion had kept pace with the donkey on one side, but had not closed with it, while the other one, waiting just outside the limits of the camp, met and pulled down its victim close to a small bush, after which they dragged the carcass about ten yards farther away before beginning to eat it. Lion have a tiresome, though logical, habit of paying their nocturnal visits not in bright moonlight when they could easily be detected, but rather at the most silent hour of some pitch-black night, such as the one just mentioned, when drizzling rain is falling and everyone is making the most of whatever shelter is to be had.

Soon after this, another new ranger, Ledeboer, who had joined the staff in 1921 and was stationed at Letaba – at that time even more inaccessible than

De Laporte and his wife at the door of their wattle and daub home at Kaapmuiden. Living in isolation and in an unhealthy climate, the wife of a game ranger endured many hardships. Once, during her husband's absence, Mrs de Laporte killed four lion that were molesting her cattle.

Satara – also went down with pneumonia, though luckily with happier results than in Lloyd's case. His wife went through an indescribably trying time. For some two months and in a leaky hut made of mud and grass, she had single-handedly had to nurse her husband at the same time as having to look after her sick baby. There was no hope of getting any medical attention, nor even the most ordinary invalid comforts. In fact, the nearest white habitation being a hundred miles away with no connecting road, it was a long time before anyone learned that Ledeboer was ill and of the straits his wife was in. However, notwithstanding being of a certain age, he completely recovered, a tribute to a brave woman and a strong constitution. To live permanently in the bush far away from any possible aid in sickness a man ought to be young, or at least of an age when the constitution is still resistive and resilient. In all the earlier years of the reserve, when we lived under exceedingly hard conditions at times, I don't remember anyone suffering from ailments other than malarial fever, which we knew how to deal with, and common colds; but the staff was mostly young then, and all gifted with exceptionally strong constitutions. After fifty a man cannot with impunity expose himself to hardships whose effects he could laugh at when he was thirty, and this is especially true of life in the wilder parts of Africa, where, in cases of serious illness there is often no medical aid available.

For a good many years the quest for the Kruger Millions, referred to in a previous chapter, had languished, and we, whose duty it was to make arrangements for the reception and control of the parties, had begun to hope that it was dead. But our optimism was, as it proved, entirely premature, and during the winter of 1920 the best equipped of all the private expeditions arrived at Sabi Bridge by train, bringing with it wagons, donkeys, tents, and very complete camping equipment, even to grapnels and cranes for hoisting up the heavy boxes of treasure from their pit when found. The delay in the arrival of some stores kept our visitors encamped at Sabi Bridge for nearly a week, and I had many opportunities of conversing with the leader and other members of the party. The mystery which had enshrouded past expeditions was as nothing to that surrounding the present one. All must have been convinced that the treasure was theirs for the taking, for not only had they provided themselves, as described, with the machinery for raising it, but they had taken precautions to safeguard themselves against subsequent robbery. Accompanying the party were two young men whose exact position rather puzzled me; they seemed in the party and yet not of it. On a certain afternoon one of them was having tea on my veranda; he flung his coat carelessly over the back of a chair, and out of the pocket, with a great clatter, fell a large automatic. He picked it up in rather apologetic fashion explaining that 'his boss liked him to carry it!' Obvious as everything seemed, it was only a day or so before he left, and after I had explained how everybody in the lowveld was perfectly aware of the nature of his quest, that the leader grudgingly admitted that 'it might be something of the kind'; but when I went on to say that we knew exactly where he was bound for, he was not only incredulous but rather indignant. 'I have here with me,' he said, 'the very man who himself saw the treasure buried; no one in South Africa besides that man knows anything whatever about it, and I am the only man he has ever told. No! Previous efforts have been founded on wrong information, but you may take it from me we are on the real thing this time.' Somewhat impressed in spite of myself by his manner, I took the first opportunity of getting the guide alone – not an easy matter, as he was usually closely watched by one or other of the party; what he said was illuminating.

'I used to be a treasure-guide here long ago. Once I was taking two men down to search for it, and one night when they thought I was asleep, I heard them plotting to shoot me as soon as the treasure was found and bury me in the veld. I cut the trip as short as I could, you may believe me, and vowed I would never go again. Now for many years I have had a business in Johannesburg. Some years ago, old Mr – (the leader) got to hear that I knew about the buried treasure, and he has never given me a moment's peace since. He won't take my word that I don't know, and has made it so hot for me, that at last I have agreed to come down and show him the place where I camped with my commando.'

'Well, and did you not see anything buried?'

'Yes, I did see a hole dug, and two boxes which looked like ammunition boxes put in; but whatever was in them I expect the people coming behind us got. Ben Viljoen did not let much go past. Man! I want to get back to my job, but I shall have no peace till I have satisfied old Mr – .'

Everything having been so carefully thought out, and so much money spent, I felt genuinely disappointed when the spot chosen for the search proved to be the same koppie near the Sand River which had been the scene of scores of attempts in the past; the soil around dug and dug again; though after twelve years of peace it had resumed its virgin appearance. As soon as the spot was reached the guide pointed it out as the site of the commando's encampment, and, holding his leader to his promise, caught the first train back to Johannesburg. The party dug strenuously day after day, and one by one the members fell away, till at the end of six weeks only the leader was left to pack up the camp, a sadder and a wiser man.

In 1923 the police were made to look rather foolish and were proportionately wrathful. A young man had made a sworn statement to the effect that having been sent to inspect a farm near the Portuguese border, he had disembarked his wagon and oxen at a siding called Rolle, and had thence trekked eastward for three days. On the return journey, while he was digging a field over, he suddenly came on a quantity of buried bar gold. The police authorities, right up to the Deputy Commissioner in Pretoria, became greatly excited, and at once dispatched an officer, a sergeant, a corporal and three privates of the mounted constabulary, with four native constables and six pack donkeys to accompany the young man to the spot.

It was the height of the rainy season, a particularly wet and unhealthy March. The stated place lay far inside the game reserve. Unfortunately the last fact appeared to be unknown in Pretoria, and the whole affair had been kept so secret that I only heard of the police expedition after it had entered the reserve. Had I been advised previously I could easily have proved to the authorities that no such party as that stated had ever come. However, it was too late to do anything. Meantime the party of police, after a week of wandering about among swamp and long grass, in which they covered one hundred and forty miles, finally came to a halt at the usual koppie near Sand River – a prominent landmark. Here the guide admitted that though he thought he knew the koppie, he did not know which way he had originally gone, and the police, furiously angry, returned to Rolle. There, under cross-examination, he confessed that the whole story was a fabrication, that he had never made the trip stated, but had believed a story told him about hidden treasure and had invented the rest, hoping to share in the reward. All the police horses died of horse-sickness and all the white men had to go to hospital with malarial fever. But for the assistance rendered by our local ranger (Brent) and two of his 'boys', who accompanied the party throughout, things might have gone even worse with them. The police are dangerous people to play practical jokes upon and the young man in due course found himself undergoing a stiff sentence of imprisonment for perjury.

The 'quest' cropped up again in later years but only as a shadow of its former self. In 1931 a man told Colonel Reitz a story of how he had been with a Hollander who had the treasure with him in a Cape cart, and if he could but locate the spot where they outspanned, he knew he could find it. This man got only so far as asking information of its whereabouts from an old native of ours called Malopene, relatively a newcomer to the locality where he was then living!

After this the National Parks Board made a fee of £25 payable before permission could be granted, and subsequently only one party thought the chance of finding £2 000 000 a good enough proposition on which to hazard £25. Later still the Board stopped granting permission altogether.

Yet it must not be supposed that the search for the Kruger millions is dead. Far from it. The story will probably still be cropping up half a century hence. There will always be those eager to believe any tale, however fantastic, provided only that it offers the chance of getting something for nothing – that seldom attainable goal towards which the great mass of the human race still strives, and will strive, as in the past.

CHAPTER EIGHT
1923 TO 1924

THE TURNING POINT; AN OFFICIAL VISIT; NATIONAL PARKS BILL DRAFTED;
CURTAILMENT OF THE SABI RESERVE; A CHECK: BOY SCOUTS IN THE
RESERVE; A SOCIOLOGICAL DISCUSSION; STRAYED DONKEYS; A NIGHT
RAID; TREKKING WITH PACK DONKEYS; VISIT TO PUNDA MARIA;
COETSER; DE JAGER; INTERVIEW WITH MINISTER OF LANDS

IT WAS MENTIONED IN the last chapter that the Pretoria meeting, at which the Sabi Game Reserve was theoretically rent in pieces, was in fact the herald of a new era; its outcome proved the truth of the adage that it is always darkest before dawn. I had several satisfactory interviews with Colonel Reitz, one result of which was that he agreed to pay a visit to the reserve during the coming dry season and to see things for himself.

Accordingly, in August 1923, he duly arrived in his official capacity, attended by Sommerville, the Secretary of the Lands Department, and his private secretary, Neser. Apprised of the intended visit, some members of the Executive Committee of the Provincial Council thought they also would enjoy the trip, and Dr Hjalmar Reitz (Colonel Reitz's brother), Messrs Stoffberg and Kretschmar with Mr van Velden, the Provincial Secretary, accompanied the Minister; the party being made up by Dr Haagner, then chairman of the Wild Life Protection Society. This was the first time since 1903 that the reserve had been visited officially by any members of the Government or provincial administration. But Cinderella was now coming into her own!

I met the party at Komatipoort and travelled up with them in their private coach to Reserve Siding, just across the Sabie, where they spent the night. All the way up in the train some of the members were excitedly commenting on such game as they could see on either side of the line and discussing the sport they expected to have on the following day! I then discovered that before leaving Pretoria the members of the executive had passed a resolution giving themselves special permission to shoot in the reserve! This would never do. It might leave all kinds of repercussions, so I lost no time in surreptitiously enlisting the remainder of the party to combat so exceedingly dangerous a precedent. I believe a heated argument round the camp-fire went on far into the night and that opinions were about equally divided for and against the shooting plan. The deciding factor, I understand, was the discovery that a great deal of the land we were going to travel over was the property of private owners, by whose consent it had been included in the reserve, and that these would certainly not tacitly permit members of the Provincial Council to exercise privileges denied to them as owners. Moreover, with a council election brewing, it was realized that the violation of the reserve's sanctity by the very people who had, or were supposed to have, the task of protecting it, would be made full use of by political opponents.

I had of course put our side wise to the fact that only the year before, Greathead and party, representing the landowners, had been refused permission to shoot on their own land in the reserve, and that Greathead, at that very moment only a few miles away on the newly opened cattle ranch, would immediately know all about what they were doing. In the background hovered the Minister of Lands, all ready to put an embargo on shooting on government land within a sanctuary! Anyhow the danger passed and we spent a pleasant week driving about in two large mule trolleys and my buckboard. We visited Salitje, Lower Sabie and Tshokwane, and, though no roads existed and the native mule drivers generally drove their teams at an animated canter through bush and long grass, no serious accident occurred, the damage being confined to one broken spring and one smashed wheel. At Salitje, on a hint from Colonel Reitz that it might further the social amenities if some gesture were made that would at once do something to assuage the disappointed zeal of the hunters and be an acknowledgment of the good-natured way in which they had abandoned their first intentions, I went out with them, and shot a wildebeest for food. Just as we had stepped up to, and were contemplating the fallen animal, there was a 'click' behind us, and Van Velden emerged from the shelter of a bush, camera in hand, announcing that he had got an excellent photograph of 'members of the Executive Committee poaching in the game reserve' which he thought might do for the press! But I think even before this, the 'atmosphere' had got its grip on the party, and towards the end of the trip, there was nothing heard except talk of wildlife preservation and national parks. Indeed I don't believe that, at the end, a single member had the faintest desire to shoot anything.

Colonel Deneys Reitz was by this time enthusiastically in the national park scheme and as a first step proposed at once to translate theory into practice by approaching the landowners in regard to the disposal of their farms. Meantime, as a result of discussions in Pretoria earlier in the year, Major Scott, chairman of the Land Board, with Mr Schoch, the late Surveyor-General, were already travelling in the reserve valuing the private farms, identifying beacons and generally getting an idea of the situation. I fancy the work of a land surveyor, at least in countries such as South Africa, must be about the most healthy one a man can lead. Mr Schoch for instance – though well past sixty years of age – could walk untiringly all day long, however rough the going and hot the sun, discarding every means of conveyance other than his own legs, and I must say all the surveyors I have happened to come across have been of the same pattern. Major Scott, who though considerably younger, possessed what one may term a 'figure' and found, I imagine, his companion a little over-strenuous.

Things now began to move. Dr Schoch, brother of the late Surveyor-General and legal adviser to the Government, an enthusiastic sportsman and then, as now, a great pillar of wildlife preservation, drafted a 'National Parks Ordinance' which, practically unaltered, later became law. The Wild Life Protection Society started an energetic campaign and the railway administration began to make 'Visits to the reserve' a prominent feature of their Round-in-Nine tours. It was clear, however, that it would be out of the question for government to acquire either by purchase or exchange the whole of the two-and-a-half million-odd acres which was the total of private land within the Sabi reserve. Fortunately, the whole of the old portion of the sanctuary – to wit, that lying between the Sabie and the Crocodile rivers, as well as the whole of the Shingwedsi reserve – was Crown land, and the private farms lay entirely between the Olifants River in the north and the Sabie River in the south. In that region there was a big block of government farms lying towards the east along the Nwanedzi River, and another, known as the 'Alexandra Block', in the south-west corner between the Sand and Sabie rivers. But to make these part of a national park while releasing the private land would have implied a sanctuary consisting of two big blocks north and south and some small isolated ones in the middle, separated from one another by so much private property as to render adequate supervision of the future park very difficult.

I had long foreseen the likelihood of a portion of the Sabi reserve having to be deproclaimed, and as long ago as 1913, at the suggestion of Mr Johann Rissik, had drawn up a plan under which the area between the Olifants and the Sabie rivers was bisected by a line which followed roughly the meridian of 31°30'. When, therefore, Colonel Deneys Reitz, asked me to draw up a new western boundary line (feeling that a preliminary to any expropriation of private land would have to be the discarding of a large part of the present reserve), it was only a matter of defining on the map exactly which farm beacons should be followed. The result was to take out one million acres of private land and some five hundred thousand which were the property of the Government, the latter including the sheep grazing area west of Pretoriuskop. The four million-odd acres which remained still contained about seventy private farms with a total acreage of roughly five hundred thousand acres – not an insoluble proposition for purchase or exchange if the Government was really determined to create a national park. I had included in my plan two little wedges on the south-west, intruding into the 'grazing area', one to take in the ranger's quarters opposite Kaapmuiden on the Crocodile River (which, however, were soon after moved to Malelane) and another – those of Ranger Wolhuter – at Mtimba. The former, the less important of the two, was duly included, but apparently, by a typing omission of two lines, the latter was overlooked, and I did not know anything about it until the new boundaries were in the *Gazette* and it proved too late to have any alteration made.

Therefore, at the end of 1923, having surrendered, as the price of achieving permanency for the remainder of the reserve, some two thousand five hundred square miles of territory – which included the best of the sable and roan antelope country, as well as that containing all the red, or Natal, duiker and nearly all the mountain reedbuck – I rested in the confident expectation that the desired legislation would be passed during the next session of parliament.

But alas for premature hopes! Colonel Reitz had asked me to come to Cape Town in January to help him with advice on technical points, and so it was a sad shock to receive a wire during that month instructing me not to come as the 'National Parks Bill had been dropped'. So there we were, in the position of having given a lot away and got nothing in return. I gathered that the decisive factor was a deadlock in the negotiations with the land companies regarding the price to be paid for their farms still remaining in the reserve. Wherever the responsibility for failure may have lain, it was most disappointing; but in reality, though one did not appreciate this at the time, it was probably just as well that the Bill did not come before parliament then. There had not yet been nearly enough propaganda in the country and the public was far from being awakened. I feel pretty certain indeed that had the Act then gone to parliament, it would have emerged in so mutilated a form as to be not fully effective for its purpose. The whole thing had been pushed on in a hurry, largely on the enthusiasm of the minister concerned, and there had been no time, by a widespread press campaign, to get the politicians and the public into the right frame of mind.

Early in 1924 there was a general election and a change of government. While the former was still pending I met one day, in the street in Pretoria, Mr Oswald Pirow, an old acquaintance, who besides being a keen sportsman and strong supporter of the game reserve, was a prominent member of the Nationalist Party, under which he was shortly to hold cabinet rank. I told him of my troubles and explained how, in my belief, they had come about. He was sympathetic and encouraging and said that if, as expected, his party got into power, he would push the national park scheme with the new cabinet for all he was worth and that he did not consider they would have any difficulty in getting legislation passed to make expropriation of private land within the reserve compulsory, if need be. He was I believe as good, or even better than his word, and I think a good deal of what happened later was directly due to his efforts.

Meantime, we just carried on. The excision of so much of the reserve at the end of 1923 had at least quietened opposition for the time being and I felt that we had breathing space in which to reconstruct plans; but nothing could be done until the new government was firmly settled in the saddle.

From 1923 there commenced an annual visit by the Barberton Boy Scouts under their scoutmaster – Mr Yates – who incidentally was a brother-in-law of Wolhuter. They used to come by train to Malelane and spend a few days camping close to the Crocodile River. We provided one or more native police to guide them and generally to see that they came to no harm. By day, walks were taken in the bush to view the animals. Firewood was collected for the camp-fire, and all the scout ritual, including night watch, faithfully performed under conditions more realistic than falls to the lot of scouts in most other parts of the world. Although I did not hear of one actually doing so, a lion was quite likely to come prowling round the camp in the hours of darkness, and the scout on night sentry could certainly listen with appropriate thrills to the voices of the wilderness during the dark watches, while all the others slept. It was a popular trip and cut both ways, being good for the boys and helpful to the reserve. These visits continued until the days when the sanctuary was thrown open to the general public, rest-camps provided and roads made – until civilization had really descended upon us, and the Wild Spirit, resentful at what she saw, sometimes hid her face. The happy culmination, in short, of my efforts during so many years.

So far back as 1920, the Witwatersrand Native Labour Association had been conveying native recruits from Portuguese Territory through the Shingwedsi reserve from the Limpopo-Pafuri river junction to Punda Maria, at first by donkey wagons and later in big Thorneycroft lorries. They had made an excellent road thence all the way to their headquarters at Soekmekaar more than a hundred miles away. In 1922 a similar service was inaugurated through Satara to Acornhoek, and at intervals of fifteen miles or so along the road, corrugated-iron 'lion-proof' shelters were erected to protect their donkeys by night – a very necessary precaution.

I recollect a Public Works Department inspector once travelling through the reserve with a wagon and a team of government donkeys. One night lion stampeded them, killed three and scattered the others, which were not recovered for some time. The inspector turned out with his rifle, but unluckily, when it came to charging the weapon, he found that he had brought cartridges for some other sized bore. I had better luck when one day my own donkeys, eight of them, strayed away from a camp on the Hlambamaduba River. I had to send back twenty-five miles to Sabi Bridge for the ox-wagon to move the camp and it was a week before the first donkey was recovered. Yet, marvellous to relate of a lion country, although it was two months before the last one was found by the ganger wandering along the railway line, all were eventually retrieved. They were picked up by ones and twos over about fifty square miles of country by the searchers who were out all the time, and except that one had been slightly clawed, perhaps by a leopard, they were all quite undamaged, although exceedingly wild. One cannot explain these things. If a valuable horse had strayed, it would probably have fallen a victim the very first night.

Similar good fortune to that which had attended the desertion of the donkeys befell for a time the tame eland, the last of the herd which was being built up before the war. Finding, no doubt, the cattle dull companions, and eager to discover one of his own kind, he repeatedly absented himself, once for three days, when he was discovered seven miles away. He never on these excursions came to any harm, yet one day when he was grazing close to the cattle with herd boys in attendance, the lions got him. We had a good deal of amusement out of this animal. When a tourist train was expected at Sabi Bridge, it became the custom to have him driven up close to the siding, where he could be seen unconcernedly grazing as the train drew in. He formed a capital advertisement of the tameness of the animals in the reserve and his photograph, with appropriate captions, such as 'Wild Animals Greet Human Visitors', must have appeared scores of times in the Johannesburg press.

After Lloyd's death the Satara house stood vacant for some time and I thought it should be repainted and generally renovated. A painter from some town contracted for the work and in the course of a tour in that direction I dropped in to see how he was getting on. I found him sitting on the veranda in a deck chair, a cool drink at his elbow, the while, close by, two natives, one of them at the top of a ladder, industriously laid on the paint. It appeared that he was either a Communist, or held advanced opinions in connection with capitalism and labour, and I spent a most interesting afternoon. Finding me to be a sympathetic listener, he explained to me at great length, and with many illustrations, how the idle rich were always 'grinding the faces of the poor beneath their iron heel', and how the poor starving working man had to work his hands to the bone while his well-fed masters sat at ease. At intervals he would interrupt the flow of his conversation to shout at the two natives, 'Get a move on you lazy brutes, what do you think I pay you for?' He would then explain what an unutterably lazy lot the natives were and how no amount of 'hiding' seemed to do them any good. After he had calmed down, he would resume about the persecution of the poor by the rich.

Next morning, when my 'boys' were packing the donkeys, my friend came to watch operations, and remarked incidentally how quick and competent at their job they all seemed to be. 'I reckon you must "hide" them a lot to make them work like that,' he added. When I disclaimed modestly any activity in that direction, he winked at me and said, 'Well, all I can say is that I knock hell out of my blighters, as much as I can, and dock their pay too, but it don't seem to do no good; rotten lot they are'. This contrast between theory and practice gave food for some thought throughout the day's march. Some short time later, I heard this man's name mentioned in connection with some labour troubles, in which I gathered he was a leading protagonist of the 'Working Man'.

About this time I made what proved to be the last of my long treks from south to north of the reserves. I took the wagon as far as the Olifants River,

187

where I left it and the buckboard with some police and dogs to guard the oxen, and thence proceeded on horseback with pack donkeys through the Shingwedsi country. On the way to the Olifants I spent a night at Satara, then unoccupied, and just as I was sitting down to a scratch dinner in the empty house, a messenger appeared to say the donkeys were lost. Having driven on with the buckboard to get in before dark, I had left the wagon and loose donkeys to follow with the police and herds, expecting them to arrive soon after sundown, as it was only seven miles from Satara to the Nwanedzi River where we had outspanned. However, it appeared that some adjustment to the wagon had to be made and the whole lot had stayed behind till it was in a state to proceed. By this time it was nearly dark, and before they had got half-way, completely so. There was no moon, and apparently, when about half a mile from Satara, the whole lot of the donkeys had suddenly stamped-ed into the night. The country around was simply teeming with lion and my heart sank as I visualized what would probably happen and how my carefully planned expedition was likely to be wrecked almost at the outset.

I collected all the police, about six of them, including the two stationed at

The warden's annual patrol, which occupied him for some two-and-a-half months, was undertaken when the summer rainy season was over but while vegetation and water were still abundant.

Satara, of whom the senior was one named Zambezi, an elderly gentleman whose waistline was not what it had once been. We had only two hurricane lamps to light our way and it was one of the darkest nights I had ever been out in. The chances did not seem too good as lion were roaring, seemingly from every point of the compass. We went to the place where the animals had stampeded, thence laboriously followed the spoor, which fortunately led diagonally towards Satara, and in the end came on the wagon road, which the tracks then followed away to the west. Clearly several donkeys were in front of us, but whether all or not, it was impossible to say. After about an hour in which we covered a mile or so, we got down into a hollow where there was a swamp and we could find no spoor leading beyond. Suddenly there was a crash and a snort close by – for a moment we thought caused by some wild animal. But as we raised the lamps above our heads, somebody called out 'Bongolo!', and sure enough, ten yards away, I could make out a pair of long ears. We spread out, and went cautiously, a lamp at each end of the line. Soon, to our delight, we found all eight animals, apparently very nervous, huddled up in a bunch among some long grass. Very carefully, in case of a fresh stampede, we got all round them, and then, having managed to catch one and get a riem round its neck, we led it off and herded the others along behind. One of the 'boys' led the way with a lantern, while the other light was carried in rear of the procession.

The homeward journey, though not much more than a mile, was full of anxiety. Every now and then there was a tendency on the part of the donkeys, which could only dimly be seen, to break away, and if one had not been led in front, I am certain they would have done so. We crept along with constant halts to make sure every one was in place on the flanks. Once indeed the whole lot, startled by a herd of zebra which thundered by in the darkness not very far away, went off down the road at best pace. We all ran our hardest, Zambezi (gallantly doing his best) blowing like a broken-winded horse in rear, the oscillating lamp which he carried showing his whereabouts. Luckily we were able to head the fugitives off before they left the road, and getting them once more safely rounded up, drove them triumphantly into camp soon after 9 p.m. It was a lucky let-off, and simply miraculous that not a single lion had come near the donkeys during the whole time they were out by themselves in the veld.

Adventures, and incidentally, my good luck, were not yet at an end. Having duly arrived at the Olifants River at about 2 p.m. one day, I found the picket and cattle kraal in a very tumble-down condition and we spent the rest of the day in strengthening the latter with thorn bushes – fortunately as it appeared later. About 9.30 p.m. I heard lion a mile or so away. Two hours later the dogs began to bark furiously, and a 'boy' came pattering over to my hut with the cheering news that a lion was in the cattle kraal! There were the usual delays of getting shoes on, lighting lamps – matches always break on these occasions – and grabbing hold of ammunition. Then I ran over, holding my little Osram electric lamp, and found the dogs barking just outside the cattle kraal – the lion, which appeared to be inside, answering them with a continuous purring growl, very low and menacing; not the most pleasant thing to hear when close at hand. Although he appeared to be inside, it seemed strange that not a sound came from the oxen. Feeling that we wanted all the illumination we could get, I lighted a carbide lamp, a task which consumed a little time. But at length, some ten minutes after the first alarm, armed with my Paradox, which I had loaded with S.S.G. (slugs), and holding the electric lamp in my left hand, I went slowly round the kraal, the dogs preceding me, and the 'boys' behind with all the lamps that could be mustered. The low growling continued, but, though quite near by its exact locality was difficult to define. When we had got nearly half-way round there was a tremendous crashing in the fence, and about a dozen paces away, a dark form bounded out across our front, at which, while still in mid air, I took a snap shot, apparently without effect, while the following second barrel was a mere hazard into the dark. A few seconds later came some deep grunts and sounds of breaking branches, then silence. The dogs ran forward, almost immediately to come tearing back on us, Belfast – a big heavy beast – nearly upsetting me in his rush. I did not think it prudent to go on, especially since the lion was now quite silent and there was therefore no indication of its whereabouts, so we all went into the cattle kraal, where to my surprise, the oxen were standing perfectly safe and to all appearance completely unperturbed. Hurricane lamps were then hung up round the zeriba, which stood right on the edge of dense bush, and as there seemed nothing more to be done at present, we all went back to bed. I slept only disjointedly, and through the night could hear what I was sure must be a second lion prowling round the camp, calling for his mate in the low unmistakable tones used by them when 'talking' to one another. I began to think I might really have killed the lion, though it seemed rather a wild idea.

At grey dawn Bles, that marvellously good lion dog, began barking continuously from one spot. So taking the Paradox again, I went out in pyjamas to find him standing over a big dead lion, just visible in the growing light. It had only gone some thirty paces before it had fallen and we had heard its dying struggles. The S.S.G. had made a splendid pattern with the heart as centre and one slug had gone through the aorta. It proved to be a very large and very gaunt male with a small grey mane, the canine teeth broken to stumps on one side. Its pads were full of porcupine quills, and its chest also, thus evidently it could not catch game and was a dangerous beast, well got rid of. In fact old Jack, living in a hut not far away, said that with another and smaller male, it had been hanging about for some time in the vicinity and only the month before had, in broad daylight, killed his donkey, menacing him when he tried to drive it off.

On examining the cattle kraal, I found that the lion had wormed himself on his belly through the thorn branches which, with yesterday's additions, were about fifteen feet wide, but had got barely half-way through when he was disturbed by the dogs. He then must have become alarmed and have lain in the middle of the fence growling at his disturbers, and making no further attempt to get at the cattle, which had neither seen nor winded him. When we began to come close, the barking of the dogs, the talking of the natives and the flashing of the lights must have been too much for his nerve, and he had dashed straight out – luckily for us not in our direction! I was impressed by two things: first, the enormous strength of an animal which, from a prone position, and at one bound, could smash like paper through at least six feet of thorn bush and packed branches, and secondly, by the great natural fear of man which a lion instinctively harbours. The thick zeriba looked as if a motorcar had been driven through it and showed that, when really meaning business, there can be few fences capable of keeping a lion in or out. Of course, had his heart not failed him, and had he come at, instead of going away from us, he would have had by a long way the best of the deal; so once again it was satisfactory to feel that the lion is not really the ferocious monster of the story books.

Having crossed the Olifants River, which in those days meant nearly a whole day's work, I went on to where Ledeboer was then living just north of the Letaba. His wife and infant were with him and the quarters not too good. No houses for rangers had at that time been provided anywhere north of the Olifants River, the area being too unget-at-able in the view of government; but the Ledeboers seemed to be quite contented pending something better being provided for them. Ledeboer said that about seven bull elephants, singly or in pairs, frequented the neighbourhood, and so tame were they that they often came quite close to his quarters, becoming truculent only if the dogs barked at them or attempted to drive them off. Once an old male had pursued his terrier almost up to the house. Natives complained that if mealies were stored in a sleeping hut, the elephants sometimes at night would remove the thatch, and insert their trunks, so it was difficult not only to raise any crops but to keep the grain when reaped. Unfortunately for the sufferers, in a game sanctuary the only remedy was to move out of the patrol area of the animals, though I suggested to Ledeboer that a few squibs and crackers might, as with lion at night, prove of some value.

The journey northwards through the Shingwedsi country was uneventful though interesting. Excepting in the vicinity of Major Fraser's old camp at Malunzane, there was not much game, and such as did occur, rather wild. On the Bububu River I saw a place where a rhinoceros had recently rubbed his horn against a tree and had broken a bush, but we could not catch sight of the animal in the flesh. This was an interesting episode, being apparently the last time any traces of rhinos have been observed in that country, and I suppose this particular animal wandered into Portuguese territory and was killed there. The native hunting camps, which had been so much in evidence along the Shingwedsi in former years, had entirely disappeared, and there were now practically no inhabitants in the area until the western border was approached.

One soon falls into a routine in trekking with pack animals and after a few days everyone knows his particular task. I would awake at early dawn and shout loudly, when the men would arise, loose the animals, and turn them out to graze, after which the camp was packed up and breakfast cooked. When the loads had been adjusted and weighed – of course they alter in weight considerably day by day, as meal and grain are consumed by men and animals – and we had finished our early meal, the donkeys would be brought in, saddled and loaded, the latter proceeding meriting time and care if delays on the march, and sore backs are to be avoided. Then, when all was ready, the horse was saddled, the donkeys were driven forth, and after a last look round I followed the line.

During the march I usually rode ahead, stopping every now and then to allow the animals to come up, as pack donkeys, though they can keep up a steady three miles an hour, lose about half a mile even on a slowly walking horse in that distance. Sometimes there were small excitements during the march, such as disturbing lion or other carnivora, finding fresh kills and so on. With donkeys I usually found it best to complete the day's trek without making a long halt with its necessary off-saddle, and just to stop every hour,

The end of a day's patrol when, 'from the recesses of the wagon appear camp-table, chair, bottle, glasses, all the things tending to mitigate the asperities of life' (page 147).

see that the loads were all right and that the pack-saddles had not slipped. Therefore we had generally completed our fifteen or twenty miles by about 2 p.m. when there was still plenty of time to select a good camping place and to allow the animals a few hours' grazing before dark. After having watered and then turned them out to their own devices, all hands would set to work to make a good zeriba which always enclosed the whole camp, leaving one entrance in which a fire was lighted at night.

As winter rain is not unknown and as it also furnished an illusion of privacy, I always carried a small bivouac tent, into which I might crawl on hands and knees, and within which all my more intimate possessions, such as firearms, ammunition, torch and reading matter were stored on top of the blankets. The 'boys' slept round a large fire, and at the farthest side of the zeriba from the entrance a long ground-rope was pegged down, to which the horses and the donkeys were tethered in line. The dogs usually barked more or less all night but one became accustomed to that, and it provided the encouraging feeling that they were doing their job. Dinner was at sundown, and usually by the time it was dark, the nosebags were off, the horses and the dogs fed, and I turned in while the 'boys' were discussing their own meal, after which they would talk a little and then one by one roll themselves in their blankets and relapse into slumber. A good life, and I must have covered many thousand miles thus from first to last.

At Punda Maria, which it had taken nearly three weeks to reach from Sabi Bridge, Coetser, the ranger, had built half a dozen wattle-and-daub huts and a sort of summer house, protected from flies by mosquito-wire gauze. I found there Mr Pirow, with Drs Schoch, Stamer and Haagner, proceeding on a shooting trip to Portuguese territory. My old friend Paul Neergaard, the local manager of the native recruiting association, was also passing through on inspection work. We spent a pleasant evening; Coetser, who, whatever his faults, was a cheery soul, producing a gramophone and entertaining us with stories of his past adventures, apocryphal or otherwise. He had been a member of the Staats Artillerie before and during part of the South African War, and one gathered that most of the republican successes could largely be traced to his efforts. He had also, it seemed, been General Botha's right-hand man, both in 1914 and afterwards in the East African campaign!

Long afterwards I learnt that, during this visit, he had committed a cardinal blunder in suggesting to Pirow, by way of ingratiating himself, that the latter should come and have a few days shooting with him in the reserve! He had approached the wrong man as it happened, and when Pirow became a member of the National Parks Board, Coetser's days as a ranger were numbered. In those days Punda Maria was very far away, and one had to do what one could and accept what was given. The mere fact of having a white officer there, even if the latter did occasionally overstep the line, at least kept the natives and hunting parties generally from doing what they liked, while one had to give Coetser the credit of being exceedingly energetic, and when he liked, quite efficient.

About a year before this, he had been ill with blackwater fever, and Neergaard hearing of it and knowing that he was far from any medical aid – indeed, in the absence of his wife, without any attention except that of his native servants – hurried down to take him to hospital, though as it happened he found the patient was already convalescent. Now Coetser was, as his acquaintances knew him, a sturdily-built, middle-aged man, with a fresh complexion and rich brown hair without a streak of grey in it. When Neergaard arrived he was greeted by a seeming total stranger: an old man, cadaverous from illness, with long snow-white hair and beard, among whose first words were, 'For God's sake, old man, did you bring any hair restorer with you?'

The year after this visit I moved Coetser down to Satara to take Lloyd's place, and Colonel Piet de Jager went to Punda Maria. De Jager had a fine military record, having been a commandant in the South African War and colonel of a mounted corps in East Africa during the 1916 campaign, greatly distinguishing himself in each. He had earned the Distinguished Service Order in the latter and several other decorations, which he once showed to me. Among them was some Russian or Serbian order, and I asked him about it. He said he had no clear idea what it was, but that General Smuts had made him a present of it, and in fact, so far as I remember, he had an inscription to that effect on the back. In person he was, although over sixty years of age, a strikingly handsome man, his features those one associates with the old French nobility, from whom I have no doubt he was a lineal descendant. Unfortunately he had been born before the days of universal higher education in the Transvaal. But he was not contented at Punda Maria; he hated the loneliness and longed to get back to his family and his farm, besides which, he suffered seriously from malaria, first contracted in East Africa and not bettered by summers spent in the reserve. In fact his best days, as with many others of us, alas, were behind him.

It is to De Jager, however, that belongs the credit of definitely having established the existence of nyala in the Pafuri bush. These rare and handsome antelope had once or twice been reported in Coetser's time, but De Jager actually found the horns of one killed by a lion and sent them to me. It is possible that the animals had come back to old haunts from Portuguese territory. On the other hand a few – too few to be noticed – may have all the time existed in the dense bush south of the Limpopo River, and on the whole I am disposed to think this may have been the case. Eland, too, were beginning to become almost numerous in the north and this species certainly was heavily recruited from across the frontier, since it is certain that there were few of any in the reserve up to 1905.

Towards the end of 1924 I called upon Mr Piet Grobler, who had become Minister of Lands, and in whom therefore all our hopes now centred. On my way to his office I put my foot on a loose flooring board and re-sprained my ankle, which occurrence I feared might be an evil omen. But for once forebodings were unjustified and the path to the goal was from this time onwards to be strewn with roses – a pleasant path on the whole, even though the roses had here and there thorns among them.

I found Mr Grobler's interest in the national park scheme had already been stimulated and he was most sympathetic, though at that time he seemed to consider the difficulties in the way of fruition too considerable to be tackled at the moment. A grand-nephew of President Kruger, who had been responsible for the inauguration of the original Sabi Game Reserve in 1898, it appeared appropriate for him to put the seal of security and permanence on what his kinsman had originated. I felt that things were going in the right direction, but slowly, and it looked as if there might yet be a long while to wait before anything practical evolved. Sommerville continued to be the Secretary for Lands, and I knew that so far as it came within his official sphere, he would do all in his power to help, though less than two years had passed since, at the memorable Pretoria meeting, he had recorded his department's desire for total abolition!

CHAPTER NINE
1925 TO 1926

THE YEAR 1925 BEGAN with the campaign against the brown locust (*Locustana pardalina*), which in the latter part of the previous year had invaded the Transvaal from Bechuanaland. This type differs in habit as well as in appearance from its cousin the red locust (*Nomadacris septemfasciata*) against which we had battled in 1906. Up to a point they resemble one another in their ways. Both arrive in enormous flying swarms, which at a distance resemble thick clouds of drifting smoke, and close at hand literally darken the sky. Where they settle for the night or rest during the day, they consume completely every green thing on which they alight. Although the swarms always persist in some general direction, they are often carried hither and thither according to the direction of whatever wind may be blowing at the time. In due course the swarm ceases its flight to permit the females to lay their eggs, which are cemented together in clusters of some hundreds each and are inserted several inches into the ground. After having deposited their eggs the old locusts are supposed to die in a short time; at any rate they are believed to survive only during one full season.

After a period, the length of which depends on whether there is in the meantime any rain or not, the young ones, known as 'hoppers', hatch out, at first only the size of the tiniest grasshoppers, and spread in little patches all over the piece of country where the parent swarm settled. After a few weeks the isolated patches of hoppers – or voetgangers, as they are usually called – having meantime grown enormously, join up and commence to trek, always heading in the same direction. They move off each morning as soon as the sun begins to warm the ground and continue steadily on all day, except for a few hours during the hottest time. As they hop along, they eat up – even more wholeheartedly than their parents – every kind of herbage in their way. They are dense on the ground, and a large swarm may easily cover a square mile of country. In about two months, varying in the case of different species, they begin to grow wings, fly off, and the cycle is repeated.

In their special habits, as remarked above, the red and brown locust differ widely; for whereas the flying swarms of the latter always rest on the ground, the former favours the branches of the trees, which frequently are borne down by their accumulated weight. The hoppers of the red species are far more active than the others and when alarmed spring into bushes and undergrowth, instead of confining themselves, like their more stolid cousins, to the surface of the ground.

Should a flying swarm of locusts be observed approaching and appear likely to pass over gardens or orchards, all hands turn out armed with tin cans, rattles, anything that will make a noise. When the swarm, with immense rustling of wings, is at length overhead, an overwhelming din aris-es; each man shouts and drums his loudest, smoke fires are lighted, long sticks thrust into branches of fruit trees; in fact, every thought-of device used to discourage permanent settlement. After a time varying directly with the size of the swarm – sometimes, where an exceptionally large one is con-cerned, two hours or more – when the danger seems over and the locusts are a mere cloud on the horizon, it is safe to disperse, though even then it is wise to post look-outs, for should the wind suddenly veer round, they are quite capable of returning on their tracks.

The usual method adopted in South Africa in the wars against locusts has been to attack them while still in the hopper stage by means of arsenical spray. This, if mixed in the correct proportion of arsenic to water as detailed in the instructions, is, in my experience, innocuous to bird and beast. In fact, I believe experiment has demonstrated that to absorb a fatal dose, a grazing animal in amount of grass, and a bird in weight of locusts, must each con-sume well above its greatest natural capacity. Unfortunately, those entrusted with the work were not always so meticulously careful as they might have been in regard to mixing the preparation of the mixture. It has even been hinted that superfluous tins of the pure poison were got rid of by emptying them on the ground. Such departures from the narrow path are sufficient to account for the considerable mortality among stock which has been an unhappy concomitant of every locust campaign in South Africa.

In the game reserve, thanks to employing only our own staff, we were able to conduct matters in a more methodical and better disciplined manner than was possible in other parts of the country. Each ranger divided his district into sections, to each of which was appointed a native policeman in charge of a squad of labourers working two or more pumps. Relays of carriers ferried water and fresh supplies of poison to the working gangs. The ranger rode round his squads daily, supervised work and checked the correct proportion of water to poison. So far as I know – and careful observations were made – there was no loss of wildlife whatever as a result of our locust campaigns. We were also able to show a return of a larger number of swarms destroyed at about one-tenth of the cost of the neighbouring areas outside our boundaries, where casual labour was employed. This was not, however, known until afterwards, and at the time some hailed the arrival of the locusts as a convenient stick wherewith to beat the reserve administration, and incidentally, perhaps, as a lever with the help of which secret desires might be gratified.

Accordingly, the headquarters of the locust bureau was bombarded with moving tales of how the insects were being allowed to breed and multiply unchecked in the reserve, with riders pointing out how essential it was that the work should be taken out of the incompetent hands of the staff and placed in those of the local residents, who would then (it followed) have the right – armed, of course – to explore its fastnesses in any direction they pleased. In response to these protests, an inspector was sent down early in 1925, who reported (unfortunately for the critics) that the reserve was the only place he had visited in which locust spraying was being carried out by a methodical system. This closed the agitation, though, of course, the next and greater campaign of 1934 saw it again revived, with similar arguments and results.

In 1925 the arsenic was issued ready mixed with sugar, which was the fruit of experience. For in 1906 each was doled out separately, the latter in the form of molasses, not very appetizing to look at, yet sufficiently attractive to ensure that a minimum of it would be mixed with the poison – it seemed a pity to waste it on locusts.

Whether arsenic spraying is really an effective remedy or not is a disputed point. For destroying hoppers in the near neighbourhood of crops there is probably nothing better. But even though ninety per cent over a large area may be destroyed – an optimistic conception – there would still, next season, appear as a result of incubation, at least ten times as many locusts as there were the season before. Some go so far as to say that by killing off a large proportion of the insects artificially, their inevitable annihilation by the parasites which sooner or later always attack them when their numbers become excessive, is proportionately delayed. For their part the tribal natives, who value locusts as food, and had in the past been accustomed to collect enormous quantities of hoppers for that purpose, have never shown themselves specially enthusiastic. I recollect an old man whose mealie lands had been partly saved, saying resignedly, 'Well, I may get some mealies, but your *muti* has killed all my sweet potatoes, and now I cannot eat the locusts to make up for it!'

Enormous flocks of insect-eating birds, storks of various species, egrets and others, constantly hang on the flanks of the flying swarms and congregate at places where the young have hatched out. Guineafowl, baboon, jackal, mongoose and many other creatures consume such large numbers of the hoppers that relatively small hatchlings may, in a wild country, safely be left to natural enemies. I have seen numbers being dragged underground by scorpions and baboon spiders; in fact, it may be said that most insectivorous and carnivorous creatures welcome the advent of the locusts as much as man deplores it.

In a sense our locust labours in the reserve were altruistic since there were present no white farmers and relatively few resident natives; such crops as the latter sowed generally dying from drought in any case. The damage that any possible number of locust swarms could do to our eight thousand square miles of grass and secondary forest could never be other than imperceptible in affecting the food supply of our wild animals. But we had to consider our neighbours. On two sides we were close to cultivated country; indeed, so well was it understood that we had nothing to fear from locusts ourselves, that it was invariably assumed by our neighbours that we were adopting a *laissez-faire* attitude with regard to them, and perhaps the knowledge of this spurred us to do our best!

Meantime public interest in the national park scheme was gradually extending; paragraphs, even leading articles, began to appear in newspapers, and the position slowly strengthened. This was just as well, for about the middle of the year there began a determined agitation against the Sabi reserve on the part of some of the settlers along the south bank of the

Crocodile River, who for various and quite understandable reasons had never viewed it with friendly eyes. During each winter lion were accustomed to cross the river and undoubtedly gave a lot of trouble by killing stock, while the waterbuck and kudu raided orchards and winter crops. The attack began in the *Farmer's Weekly* and pictured the condition of things in so lurid a light that the periodical devoted a leading article to it, as subsequently did one or more of the leading Johannesburg dailies.

> I would like [wrote this correspondent] to draw your readers' atten-
> tion to the scandal of the Sabi Game Reserve, where they have been
> breeding lions for the last twenty-five years. I have lived opposite
> the reserve since 1914 and have noticed a great shrinkage of game.
> Zebra used to cross over in droves, and it was a common sight to see
> them in the reserve, but I have not seen one since 1922. Blue wilde-
> beest is another species which is disappearing from the Sabi Game
> Reserve. Of all the white elephants, and for sheer waste of money
> and game, and mismanagement, I think the conduct of the Sabi
> Game Reserve 'takes the cake'.

Others joined in to the effect that if any game was to survive all the lion must be destroyed at once. One, better informed than the others to the extent that he had heard some rumour of the national parks movement, wrote in a popular weekly that if the scheme bore fruit the farmers were ruined. 'Sir,' he ended eloquently, 'I have lived here for thirty years, and we might have had a happy paradise of smiling homesteads, and what have we got instead? Lions!'

The general object appeared to be to obtain permission for 'certified sportsmen' (an embracing term) to enter the reserve and shoot the lion, and one wondered – knowing something of those who were likely to volunteer for the work – what proportion lion would bear to game among the slain! However, supporters of the reserve began to enter the lists, and after rather an acrimonious correspondence extending through the press over some months, the attack gradually died away. While the battle was in full swing, however, I was really alarmed by the action of the Wild Life Protection Society, always our strong supporter, which, through some misunderstand-ing, actually wrote officially to the provincial administration favouring the plan of allowing 'certified sportsmen' to assist the staff in destroying lion. In due course the letter was sent to me for comment and its contents justified a hurried journey to Pretoria, followed by an emergency meeting of the society, where everything was satisfactorily explained and straightened out. The fact was, I knew the inwardness – and the probable result if it were adopted – of the 'certified sportsmen' suggestion, and the society did not.

It was clear, nevertheless, that the lion menace did really form so genuine an excuse for agitation against the reserve that some drastic step should be taken immediately to remove it, especially at this crucial period when the whole future of wildlife preservation seemed to be in the melting-pot. Indeed, had this agitation occurred some two or three years earlier, I believe the results to the sanctuary, and therefore the future national park, might have been serious. Fortunately, things had already moved too far in the right direction to render it more than disquieting. I secured the services as a ranger of Mr Harold Trollope, in place of a recently appointed individual who, after a couple of months at Malelane, was prostrated through nervous breakdown, caused by what to him seemed the loneliness of the life.

Mr Trollope was a hunter of wide experience and, moreover, a man of tact and organizing ability, which made him an ideal ranger. His first task was to alleviate the lion menace in respect of our neighbours, and so well did he succeed that within a couple of years, after which, to my regret, he terminated

Harold Trollope, appointed game ranger in 1925, was an excellent shot and an experienced hunter. He successfully eliminated almost all predators from the Malelane section of the game reserve.

his service, he had not only completely cleared his own area of all lion, but had even, as some of the neighbouring rangers rather plaintively remarked, 'left not one' in their sections either. He shot all his lion single-handed, preferring to gallop after them on horseback where the country permitted, and shoot them at bay or in the act of charging. He was a dead shot, possessed of the coolest nerve, and so successful was he, and so entirely confident in himself, that latterly he used to go out of his way deliberately to invite charges, finding the sport not sufficiently exciting otherwise. Yet, I think he was lucky. However cool a man may be, and however steady a shot, if he makes a habit of this kind of thing, the day is apt to arrive when something wrong in the mechanism of the rifle, perhaps some flaw in the cartridge, may cause a misfire; or possibly some slight and perhaps unnoticed physical depression due to a cold, even a disturbed night, may affect the nerve at the crucial moment and make all the difference between a dead lion and a dead man.

One tragedy marked Trollope's tenure of office as a ranger. He had allowed his father-in-law, Mr Glen Leary, a retired magistrate and a man of some seventy years of age, to accompany him on a leopard hunt, not far away from his station. It appears that the dogs bayed the leopard up a dry spruit, and Trollope, leaving his father-in-law posted in a position of vantage, whence he could command the line by which the animal might break back, ran on after the dogs. After a time, Mr Glen Leary, becoming dissatisfied with his position, left his post and walked a little distance forward to a point whence he fancied he could see better what was happening. Unfortunately this brought him into long grass, through which, at that very moment the leopard was already stealing back. Mr Leary was right in the animal's path and did not see it until it was almost on him. He fired one ineffective shot, was immediately borne backwards and fell into the bed of the spruit with the leopard on top of him. Though Trollope and the dogs arrived on the scene a few moments later and the animal was at once dispatched, it was too late. Mr Leary had sustained terrible wounds from which even a young man would hardly have recovered, and he died long before he could receive any professional medical attention. The tragedy was rendered all the more distressing in that Mr Yates, who had also been of the party, was standing close by, totally unarmed and while witnessing the whole incident, was powerless to render any assistance.

During 1925 the Prince of Wales visited South Africa. It had been intended to provide a big game shoot as part of the programme, and I was given authority to take the necessary steps for getting the Alexandra Block – until

1923 included in the reserve – in readiness. It had suffered to some extent from poaching, but two months of intensive policing had, by June, put an end to anything of the kind, and it was still full of game – sable, waterbuck, tsessebe and roan, as well as wildebeest and zebra, with a fair sprinkling of lion. However, at the last moment the shoot was off, which perhaps was a good thing, since the whole area was likely to have become a huge camp of local people, who were determined to trek in for the occasion with every conveyance at their disposal and would have been impossible to keep away without an army of police. So, on the whole, I hardly think the shoot would have been a success, and I was able to console myself that I had at least escaped the obloquy which in that event would certainly have fallen upon me.

A month or so later, members of His Royal Highness's personal staff, Captain Dudley North, R.N., Sir Godfrey Thomas, and Captain Piers Legh, took advantage of a few days' pause in the exceedingly strenuous tour and came by special train to Newington, where, going into camp with Colonel Hoare and myself, each was able to secure a few presentable trophies. On their departure they most considerately turned over to us practically all the pantry stores still remaining in the Royal train, which, deposited in the veld, formed an imposing pile about six feet high. It was a day or so before we were ready to get the things sorted out and cleared away. Meantime we became conscious of a penetrative and growing odour which emanated from the mass. We organized a search, and at the very bottom of the pile discovered a magnificent cod-fish off the ice, which, alas! by the time we had spoored it to its air was past any hope, and Hoare and I still think with regret of what our dilatoriness cost us.

His Royal Highness himself had merely passed through by rail on June 16, but I had the honour of being asked to meet the train at Komatipoort and travel up with it as far as Sabi Bridge. Komatipoort was duly beflagged for the occasion, and besides the local residents, nearly the whole of the British colony from Lourenço Marques was present. Though it was not the first time a member of the royal family had visited the lowveld, some of the residents appeared determined to make the most of this occasion. A number had travelled to Barberton for the forenoon reception at that place, and when the pilot train steamed into Komatipoort several enthusiasts emerged from it, having somehow secured passage that they might enjoy being presented for a second time.

To me the halt which the royal train made at Sabi Bridge, short though it was – merely the dinner hour in fact – meant a good deal. It seemed as though at exactly the right moment the heir to the throne had paused to bestow a word on my poor Cinderella, just as she was preparing to enter the ballroom, and it appeared the happiest augury for her success, in her still uncertain future. The latter half of the same year saw strenuous and growing propaganda for the national park, designed on the one hand to stimulate the Government and on the other to interest the general public. The Wild Life Protection Society, through its able Secretary, Mr J.W.H. Wilson, wrote and circularized constantly, while individual members, prominently Mr H.B. Papenfus, K.C. (at that time a member of parliament), exerted themselves in every possible way, on platforms and by organizing deputations, to bring about what we wanted. For some years past (since 1920), Colonel F.R.G. Hoare of the Union Defence Force had been accustomed to spend a few weeks with me annually in the reserve, taking photographs of game with a long-lens camera, and had obtained some startlingly successful results at that period before wild animal photography had developed as it since has done. The time was coming when practical use was to be made of these fine pictures of wildlife. Mr Paul Selby, an American and a member of the Wild Life Protection Society, also began, about 1924 or 1925, to pay visits to Pretoriuskop, when, using a fixed camera from a Ford lorry, he got a series of fine game pictures, one of which he presented annually to each member of the society. It was rather amusing, in view of later experiences, that Mr Selby should have expended immense time and trouble in camouflaging his lorry with green branches, lest animals might see in it a suspicious object. He, no more than the rest of us, foresaw that within a few years cars and lorries would be driving through the same area in thousands, accompanied by a maximum of dust and noise, with hardly an animal troubling even to raise its head from grazing to take a bored look. Of course, I knew that the game was much tamer than any outside person suspected, and I remember how Colonel Hoare, after taking vast pains to stalk a giraffe, felt almost hurt when the animal, having discovered him, deliberately walked close up to have a better look.

Some time before the period of active propaganda had commenced, Hoare had sent a selection of his best photographs to the publicity department of the South African Railways with the idea that the reproduction of some of them among the scenic pictures, which form so pleasant a feature of the railway compartments, might assist the spread of interest in the Sabi reserve. Nothing happened then, but some years later, when the Kruger National Park was growing in popularity day by day, he was advised by the administration – which had apparently overlooked his first effort – that, according to report, he had taken some good pictures of wild animals, and would he send them some. Naturally the value of anything must be in exact ratio to public interest in it, but from our point of view the most valuable time for exciting interest had then passed. I believe Hoare sent some duplicates, and that they duly found their place. Mr Selby was asked to supply a set of his photographs to the Houses of Parliament, which he kindly consented to do, and they there proved of the greatest value in giving members some idea of what was to be seen in the reserve.

The land companies maintained a waiting attitude. They were very willing to sell their farms still in the reserve to government but at their own price; otherwise they were determined to insist upon their full rights, which included the killing off of the wild animals so far as these might be considered a menace to ranching or agricultural development. Indeed, they could not anticipate being able to sell their land at all to would-be farmers without some such guarantee. So a good deal was still written and said about the wonderful capacities of the locked-up country to form a farmers' paradise, provided only the wild animals, especially the lion, could first be got rid of. Much of this was of course mere bluff, intended to force the hand of government and get from it the best price for the farms. But to me it was disquieting, for it seemed clear that if we could not interest the Government and the public sufficiently to part with a considerable sum of money on what was really still rather a speculative bid for popularity, the reserve might yet be abolished, or, more likely, perhaps reduced merely to the unconnected blocks of government land.

Our efforts to establish a national park were beginning to excite notice in countries outside South Africa. About this time I received a letter from Dr W.T. Hornaday, so well known for his campaigns on behalf of wildlife in the United States of America. He wrote, *inter alia:*

> I do *hope* to Heaven you will gain your great objective in the nationalizing as a Park of the Sabi reserve. Stick to it! The stake is a great one. When it is really done, it will be an imperishable monument to each and all of you who have worked and fought for it. I am sure you will none of you give up until you get it.

In August, Sir William Hoy, the general manager of the South African Railways, by then a keen national park partisan, had the lucky inspiration to depute Mr Stratford Caldecott, an artist, to be railway publicity agent for the advertisement of the Sabi Game Reserve as a potential public asset and sent him to me. Caldecott was without any previous veld experience whatever, but in the two months which he spent at Sabi Bridge, he contrived by enthusiasm and natural ability to acquire so complete an understanding and knowledge that he became, at a critical time, one of our most doughty and successful champions. In fact, until his lamented and premature death in 1929, there was no single man in South Africa who worked more strenuously and successfully for the cause of wildlife preservation in the sub-continent. During his visit we discussed from every angle how best to excite public interest and create an atmosphere which, when the time came, would allay opposition and make the Government's task as easy as possible.

It must be remembered that at this period we had no idea how the public would accept the plan of permanently alienating a very considerable portion of the Transvaal – a portion which by some had been publicly declared to be a land 'flowing with milk and honey' and a 'real farmers' paradise' (full, also, of payable minerals) – from the field of agriculture, pastoral and mining development. It was obviously the case also that land in which to place the rapidly growing native population was becoming dangerously scarce in the country; in fact there were a great number of interests with which the creation of a large national park would be likely to collide. It did not signify that the veld was too poor to support even a small native population (much less a colony of white farmers) and that its mineral possibilities were of no account – the public did not know the truth and it would not be difficult to work up an agitation against 'wasting magnificent country upon wild animals'. If any such agitation, with determined promoters having some axe to grind, really got going, it might be difficult for the Government to act.

We talked of all these things fully, and among the many helpful suggestions which Caldecott made there was one which, in importance and in the immense influence which it exercised sentimentally, stands out in front of all others. We were talking of the early beginnings of the reserve and I was showing him a copy of the first proclamation of 1898 signed by President Kruger. He looked hard at me and 'catching on', I said at once, 'Of course you are right, that is the obvious name – "The *Kruger* National Park"!' Few would be willing to oppose the founding of an institution linked with the name of the great president and one felt that much of any possible opposition would thus automatically collapse. In truth also, it was the appropriate term, for, as the records show, many years before the Sabi reserve became a fact, the president had more than once spoken to apathetic gatherings of the necessity of game sanctuaries.[9] Later, when the time seemed ripe, I asked some who were likely to have influence to suggest it to the Minister of Lands, and I believe that is how the park came to be known as it is today.

Immediately he got back to civilization Caldecott got busy. His well-known giraffe poster found place at every railway station in the Union; but it was as a writer, rather than as an artist, that he discovered his best use. He brought to the articles which he began to publish in newspapers and periodicals, all the fire and enthusiasm of his artistic genius. He gave interviews to reporters, addressed meetings, button-holed the man in the street. After Caldecott had been back there for a month there could hardly have been a man, woman, or child in Cape Town who had not heard, or read, or seen pictured, something about the Sabi Game Reserve!

As the year drew on, the Johannesburg, Pretoria, and Cape Town press devoted more and more space to the reserve and its future. *Die Huisgenoot* of Cape Town published little monthly articles, descriptive of animals to be found therein. The principal newspapers of the country were entirely favourable, frequently enthusiastic. Only our local press was editorially inclined to be captious. *The Goldfields News* of Barberton, for instance – a long established and highly respected weekly – faithfully representative of moderate local opinion, after expressing a doubt whether, in view of the well-known manner in which wild animals conceal themselves, visitors would see any game at all in the future park, proceeded in a later issue to say:

> We are satisfied that many civilized persons are quite indifferent to the matter of wildlife preservation, feeling no doubt that the hardships of the human race are more important ... We were afraid that what is to be seen in the reserve will not attract many people there beyond the enthusiasts, but we may be wrong, and only a matter of five or ten years' trial could serve to show whether our fears are groundless. Nevertheless we should like to see the scheme given a trial even if the taxpayer is out of pocket, and even if the Eastern Transvaal would gain more by the land in question being cultivated.

As with the scorpion, the sting of the above is in the tail! Yet, even an approval so grudging bore tribute to the atmospheric change; only a few years earlier nothing less than a scathing root and branch condemnation could have been in keeping with local feeling. In time to come, when the

Kruger National Park had attained widespread fame and popularity, it was not a little amusing to note how some, even of those who had been most actively hostile, endeavoured to acquire credit for having been among the first to push on the scheme. Truly indeed nothing succeeds like success!

Mr Piet Grobler, as Minister of Lands, had by now devoted himself to ensuring the measure being successfully carried through parliament. Himself a grand-nephew of President Kruger, he felt it fitting to be carrying on the work initiated by his famous relative, could he establish so lasting a monument to his memory as a great national park, which might be expected to rival, even to surpass, the famous institutions of the United States of America. He had devised a noteworthy alteration in the original Bill, framed in 1923, by placing all future Union national parks under a board of ten trustees, who would be unpaid and selected, it was hoped, purely on account of their love of wildlife and its preservation. Each province which came to be in possession of a national park would elect a representative to the board, and the Wild Life Protection Society would have a similar right; the remainder of the members were to be nominated by the Minister personally, while a secretary would be provided from the staff of the Lands Department, thus acting as a connecting link with government. Dr Schoch, to whose quiet work behind the scenes so much of our success had from the beginning been due, set to work altering the original Bill to meet new requirements and conditions. Major Scott submitted his valuation roll of private farms, and negotiations began with private owners, some of whom were exceedingly difficult to trace. Government fortunately still held a good deal of unallotted land in the Barberton, Pilgrim's Rest, and Soutpansberg lowveld areas, which was available for exchange. All through October and November the Lands Department officials were busy on initial spade work, and by December things were so far advanced as to justify Mr Grobler in asking the representatives of the big landowning companies to meet him for a final settlement. The interview took place at Corner House, Johannesburg, on December 9, 1925, and may – so far as the Kruger National Park is concerned – be regarded as historic. Besides the Minister, there were present Mr Schneider as the official representative of the Lands Department, Major Scott (Chairman of the Land Board), Mr H.B. Papenfus, K.C., M.P., and myself, on the one side, and on the other the land company representatives, Messrs Percy Greathead, Pott, Heard, Owen, Colonel Llewellyn Andersson and the Secretary of the Transvaal Landowners' Association.

Mr Grobler opened the proceedings with a most able and conciliatory speech, in the course of which he pointed out that the national park idea was one outside politics; that it was the duty of all to make sacrifices and thereby to render it a success. He said the Government was prepared to deal generously with the private owners in the matter of exchange of their farms in the present Sabi reserve, for land lying outside, and that a sum of money would be set aside to buy out those who did not desire such exchange. At the same time the Minister made it quite clear that the Government was in earnest, and that if owners would not accept the terms offered, it meant to reserve the right of compulsory expropriation at its own value. He then proceeded to define more exactly his proposals, which were very well received; the landowners' delegates pointing out that they yielded to no one in their eagerness to see a national park established, provided only their interests received fair consideration and treatment. Mr Papenfus, who followed, pointed out

Until the 1920s wildlife protection was confined primarily to those game species – principally antelope – which were hunted by sportsmen. Lion were regarded as vermin and shot. Here Stevenson-Hamilton poses with two dead lion.

that the national park scheme would form a great national asset in replenishing the game in parts of the country whence it had disappeared, and would be a place of rest and recreation for citizens of the Union as well as an attraction for overseas tourists.

I felt after this meeting that success was assured – only a matter of time and a little bargaining – so I left it with a light heart. Mr Grobler was, however, only at the beginning of his own difficulties, and certainly during the next few months had a most troublous and harassing time in obtaining the necessary money grants from parliament, and convincing colleagues of the necessity for being generous. In fact, I think it was solely his enthusiasm which made it possible for him to overcome all difficulties and get the Bill laid on the table during the first session of parliament; there were many ups and downs and all sorts of unforeseen difficulties to be overcome. Also, speed was desirable before any opposition had time to gather and organize. Already early in 1926, Colonel Deneys Reitz, addressing a meeting of the Kruger National Park Committee in Cape Town, observed that he had recently met a deputation of two hundred sheep farmers, who were indignant at the idea of making the Sabi Game Reserve into a national park, and he thought for that reason the matter should be pushed on without delay.

Luckily, our most dangerous opponents woke up to what was going on too late for their voices to carry the weight which might have attached to them earlier. Veterinary departments are the natural foes of wildlife preservation. To them wild animals represent merely so many potential carriers of disease germs, which may affect cattle or other domestic stock, with disastrous results to the farming industries, although in nearly all cases of epidemic disease in the past – rinderpest for instance – the infection was communicated by the cattle to the game and not vice versa. Also, in the case of east coast fever, which has overshadowed stock-farming in South Africa for thirty-five years, the game acts as a cleansing agent to the ticks just as do horses, goats and sheep, which also are immune. Yet when a case has to be stated, such facts are easily glossed over and great play is above all made with the tsetse fly menace, no doubt because there really is some foundation for the belief that the insect follows game, and it is an ingrained article of faith in the mind of the average South African farmer that game is responsible for its presence.

It is useless to point out that there are many places in Africa where fly exists without any game being available for its support, and conversely others where game exists without attendant fly – in fact, that the latter seems dependent rather on locality, than on the presence or absence of large animals, though it feeds greedily on their blood when available. Yet the fact remains that tsetse fly did swarm in certain portions of the Sabi Game Reserve prior to 1896 (the rinderpest year) and disappeared through some unknown agency due to that epidemic within the short space of six months; so completely moreover that it has never been heard of again, either in the reserve or in neighbouring parts of Portuguese East Africa. The nearest tsetse fly to the north is along the greater Sabie River in Zambezi Company territory and to the south in Zululand, in each case a distance of about two hundred miles. I do not attempt to hide that I have frequently visualized the possibility of a return of the fly to its old haunts from one or other of these reservoirs, not indeed brought by game, but far more effectively and quickly under the hoods and on the bonnets of motor cars. Still this is a danger that could and should be effectively guarded against. The veterinary department, however, appeared to base its fear on a return of fly from Portuguese country to our east across the Lebombo, which I knew to be out of any present question, since the fly disappeared from all that eastern country at the same time and in the same manner as it did from the Transvaal lowveld.

Anyhow, as I remarked above, the heavy artillery came into action too late to turn the tide of the battle. Dr Viljoen indeed wrote to the press practically advocating the extermination of all game, and the abolition of all game reserves in South Africa where there existed any danger from tsetse fly. His opinion, backed by expert knowledge, must have carried a good deal of weight had it been advanced earlier. Sir Arnold Theiler, just on the eve of retiring from his post as chief of the Bacteriological Department, where his researches had covered him with fame and made Onderstepoort world renowned, confided to me that his anxiety lest a great permanent wildlife sanctuary right up against the frontier of a foreign country, within which, in the nature of things, we could have no control over diseases, would prove a permanent danger to farming operations in the whole Transvaal by providing a corridor through which various plagues could be introduced. Stock movements may be controlled, but not those of the wild creatures.

Others of the department, such as Drs Claude Fuller and Lounsbury, did not conceal their conviction that tsetse still lurked somewhere within the unknown depths of the Sabi reserve, and that I was either ignorant of the fact or was deliberately overlooking it. But, by this time, things had gone too far; our resistive powers had greatly increased, the public was getting interested and the Government was committed. A stone which might have knocked the

Sabi reserve flat in its weaker days, now glanced harmlessly off its new armour. However justified in theory might be the alarm of the veterinary authorities, they lacked local knowledge, and were thus incapable of forming an opinion on border matters to which, for practical purposes, value could be attached.

During the early months of 1926 one could hardly take up a newspaper without seeing something or other about the Sabi Game Reserve, nearly always favourable, though sometimes giving views of opponents usually concerned about east coast fever, rinderpest, or tsetse fly. Still there was always a feeling of uncertainty. Political measures might crowd out our Bill, and if put off for another year, it might lapse entirely. It was therefore of the greatest importance that the measure should not be deferred beyond the 1926 session of parliament. Among our then many prominent supporters in the public press and otherwise, must be mentioned Dr Leonard Gill and Dr E. Warren, of the Cape Town and Pietermaritzburg museums respectively, the Wild Life Protection Society of South Africa (of which Dr Haagner, Director of the Pretoria Zoological Gardens, was chairman), the Government Publicity Executive (Railways), the National Society, the University of Cape Town, the Rotary Club, and the Transvaal Landowners' Association (the last-named, now that their requirements had been satisfied, wholeheartedly with us). The National Park Propaganda Committee, organized by Mr Caldecott, was untiring in effort.

I should like to proffer thanks here and now to everyone who at that time contributed to ultimate success, but unfortunately, remote as I was most of the time, I was not always in a position to note the names of all the allies who constantly helped by their public letters. The name of Mr Astley Maberly, the artist, who subsequently spent many months in the park and made many beautiful drawings of its animals, takes, however, a high place. Mr Yates continued, with unquenchable ardour, to fight locally a solitary battle. We had of course numberless friends, who, from their official position, could work only behind the scenes. The principal newspapers of Pretoria, Johannesburg and Cape Town, representing all shades of opinion and both sections of the people, by leading articles and paragraphs, did everything possible to guide public feeling in the right direction. I gathered privately from official sources that matters were proceeding satisfactorily, if slowly, towards buying out the smaller private landowners; the principal reason for delay being the difficulty of getting in touch with all those concerned. Owing to the principle of inheritance embodied in the Roman-Dutch

Law, many of these unoccupied farms had, in the course of years, become the property of a dozen or more owners, some of whom could not be found.

During April all doubt came to an end. The Select Committee on Crown Lands made a unanimous report, approving of the exchanges of land necessary to constitute the Kruger National Park. The details had been settled between Major Percy Greathead, representing the Transvaal Consolidated Land Company, the largest individual owner of land in the Sabi reserve, and Major Scott, Chairman of the Land Board, representing the Government. By this arrangement the land had been classed under various grades, and the basis of exchange proceeded on the lines of exchange for equivalent units of government land lying outside; so that where a piece of higher grade land, for instance, was estimated at twice the value of another area of lower grade, two units of the latter were given for one of the former. In the result the company surrendered 196 000 acres of land in the reserve for 135 000 acres of government land outside. The residue of the exchanges to other companies and private persons proceeded on the same lines. Some owners preferred cash payments, and about £40 000 was expended by government in this way. Mineral rights went with exchange and sale on both sides. Some additions were made to the reserve, which partly compensated for the 1923 reductions. Notable among these was the inclusion of the area of government land lying between the Olifants and Letaba rivers, which, as a proclaimed mining area, had cut in as a wedge between the Sabi and Shingwedsi reserves, forming a source of endless inconvenience to administration. On May 31, 1926, Mr Piet Grobler, as Minister of Lands, moved in parliament the second reading of the National Parks Act. He made an eloquent speech. He began by contrasting the wealth of animal life, as seen by the early pioneers of South Africa, with the poverty to which it later was reduced. He recalled how the republican government under President Kruger, becoming alive to the necessity, had established the Sabi Game Reserve in 1898; how this had been revived by the provisional government after the South African War, and how the game had subsequently responded to protection. He pointed out what had been done in America and how popular the national parks in that country had proved to be. He then outlined his programme for control, administration and the acquisition of the necessary funds for upkeep. In the course of this he explained fully his own excellent plan for putting the future park under a board of control, instead of under a government department. What he said deserves record as an exposition of true foresight and a deep knowledge of requirements:

As long as the (park) boundary is in the hands of the Government, the Government will always be exposed to being pressed by supporters to alter the boundary. Politics must be kept out of it. The danger is especially great that before a general election political influences will be brought to bear on the Government. Therefore, I propose the appointment of a board of control, representing the interests of the whole people. That board will have full control in its hands. It will be incorporated, and can sue and be sued. It will appoint its own officials, make its own regulations, control the park, and in a word, act as the controlling body which has charge of everything in connection with the park. The board of control will consist of ten members, serving for five years. Every year two will retire. I propose that eight members shall be appointed by me, one by the Transvaal administration (because the park is in the Transvaal) and one to be appointed by the Wild Life Protection Society ... Eventually we shall get so far that each province will appoint a member, the Government four, and the Wild Life Protection Society the tenth. Honourable Members will see that it is proposed that the members of the board shall not be paid except for current expenses, such as travelling expenses. I want to say that the persons on the board shall not make anything out of it.

The motion was seconded by General Smuts, leader of the opposition, who, after saying how grateful the public should be to Mr Grobler for introducing such a Bill, which moreover perpetuated the name of President Kruger in connection with game preservation, went on to make some only too true remarks:

We have in South Africa a number of people who take little interest in these things. There exists a feeling among a part of the population that we cannot develop the country and at the same time keep the game alive and increase it. They seem to have declared war against the game, and they devastate and exterminate it, with the result that fauna of the greatest and rarest value are more and more exterminated, which still continues to-day....

Mr H.B. Papenfus, K.C., who, as has been previously stated, was one of the foremost in the natioal park movement followed with a clear and instructive speech, founded on a personal knowledge of the reserve and its conditions. In the course of it he quoted some words frm the last message of Captain Scott when dying in the Antarctic: 'Make the boy interested in natural history if you can. It is better than games.' Other members, including Colonel Reitz, followed, and the Bill passed its second reading without a dissentient voice.

I was at Sabi Bridge, feeling rather depressed as the session progressed towards its close and nothing happened about the Bill, when the telegrams began to come in. Papenfus wired his own and General Smuts's congratulations; and Caldecott said *'Finis coronat opus'* [10] in his, which was nice of him. Later many people wrote, including General Smuts, who himself in its earlier days had been in no small degree responsible for keeping the Sabi Game Reserve alive. They all said so many kind things that I began to think I should have to buy a larger size in hats.

It was difficult to believe that all the troubles were over and that Cinderella had really become a full-blown princess. How would she bear her new dignity? I wondered who the members of the board would be. Everything seemed to depend on its personnel. Then I thought I had better go to Pretoria; so I sent a wire to say I was coming, and went hotfoot on its trail before I could be stopped. This was just as well, for on arrival I discovered that my department, rather ruffled at all these events affecting one of its charges having taken place without its having been officially consulted, had telegraphed to say I was not to come, and further, was, until the situation became clarified, stopping supplies as well, which included the contract for the badly required house at Letaba, where Ledeboer's mud hut was leaking at every point.

The department really had some cause to feel hurt. For a long time past I had been consistently breaking most of the rules in the code of official etiquette in the most scandalous manner. I had intrigued with any department of the Union government which seemed likely to be of assistance, had button-holed ministers, inspired press articles and every other kind of propaganda, all without the authority – even the knowledge – of my own department. In fact, I had been doing almost everything that a properly conducted official ought not to do. But then I suppose I never really belonged to the regular army of officialdom, very few members of which need always be on the alert for threatening danger to their particular branch of the public service, and prepared to struggle in its defence. I, on the other hand, was always thinking of and fighting for Cinderella, and I did not care how many rules actual or implied I broke on her behalf so long as I could serve her. Now I began to think she might not need me any more.

I saw Mr Grobler and congratulated him. He was insistent that we must not kill any more lion and I found he had been converted to this unexpected view by reading Pienaar's *History of a Lion Family*, a moving little work, written originally in Afrikaans, but sufficiently touching even in the English translation. I hung about the Lands Department until the names of the selected National Parks Board were known, and eventually I got them 'hot out of the oven' from Sommerville.

The Chairman was Senator W.J.C. Brebner, of Scottish parentage, a close friend of General Hertzog and a leading light of the present government party. He lived in Bloemfontein and so might be said to represent the Orange Free State on the Board. Colonel Deneys Reitz was an obvious choice from his previous position as Minister of Lands and the tremendous lot he had

The National Parks Board of Trustees at its first meeting on 16 September 1926. Front row, left to right: W.J.C. Brebner (Chairman), P.G.W. Grobler (Minister of Lands) and D. Reitz. Back row: R.A. Hockly, A.E. Charter, W.A. Campbell, G.S. Preller, C.R. de Laporte (Acting Warden, Kruger National Park), A.K. Haagner, J.A. de Ridder. Trustees not included in the photograph were Sir Abe Bailey, O. Pirow and H.B. Papenfus.

217

then and since done to bring the national parks scheme into the region of practical politics. It is the case, indeed, that amid the shower of congratulations which descended upon those who had been primarily responsible for final accomplishment, he scarcely received his due share of recognition. There was some tendency to overlook how it was Colonel Reitz who had sponsored all the initial steps towards the creation of a national park. He had caused the parks ordinance to be drafted, had ordered the farm survey – so efficiently carried out by Major Scott and Mr Schoch – and, by excising from the Sabi reserve all the privately owned land that could be spared from the sanctuary without affecting unduly its value as such, had made it possible later for the Government to find enough land outside to exchange for what still remained. In fact, it was he who set the stage for the events of a few years later, and by doing so not only lightened the tasks of the later actors, but considerably accelerated the happy culmination. Mr Oswald Pirow had probably been more deeply responsible for our ultimate success than was known, and moreover was a keen sportsman and a man thoroughly conversant with the ways of the wild. Mr H.B. Papenfus was another clearly indicated and well-selected member. Then there was Mr R.A. Hockly, a well-known Cape sheep farmer and an old friend of the reserve; Dr Gustav Preller, editor of *Ons Vaderland* newspaper in Pretoria, which had been lending valuable support to the movement; Sir Abe Bailey, a keen sportsman and representative of land company interests; Mr W.A. Campbell of Natal, a strong game protectionist and a man of influence; Dr Haagner representing the Wild Life Protection Society, and finally Mr A.E. Charter of the Transvaal administration to represent the province, and at the beginning to lend to the board the benefit of his long experience in the handling of the reserve and its warden. Mr de Ridder of the Lands Department was the Secretary.

On the whole an excellent board, whose selection, with a deaf ear to the demands of party politics or racial discrimination, reflects everlasting credit on Mr Grobler, and forms yet another tribute to the splendid enthusiasm and determination to inaugurate and make a success of the Kruger National Park which he displayed from the very beginning. No one else had done more than toy with the surrounding nettles; only when Mr Grobler came along were they firmly grasped and the path made clear. He deserves always to be remembered as 'Cinderella's Fairy Godmother', or perhaps I ought to say 'Godfather'!

Now that the long struggle was at last over and there seemed nothing more left to fight for, the inevitable reaction, with its accompanying sense of depression, set in. After the constant anxieties and the many reverses of the past twenty years, success, as in the Great War, had come rather suddenly and unexpectedly at the end – so suddenly as to be almost a shock. I began to consider what I had better do. According to the terms of the new Act, the board was to take over control from the Transvaal administration at the beginning of 1927, when all the present game reserve staff would automatically be retrenched from the government service, with such pensions and gratuities as were individually due. I might be asked to stay on; on the other hand, I might not, and in the latter event I felt I would rather be far away at that moment. Even were my appointment renewed, it seemed to me that the future loomed rather blank and dull; further service would be in the nature of an anticlimax so far as I was personally concerned. I felt I ought to say, 'Here is the young lady who has been my charge; I have done what I can to make her worthy of the position she is to hold; it is for you to see that she maintains it with dignity' – in fact, that the time had come to sing *'Nunc Dimittis'*.[1] It is all quite amusing in retrospect, but at the time – suffering no doubt from reaction – that is how I felt about the situation. So I made up my mind to ask for what leave was due to me and depart before the new board took over, relegating the next move, if any, to that body, to be answered as might then seem best.

Meantime I wanted to see as much as possible of my old haunts before saying good-bye and spent the greater part of the winter trekking about. Colonel Hoare stayed a month with me and we climbed about among the boulders and euphorbias of Ship Mountain, seeking unsuccessfully the water which formerly, tradition says, was found at the top; shot crocodile in the Nwaswitsontso gorge and did a little lion and other wildlife photography, on one occasion getting a lioness, followed by seven small cubs, driven past Hoare's camera with quite successful results – a second lioness no doubt lurking behind out of sight as rearguard.

The executive committee of the provincial council also came along in a special train to bestow a valedictory blessing. Mr Hofmeyr, the Administrator, who was paying his first visit, seemed rather doubtful about the success of the national park, while Charter was frankly pessimistic, a not unnatural attitude on his part, since most of the complaints about the Sabi Game Reserve had in the past come to his office, and he must have found it hard to conceive that such a grimy Cinderella could ever become popular with the general public. In fact, I was not myself any too sure; nor did this factor in my eyes bulk as a matter of paramount importance, except in so far as it might affect the future of the animals, to the preservation of which the Act had lent an element of permanency which was previously sadly absent.

In September I packed up and departed. On the way through Pretoria Mr Grobler sent for me; he said a rumour had reached him that I contemplated cutting my connection with the game reserve and he begged me to reconsider the matter. He pointed out that the board would at first be floundering in unknown waters, that my experience would be useful, and that I ought to see it at least fairly started. He added some very kind personal remarks to the effect that he personally would much like me to remain. This put rather a new complexion on matters; I began to feel that I might perhaps be wanted to carry on after all, and that if so, it might be my duty to go back. In due course a cable, sent by the board as soon as it took office, did in fact arrive, and under the circumstances, and with the Sabi unceasingly pulling me by invisible cords which became harder and harder to resist, there was only one thing to do, and so I faced quite cheerfully an anti-climax even worse than that I had previously reckoned on.

PART TWO

❖

THE KRUGER NATIONAL PARK

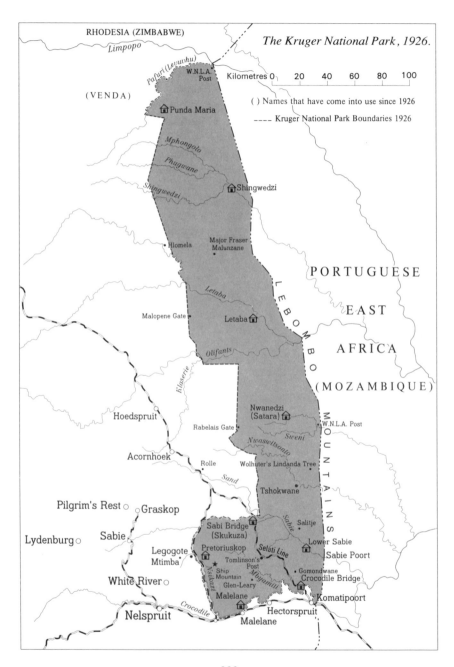

RHODESIA (ZIMBABWE)

The Kruger National Park, 1926.

Limpopo

(VENDA)

Pafuri (Levuvhu)

W.N.L.A. Post

Kilometres 0   20   40   60   80   100

( ) Names that have come into use since 1926

---- Kruger National Park Boundaries 1926

Punda Maria

Mphongolo

Phugwane

Shingwedzi

Shingwedzi

• Hlomela

Major Fraser
Malunzane

PORTUGUESE

Letaba

Malopene Gate

Letaba

EAST

Olifants

AFRICA

Klaserie

(MOZAMBIQUE)

Hoedspruit

Nwanedzi
(Satara)

L E B O M B O

W.N.L.A. Post

Rabelais Gate

Sweni

Nwaswitsonto

Acornhoek

• Rolle

Wolhuter's Lindanda Tree

Sand

M O U N T A I N S

Tshokwane

Pilgrim's Rest

Graskop

Sabie

• Salitje

Sabi Bridge
(Skukuza)

Lydenburg

Sabie

Pretoriuskop

Selati Line

Lower Sabie

Sabie Poort

Legogote
Mtimba

★ Tomlinson's
Post

Mbyamiti

Ship
Mountain

• Gomondwane
Crocodile Bridge

White River

Glen-Leary

Nsikazi

Malelane

Komatipoort

Crocodile

Malelane

Hectorspruit

Nelspruit

222

CHAPTER TEN
1927 AND AFTER

EARLY DIFFICULTIES AND SMALL BEGINNINGS; CAPTAIN HOWE; REST–
CAMPS, ROADS AND PONTOONS; CHANGES IN THE BOARD AND STAFF;
TOURIST TRAFFIC AND REACTIONS OF THE ANIMALS TO IT; OPENING UP
OF THE NORTHERN AREAS; CAUSEWAYS AND BORE–HOLES

I RETURNED TO FIND Cinderella greatly prospering under her new conditions, her guardians, the board of trustees, doing everything in their
power to deck her out in garments likely to make her yet more attractive to
her prospective bridegroom, the Prince – in other words, the Public. To
some minds it may have appeared like painting the lily, but it had to be recognized that without a good many artificial aids the Prince would not have
those opportunities of better acquaintance conducive to making her his companion for life.

Funds were the primary problem. The board found itself in the difficult
position of having to make good roads, build rest-camps and bridges, as well
as add considerably to the staff, while having at its disposal from government the same funds that had barely sufficed to finance the administration of
the game reserve; that is to say, enough to pay the salaries and wages of the
present employees, with a few hundred over for contingencies. According to
the Act, the board was to find the money necessary for future development
from voluntary subscriptions, donations and bequests from the public, fees
or other moneys received or raised under the provisions of the Act, fines for
contraventions of the Act and its regulations, and from any contributions
made by a provincial council. The Government, as represented by the
Minister of Lands, was authorized to pay for management, control and main-
tenance, but nothing towards capital expenditure or permanent improvements, other than those connected with the official residences of the staff.

So far the public showed no signs of making any voluntary response, nor, indeed, could we reasonably have expected it to do so at that stage. After an initial deadlock, it was arranged that the Union government should contribute £7 000 per annum towards administration, and that the Transvaal Provincial Council should aid with an annual grant of £3 000 but this provided nothing for development. Happily, benevolence reigned, and Mr Havenga, the Minister for Finance, arranged to find a special sum of £7 000 from treasury funds by way of giving the board a start. A godsend indeed, and with its aid, by the middle of 1927 a beginning was made on road making. Up to then the only road in the Kruger National Park capable of taking motor transport was a circular route from Crocodile Bridge to Lower Sabie, constructed by De Laporte a couple of years before for the use of his own motor car within his particular district or section. There were no roads connecting us with the outside world. In fact, De Laporte's car and the secondhand Ford 'tin Lizzie' which I acquired late in 1927, had both to be brought in by train and to depend for necessary repairs upon such talent as the staff itself could provide.

The first essential, to my mind, was proper administrative communication, and the earlier roads were constructed less with a view to later convenience for the public, than to linking up the various section rangers with headquarters. Since the rangers' stations, generally speaking, ran in a line from south to north, these administrative highways would later become the main trunk arteries through the park, and in fact did become so. So I started first on a road from Sabi Bridge to the Olifants River, followed by one to Pretoriuskop and then one to Crocodile Bridge. Wolhuter made a circular route round Pretoriuskop and this actually became available for the public as early as 1927, thanks to a rough track just traversible by cars, which already existed to the boundary of the old reserve from White River, and which had, in the past, more or less linked us with the outside world. The few people who, in the first year, visited the park at Pretoriuskop were expected to make their own camps and generally to fend for themselves within the thorn zeribas which we constructed to protect them at night.

The board soon decided to charge an entrance fee of £1 per car and drew up a code of regulations founded on those which had previously been in force for the reserve, with necessary amendments and additions. It had rather been anticipated that – at least in the earlier stages – all tours by members of the public would have to be personally conducted; for by the Act, firearms were not allowed in the park and it was not known what the reactions of the

*When the national park was first opened to tourists no accom-
modation facilities were provided and visitors were free to
camp wherever they pleased. They had to protect themselves
by carrying firearms and by constructing their own barriers
around their tents.*

lion would be to motor traffic. However, it was quickly realized that personally conducted tours would not be practicable, and the board found a loophole in the Act which enabled it to permit one firearm per car to be carried
for purely protective purposes. To guard against misuse the breech was
secured by a piece of wire and a lead seal, without breaking which the
weapon could not be used.

At first visitors in every case came armed, but later, as the gentle and
friendly nature of the local well-fed lion became better known, the number
of cars which carried lethal weapons dwindled to less than twenty per cent.
As a matter of fact, in a sudden emergency a loaded firearm in a motor car
may be more dangerous to the inmates than to anything outside, nor can a
weapon longer than a pistol be manipulated with ease and certainty inside
the restricted space of such a vehicle, especially when the bearer is excited
or in a hurry. Of course to be of the slightest use against rapid attack a
firearm must be already loaded, which renders it a constant menace. Still,
the fact of having a gun at hand, however potentially ineffective for the purpose designed, and however personally unqualified to make the best use of it

the holder may be, no doubt does convey a certain sense of security, and mainly for that reason (and not to discourage visitors from coming to the park) it was thought wise to make the concession.

Late in 1927, as just retribution for having played fast and loose with a bad attack of malaria, I went down with the first serious illness of my life and had to go for an overseas trip. In my absence Captain Howe of the South African Police was brought in temporarily, and carried on the work of warden for nearly a year with energy and efficiency. During this period the road mileage was increased enormously and small beginnings were made in erecting shelters for tourists. This last was most necessary, for the traffic was increasing by leaps and bounds. In 1927, when Pretoriuskop alone was open, three cars entered; in 1928, still at Pretoriuskop only, the number was one hundred and eighty; in 1929, when it was possible to travel over most of the area south of the Olifants River, the total rose to eight hundred and fifty. Since there was hardly any special accommodation available, the rangers were obliged to surrender their own quarters to the visitors, who camped out in every room and on the verandas, the rightful owner having to sleep as best he could outside. As one ranger remarked, 'I did not mind so much their using my soap, towels, plates, knives and forks, but I do wish they had not used my toothbrush!'

Some remedy for this unsatisfactory state of things had to be found before the 1930 season. Further, the rangers, in default of any assistance, were obliged to give up their proper duty of looking after their sections for that of supplying petrol to tourist cars, checking permits, answering questions as to routes, and generally doing every sort of work except that for which they had been appointed. The fact was, as I had already pointed out, the place had been thrown open to the public long before it was ready for their reception. We should have been given at least two years of preparation. Practically everything remained to be done in order to transform, so far as possible, the wild, trackless, primitive bit of Africa which the Sabi reserve was in 1926, into a mild imitation of the American Yellowstone Park, with hardly any money for the purpose. The cumulative torrent of visitors, with the consequent absorption of the ranger staff in meeting their requirements, did not render our task of development any easier.

Meantime several changes had taken place both in the personnel of the board and of the staff. In the former, Dr Haagner had given place to Mr Selby as representative of the Wild Life Protection Society, and Mr Charter had retired in favour of Mr de Souza, representing the Transvaal Province,

the latter, later, made way for Mr Ludorf, who, it will be recollected, officiated as chairman of the memorable commission of 1917, the first public
body to recognize Cinderella for what she really was. In 1930 Mr Selby was
succeeded by Colonel F.R.G. Hoare, who possessed long and intimate
knowledge of the old Sabi reserve. In 1928 Mr F.S. Potgieter of the lands
department had taken over the post of secretary to the board. It was a fortunate appointment. For about eight years he carried out his duties, which
necessitated no little organizing ability and limitless tact, with a success
which earned him equal popularity with the public, the members of the
board and the staff of the park. That he might become thoroughly efficient
by knowledge of requirements at, as it were, both ends of the string, he spent
the greater part of two summers in the warden's office at Skukuza, and to
this may largely be attributed the later uninterruptedly smooth functioning of
the whole machine. With constantly increasing work, his own office in
Pretoria gradually perforce grew from a single-man business, to one employing half a dozen clerks and typists. Upon his greatly regretted resignation in
1936, he was succeeded by Mr van Graan, transferred from the South
African railways administration.

Of the staff, De Laporte, De Jager, Trollope and Coetser had retired, and
we had a number of new rangers: Tomlinson, Crous, McDonald, James,
Botha and Steyn. There were now seven section rangers and one at headquarters, besides the warden. I was particularly sorry to lose De Laporte, my
second-in-command, who had been with me through all the ups and downs
for some twenty-five years and was a man who could be ill-spared; but his
own and his wife's health necessitated a change to a less trying climate, and
in fact he had been getting restless for some years past. Only Wolhuter now
remained of our original little band.

There had at first been some idea of placing all the arrangements for visitors to the park under the South African Railways Publicity Department,
which controls the general tourist traffic of the country, and of retaining
directly under the board only the policing, care of the fauna and flora, and
administration of resident natives – in fact the same duties as the staff had
hitherto carried out. But at the time the railway administration was unwilling
to add to its commitments, and no doubt, as things eventually turned out,
it was best that the entire control should have remained vested in the
board. An attempt had also been made to come to some arrangement with the
same department by which we might utilize the two existing railway bridges
for the transit of motor cars over the Crocodile and Sabie rivers, but the

expense proving prohibitive, the board had to fall back on its own resources.

Mr Selby, who was manager of a gold mine in Johannesburg, was in a position to place at our disposal a large quantity of derelict material, such as wire rope, piping, and so on, which was ideal for the building of the concrete rondavels which the board had decided upon for tourist accommodation. He also supplied from the same source the wherewithal to construct pontoons, and by the aid of these it became possible to transfer motor cars across the various rivers, which hitherto had barred any traffic from north to south. Before the opening of the 1929 season such ferries had been put in the Crocodile and Sabie rivers, and by the end of the same year the Olifants was similarly conquered. For the Sand River, a shallow, swift running stream, we improvised a corduroy crossing of gum poles wired together and anchored to the stream-bed. It was an alarming method until one got used to it, for the bridge swayed and sank to the shallow bottom of the stream with the passage of every car.

By 1930 we had built half a dozen rest-camps, consisting in all of about a hundred concrete huts. The design of these was ingenious. Circular wooden moulds in sections were made, and the concrete poured in after the usual fashion, while the roof-stays, of iron piping or wire rope, had their lower ends embedded in the walls and their upper extremities secured at the apex of the roof by a metal cone. They were thatched with local grass. Rather unfortunately perhaps, the designer of these otherwise excellent huts suffered, in common with many people at that time, from a severe lion complex. He pictured the lions as ravening monsters, whose most ardent desire in life was to rend in pieces defenceless tourists. So instead of having windows, by which of course the lions might easily enter, he arranged that the walls should not meet the roof, and that there should be an air space of about a foot between, which it was considered the lions might haply not observe, while seeking entrance elsewhere. To serve the double purpose of lighting the interior, and to allow the inmates to gaze fearfully out upon the raging but baffled beasts outside, a round hole was cut in the middle of each door. In practice, I regret to say that these holes were used rather by inquisitive persons desiring to see what was going on inside than by the inmates for the purpose intended, and were generally found stuffed up with old socks, shirts or paper. The ventilation scheme, too, proved unpopular. The visitors complained that the huts were too cold, and in response to clamour we had to brick up, or otherwise close them, and as windows could not be made without seriously damaging the structures, they suffered from lack of ventilation and were exceedingly hot in warm weather, or whenever the door had to be closed. In later attempts we decided to brave the lion menace and to make proper windows, which could be opened or closed at will.

For the first year or two permits to enter the park were issued by agents on application at places all over the Union. At the entrance gates, through lack of funds, we could station only native policemen, who checked or were supposed to check the permits for each car. As these 'boys' were invariably entirely illiterate, and could as a rule speak no language except their own, it was not the most satisfactory system that could be devised. So I hit upon the expedient of employing white gate-officers, and paying them on a percentage of takings, at the same time withdrawing the issue of permits from the hands of the agents and having payment made only at the entrance gates. The board agreed to the change and it worked well from the beginning. The 'tourist officers' as they were called, were employed for one season only and re-appointed at the beginning of the next one, if satisfactory. The control of the larger camps was placed in the hands of contractors, who were allowed to conduct catering, sell petrol and maintain trading stores as their financial assets. For the smaller camps we appointed our own officers temporarily, on a percentage basis, with the right to cater in light refreshments. A still later development when funds increased was the placing of all tourist officers on a fixed salary, which at the beginning was not a practical proposition.

During the first couple of years we specified no restricted seasons for the entrance of visitors. The result was that while the traffic in the hot weather was so small as not to justify the expense of the staff which had to be provided, cars were constantly getting bogged in lonely places after rain and frequently had to remain out all night; also, a considerable percentage of these summer visitors contracted malarial fever, and some even died. The culmination was the misfortune which overtook a party of American tourists from one of the 'luxury cruisers'.

In March 1929 a special train arrived one morning at Crocodile Bridge and the two lorries brought with it were duly disembarked. It had been arranged that the passengers should travel by road in two divisions. The first contingent was to leave in the forenoon on the lorries, travel the thirty-eight miles round trip via Lower Sabie and come back to the train for luncheon. The second lot were to repeat the process in the afternoon. It was a very hot, still day and the ranger who had met the train – McDonald – warned the railway official in charge of the tourists that there was likely to be a thunderstorm later. However, it was decided that the trip must not be postponed and so the first two lorries duly set off. Before they had gone more than a few miles, stopping of course to look at game on the way, the sky quickly clouded over and a tropical thunderstorm burst over them. Endeavours were made to proceed but soon – the soft road having become a quagmire – it was decided to retrace steps.

It was then found that a dry spruit crossed on the outward journey, was now a roaring torrent. The first lorry, emptied of its passengers, essayed the crossing, but promptly upset and lay on its side, effectually blocking the way for further traffic. The rain still came down in torrents, the second lorry was bogged and the afternoon was drawing on. Lion began to roar; the party took to the trees – the ladies in the summer frocks which they had donned for a day's outing in tropical heat. It may be added that the trees were mainly *Acacia*, provided with every imaginable type of sharp thorn, hooked, straight and combinations of both.

In this regrettable predicament the ranger discovered the party shortly before it became dark. Guessing what would happen as soon as the storm had abated a little, he had set to work to collect a gang of natives, loaded them with blankets and food, and appeared, *deus ex machina*, in the midst of the almost despairing holiday-makers. He led them to the Gomondwane picket, where were a couple of huts normally occupied by native police, and installed them therein, ladies in one and men in the other, that the *convenances* might receive due respect. Large fires were lighted inside, wet clothes were dried, and in an atmosphere of mingled wood-smoke and steam, singing lustily to keep their spirits up, the passengers from the 'luxury cruiser' spent a night, which if not entirely of the most comfortable, at least provided them with a taste of African life at first hand, an experience they could hardly have anticipated when they left New York, and one which I have no doubt many of them later delighted to describe in detail to their friends at home

The aftermath was several cases of malaria and some temporary damage to South African tourist traffic through the rather sweeping condemnation in some of the American journals of South Africa generally as a kind of death trap. After this episode the board decided that it was necessary to close the park to the public during the rainy season, and from 1930 onwards it was open only from the end of May until the end of October, during which months there was a reasonable chance of little or no rain falling and the malaria menace was practically absent.

It was soon found necessary to prohibit night travelling. In the early days people used to go out joy-riding, sometimes with small children, at all hours of the night and often through car trouble get marooned miles from anywhere. It was also realized that game animals became so dazzled by the headlights that they were quite incapable of getting out of the way of cars and were frequently run down and killed in consequence.

It became evident, almost from the start, that the park was going to be a great success. It fulfilled a want and gave the holiday-making public something entirely different from anything it had experienced before. It cost a good deal less to spend a week in the midst of unique surroundings where wildlife went on much as it may be supposed to have proceeded in the Pleistocene, than to put in the same period at a Durban or Cape Town hotel. The animals, on their side, responded nobly. Having quickly discovered that the unknown monsters which came roaring along the roads amid clouds of dust were innocuous, they very soon ceased to pay more than cursory attention to them and went on with their daily routine as if the intruders were not there – or nearly so. Impala, usually among the most wary and timid of antelope, crowded on the roads in front of the cars like sheep, often, indeed, barely escaping disaster under the wheels.

One curious trait, common to nearly all the larger herbivora, the fundamental motive for which I have never fathomed, is their overwhelming desire to run across the road in front of a car. A herd of wildebeest or zebra will gallop alongside for a considerable distance, until the car slackens speed, or a turn in the road gives them an advantage, when they will dash furiously across it to the other side, the hindmost often barely clearing the bumpers, while the gravel and dust displaced by their hoofs rattle against the windscreen. It will no doubt have often been observed that the domestic hen is filled with the same strange ambition.

But the lion gave us the greatest and most satisfactory surprise of all. When it was first decided to allow tourists to enter the park unescorted in their own cars, it was not known how the lion would take it. Personally, I thought it likely that they would give the roads a wide berth; being highly intelligent creatures, it was hardly to be supposed that they would deliberately put themselves in the way of possible danger. On the other hand, those whose ideas of them were culled from travellers' tales and nursery stories, quite naturally pictured them as ravening, raging, homicidal maniacs, whose chief aim in life being to lap human blood, were only too likely to tear our visitors from their cars.

The lion soon proved both opinions to be mistaken. Having made up their minds that motor cars were neither good to eat nor a potential danger to themselves, they almost completely ignored them. At first I was convinced that their intelligence did not suffice to connect these vehicles with mankind; that the smell of the petrol and oil drowned the human odour; that the semi-obscurity wrapping the people inside, their heads only visible from the level of a lion's eyes, effectually concealed their identity. I became further confirmed in my belief after having tried occasionally the experiment of getting out of the car on the opposite side of it from the lions and then suddenly showing myself in the roadway. When I did this the previously sleepy and unconcerned animals always sprang to their feet and with grunts of alarm made off at full gallop, indicating thus to my mind that once they recognized a human being, their natural fear of him immediately showed itself.

Nevertheless, later observation led me to alter this opinion. There was, I began to realize, something more subtle in the lion's attitude than I had previously suspected. It is difficult, perhaps impossible, even for those who have had much contact with wild animals, to guess how their minds work, or to imagine how ordinary things appear to their eyes. But it may be hazarded, since all animals judge externals from their own experiences of them, when not from the examples of their fellows, that the lion perfectly well realizes there are human beings inside the cars, but, by some queer train of reasoning, never having known them to be enemies while sitting in one, he thinks that, so long as they stay like that, they remain automatically friendly, but

Although wary of people on foot, lion were unafraid of motor vehicles and provided excellent photographic and viewing opportunities.

the moment they get out, they resume their natural hostile role. Sometimes I have got out on the running-board and seen the lions spring up ready to bolt, only once more to lie down quietly the moment I again re-entered the car.

The ordinary bush lion does not regard man, any more than he regards dogs and jackal, as his natural prey. The man-eater is an anomaly, originally driven to an unnatural diet by circumstances, and persisting in it from depraved instinct like a habitual criminal among human beings. So, our lion having argued out the position in their own queer way, decided that so long as the people stayed in their cars they might be permitted to drive up to within a few yards, talk, gesticulate, shout if they liked, without necessitating any interruption of the midday siesta. Sometimes a younger animal would, in play, run after a moving car, greatly of course to the terror of the occupants. But if the car stopped, the lion would stop, too, and sit down on his haunches in the middle of the road, speculatively regarding it. If, presently, no movement was made, he would get up, shake himself and stroll off as one saying, 'Well, if you don't want to play, I'm off'. In most cases, however, the driver at once pressed the accelerator and arrived at the nearest rest-camp with a horrifying tale of how his car had been charged, and how narrowly all in it had escaped.

More than once it has happened that after dusk a herd of impala has dashed across the road in front of a car in the usual way, and that the last one has either struck the running-board or perhaps cleared the radiator in one of the magnificent leaps which distinguish the species. The tale has invariably been that a lion was chasing a buck across the road and sprang on to the front of the car. I fancy the people inside, excitement blinding their senses, have really believed that is what has happened. The animal was of a sort of yellow colour, and it sprang at the car – of course it was a lion. I am bound to say that examination of such cars never disclosed marks such as one might suppose would be caused by the claws of a frightened or annoyed lion clinging to its body. Still, it always made a good story for the tourists' friends. After having spent more than thirty years looking after the Sabi and Shingwedsi reserves, and having travelled through them under all possible conditions in the old style, and thousands of miles annually in the new, I have never in the whole of that time, encountered a tithe of the adventures and hairbreadth escapes which appear to befall some tourists driving along the roads in the course of the short space of a two days' visit.

Now and then, however, they really did have adventures. A party decided to picnic at a certain beauty spot and after luncheon decided it would be nice to go for a short drive, leaving their property on the spot; not a particularly prudent thing to do anywhere, it might be supposed, though no doubt they thought that in the absence of the human element all would be well. On their return an hour later, they found a large family of lion in possession. The remains of the cold viands were being consumed and some of the younger and more playful animals, having torn open dress and suitcases, were running round bearing in their mouths various articles of apparel, while their playmates excitedly pursued them. Frantic sounding of the hooter had no effect whatever, and unwilling to take more drastic steps, the party made for the nearest rest-camp, where a fairly uncomfortable night was spent. In the morning the lions had indeed gone, but a sad state of things greeted the eyes of the tourists. Articles of apparel, torn to shreds, decked every bush in the vicinity, the remnants of the luncheon well trodden in among the general litter; the leather suitcases, used as whetstones for sharpening claws, had failed to withstand the strain. Sadly they gathered up what was left and discussed the possibility of suing the Board of Trustees for damages. Of course, a troop of baboon would act in much the same way and it is unfortunately little safer to leave unguarded property about among wild animals than among tame human beings.

Visitors were found ready to believe almost any story so long as it had some 'kick' about it. One yarn, which found considerable credence in the early days, was to the effect that while a car was proceeding on its lawful occasions, two lions, one from each side of the road, simultaneously charged it. Unfortunately for the lions, though fortunately for the car and its occupants, they slightly misjudged the pace at which it was going, missed it by a few feet and, colliding head on with one another, were left lying senseless in the roadway!

It was current talk among the staff that the lion were just as much interested in watching the tourist cars pass along the roads as the occupants of the cars were in gazing at the lion lying at the sides. It is true that while on certain roads visitors could rely on seeing lion daily, sleeping or lazily watching the traffic from a few yards away, from the end of the tourist season until the park opened again the following year, it was the exception for any of us to find them thus posed. During one season a lioness brought up her family on a little island covered with long grass, and situated in the middle of a large natural pan, itself partly overgrown with coarse herbage – a place tourists were wont to refer to as the 'lily pond' in reference to numbers of waterlilies growing there. Sometimes the troop to which the lioness belonged would join her on the island for the day. This being the only water available for a good many miles round, a considerable amount of game drank there. The wildebeest, zebra, kudu, warthog and impala which formed the majority, were rather at a disadvantage, owing to the road which ran along all one side of the pan becoming a parking place for tourist cars, their occupants patiently waiting, often through many hours, for something to happen. It frequently did. The game having access only at one point to the water, a day seldom passed without toll being paid for its use. The lion took no notice of the cars and pulled down their prey often within less than a hundred yards of them, consuming it forthwith in full view of the excited spectators, while jackal carrying bits of stolen meat in their jaws sometimes fled away through the midst of the cars. In this easy way people from the towns, who had most of them never before seen a wild beast out of a zoo, were able to note (if they liked) exactly how lion kill their prey, an experience often denied even to the most experienced hunters in the past.

Enjoying complete immunity, lion become more and more diurnal animals. It became clear that under entirely natural conditions, and in the absence of man as a menace, the lion is by far the least nocturnal, as he is the least cat-like, in disposition, of the cats. Where accustomed to being on the alert for danger, lion by day like to lie up in patches of dense bush or other covert surrounded by more or less open country, or on the tops of rocky hills and knolls, whence, themselves well hidden, they can note equally the movements of prospective prey and any sign of approaching danger. After a few years of peace, and having become thoroughly accustomed to the passage of cars, we found they had largely changed their habits and now rested for the day under any odd bit of shade, oblivious of whether they were screened from observation or otherwise. In fact, in early mornings, when the grass was damp, and in late afternoons when the sun had ceased to trouble, their favourite resting-place seemed to be the middle of the road. They quickly found out that if they completely ignored them, approaching tourist cars would, after a lot of hooting and backing, finally turn round and go off in the other direction, leaving them to rest in peace. I learnt that the best way, if the road was thus blocked, was to approach slowly but determinedly in low gear, when, at length separated only by a few yards from the bumper bar, they would heave themselves up resignedly, move away a few steps and collapse at the side of the road, usually going to sleep again at once. I never knew them to display any resentment when thus disturbed. Intelligent animals! Doubtless they realized they were trespassing.

The mental reactions of the public were in their way no less interesting than those of the lion. Some who had at first entered the park with considerable trepidation, firmly convinced that they were jeopardizing their lives or at least running very considerable risks, after a time developed a tendency to go to the opposite extreme, and regarded the lion much in the light of large domestic cats which might be stroked with impunity. This last complex was fraught with even greater danger than that of unreasoning fear. Impelled by the latter, a nervous visitor might, believing himself to be in extreme peril, discharge his firearm (if unfortunately he happened to have one in the car with him), when, even did he not hit one of his companions, he might chance to wound a hitherto peacefully disposed lion; but the odds were in favour of his missing both.

On the reverse of the medal we have found people doing things that should qualify them for mental homes. Having observed a recumbent lioness accompanied by small cubs, mildly gazing at the car from a little distance, an enthusiastic young lady has been known to exclaim, 'Oh, the darlings! I *must* get a close-up of them,' and excitedly springing from the car, run towards them with camera in hand. Greeted immediately by an ominous growl, she had then scuttled wildly back to shelter, thus incurring even graver danger than when facing the animal.

Not the least remarkable point in the general attitude of lion to motor cars is the complete trust in them which lionesses, even when guarding quite small cubs, have displayed. I have seen several of these little animals frisk across the road close in front of a stationary car, while their mother, already crossed over, waited patiently by the roadside until they joined her, displaying throughout hardly any trace of nervousness, and none of animosity – though no doubt had anyone incautiously stepped out of the car her reactions would have been of quite a different nature.

On a certain bank holiday the occupants of a car noticed a large male lion extended on his side motionless near the road. More cars came up and parked themselves until there were about a dozen altogether. Still the lion never moved. A number of men climbed out, discussed the situation and finally arrived at the conclusion that he must be dead. So the boldest spirit, picking up a stick, approached a few yards nearer and hurled his missile with such good aim, that the lion sprang to his feet with a roar, and the whole audience rushed headlong for their cars. It certainly says a great deal for the amiable disposition of the park lion that this animal simply stood staring at them in astonishment, for it is hard to imagine any stronger temptation to a

*Initially the staff of the Kruger National Park were few and
ill-equipped to control large numbers of tourists, many of
whom foolishly left their cars to obtain better views of lion.*

lion than that offered. Another time a man, seeing a single male busy on a
kill near the road, desired apparently to display his valour by getting out,
making short rushes in the direction of the lion, and when it growled, running back to the car. With better luck than he deserved, he continued to
repeat the performance until someone came along and stopped him. It is
almost inconceivable that persons evidently considered sane enough to be at
large, should act as described above. Amid unfamiliar surroundings some
appear to lose all sense of proportion. Experienced hunters would shudder at
the risks to which the utterly inexperienced sometimes lightheartedly expose
themselves.

To the majority of the visitors the main, one might even say the sole,
attraction of the park has been the lion. The bulk of the tourists have always
hailed from the larger towns, and few of these can have ever before seen a
wild animal, except behind bars. To most even the names of the various antelope are seemingly unknown – wildebeest, for instance, are often thought to
be buffalo; impala are usually referred to as springbok; once a warthog (at a
distance, no doubt) has been set down as a rhinoceros. One lady asked a
ranger how we managed to keep fish in the rivers with so many hippos
about; another enquired whether giraffe took a heavy toll of the smaller ante-

lope. It is hard to realize how deep was the ignorance of natural history prevalent among the townspeople even of South Africa. I am sure that the Kruger National Park (in addition to its most important educative work in teaching people that wild animals are worth preserving for their own sakes and not merely to provide so much meat and leather) has done more than all the zoos and natural history books put together to implant some knowledge of the habits and appearance of the various creatures, even though little but lukewarm interest be taken in anything but lion, with giraffe, elephant and hippo tying as bad seconds. When two cars meet on the road and the occupants stop to exchange news, the first mutual question invariably is, 'Did you see a lion?' – sometimes, 'Did you see anything?' which has the same implication. I once asked a man if he had come across much along the road. 'Not a blessed thing,' he replied. 'But,' I said rather surprised, 'I have just been along there myself, and I saw any number of impala, some waterbuck, and a few rather fine sable antelope.' 'Oh, those,' was the contemptuous rejoinder. 'Yes I saw *them* all right, but I did not see a single lion!'

Now the lion is certainly a most intelligent and interesting animal, highly sensitive, displaying in his methods of hunting a tactical co-ordination which can be the outcome only of well-developed reasoning faculties, and possessing exceptional powers of communication with his fellows. But it is unusual for visitors to see him otherwise than somnolent, or at best lethargically pacing along, apparently almost too tired to lift his feet. It is possible to see lion to equal advantage in any zoo. Whence, then, comes the immense popularity of this animal as a sight-seeing attraction? Presumably it is to be found in the fascination, the instinctive sense of imminent peril experienced by the initiated visitor who, brought up on stories of the ravening monster of legend, finds himself for the first time face to face with one of these terrible creatures and separated from its possible wrath by nothing more substantial than the window-glass of his motor car. It is a very natural state of mind under the circumstances, and a rich compensatory harvest is no doubt reaped later in that most exhilarating of all feelings, the memory of danger met and happily surmounted. Many people keep a careful record of every lion seen, and at night in the rest-camp the tallies are produced and eagerly compared with those of other enthusiasts.

It was interesting to observe the effects of a certain amount of familiarity with lion upon some who had, on meeting them for the first time, become highly excited, not to say nervous. They seemed to pass, without any intermediate phase, from their first condition to one of complete confidence in the benevolent nature of the lion and in their own capacity to deal with the animal under all circumstances. After a few visits to the park, and after having taken some photographs at close quarters, they felt that the nature of the beast was to them as an open book that they were qualified to lecture on its habits – perhaps that they had established mental contact and possessed some mysterious, hypnotic gift which gave them power to charm. Such people are apt to persuade themselves that under no circumstances can a lion be dangerous to them.

I have always felt a little nervous as to the possible outcome of this over-confidence. Although the unmolested lion, even after having to some extent discarded its natural fear of man, is usually content to leave him alone, as not forming an item of its natural prey, yet it is, after all, a formidable beast of rapine, whose mental reactions no human being can presume to fore-shadow or fully to understand. There are also a good many persons who hold precisely opposite views, who hate and fear predatory animals and think they should all be exterminated everywhere. They look on them as criminals, mainly it seems because nature condemned them to eat raw meat. The old hunters and lowvelders had no doubts on the subject, and in their case it was quite a logical expression of opinion. Lion were thieves that killed and wasted creatures which ought to be turned into meat and leather for the financial profit of the human predatory animal; to preserve game and lion at the same time seemed ridiculous in their eyes.

I had perhaps some excuse for feeling relieved when each season closed without someone or other having paid the penalty of folly, though actually, during the first eight years during which tourists were let loose among unconfined wild animals, there was only one accident, and this not in respect of a beast of prey, but of a herbivore, a bull sable, in fact. A visitor, seeing it standing motionless behind a tree, thought he would get closer for a photograph, and against the regulations he got out of his car and walked up to within a few yards of the animal. He did not know, of course, that it had recently been badly wounded in a fight with another – so crippled, in fact, that it died from its injuries a few days later. When he was about six paces from it, it put its head down, charged him, drove one horn through his thigh and undoubtedly would have killed him had not his wife and a native servant rushed to his assistance and pluckily driven the beast off with sticks and stones.

To induce the more unthinking to behave sensibly, as much in their own interests as in those of others, we at first contented ourselves with hortatory notices embodying good advice; but as these remained apparently unread and certainly unregarded, we had to strengthen the position by regulations, for breaking which there was a specified fine. The commonest offences were those of getting out of cars in the presence of game, thereby invariably disturbing it (in the case of lion, an invitation to danger), and leaving the roads, which usually implied pursuing animals, such as giraffe, across country. With the game thus driven away from the vicinity of the road, people following behind became annoyed and the abuse had to be stopped.

At the same time it was always difficult to obtain information from the public definite enough to justify a prosecution. Seldom had the number of the offending car been noticed, neither was any recognizable description of it, nor of its occupants, forthcoming. It was of course quite reasonable that people living at the other end of the country should dread the prospect of being brought long distances to be witnesses in a petty police court case, and it was never generally understood that under the excellent system known as 'admission of guilt' there was no necessity either for accused or witnesses to appear in court at all. To help people's memories we had large notices, 'Stay in Your Car and Keep to the Road', put up at intervals where most likely to catch the eye, and smaller ones to the same effect attached to the windscreen of each car as it entered the park. Naturally the limited staff could not be everywhere at the same time and the game went merrily on. Yet while these aberrations were not unusual on the part of a minority of the more thoughtless and selfish, the great mass of the visitors behaved in the most exemplary manner, equally on the roads and in the rest-camps, which in view of a natural tendency to imagine that the restraints of civilization are dead letters in the wilds, is a tribute to the general law-abiding nature of the population of South Africa.

Year by year we increased our camping accommodation and our road mileage as the park became progressively better known and more popular. In 1928, 122 miles of road had been completed; in 1929, 382; in 1930, 450; and by 1936 approximately 900. The tourist traffic rose in like proportion from three cars with a dozen visitors in 1927, to over 6 000 cars and lorries, carrying about 26 000 people, in 1935. The park opened on May 31 and closed on October 31 each year. But Pretoriuskop in the extreme west, lying just under the foothills of the Drakensberg, with its large rest-camp and one hundred miles of surrounding road, being considered practically free from malaria, remained open to the public throughout the twelve months – something had to be done for overseas visitors. Unfortunately the healthy lowveld winter synchronizes with the European and North American summer, when people have no incentive to seek warmer climes. Consequently, South Africa becomes popular only after Christmas, and in view of past experiences, it was out of the question to keep open the lower-lying parts of the park in the rainy season, with limited visibility, malarial fever rampant and roads often impassable. Fortunately, Pretoriuskop was blessed with a sandy soil, a good climate and sweet grass which attracted game in great numbers during the summer months.

In 1931 it seemed the time had come at last to open up the long neglected Shingwedsi area. I had always felt that its day would come, and I had strenuously opposed all suggestions to excise any part of it from the sanctuary. For some years past it had been carefully nursed and was now beginning to show sufficient head of game to justify public admittance. Although the animals were less plentiful than in the south, species not found there, such as elephant, eland and nyala, existed, while roan antelope, tsessebe and reedbuck were relatively common. The country itself was attractive – especially in the extreme north, where huge baobabs, and sometimes palm-trees of good size, were features of the landscape; the handsome mopane was everywhere predominant. Some of the views, too, especially along the Pafuri River, were delightful.

In order to develop this area, about a hundred miles of new road had to be constructed, and some means of crossing the Letaba River had to be found. Previously it had been possible to visit the country only either by laboriously

Being in the extreme west and therefore free of malaria,
Pretoriuskop (shown here in the 1930s) was the only camp
open throughout the year.

241

trekking up with donkeys from the south (a method of progress which, however delightful in itself, was unsuited to our new conditions), or by travelling twenty-four hours by train to the nearest point on the railway, thereafter inducing one of my friends of the Witwatersrand Native Labour Association, first Mr Neergaard and afterwards Mr MacKay, to run me down by car, an unwarrantable trespass on their kindness. Under the able direction of Ranger C.G. Crous, the road as far as the Shingwedsi was completed within a year, and that from Punda Maria southwards – already partly made – was efficiently finished by Ranger Botha.

At one time it looked as though the work might be badly held up. The native labourers began to go sick one after another from a mysterious disease which puzzled the staff, and which was at once attributed by the men themselves to the results of witchcraft. We were threatened with wholesale desertion. Then just at the right time, the local health officer happened to come along and diagnosed it as scurvy, apparently due to a uniform diet of maize porridge. I had always vaguely believed that scurvy was purely a seafarers' complaint and that to contract it a diet of 'salt horse' and weevily biscuits was essential. However, the diagnosis must have been correct, for as soon as we were able to administer fresh vegetables and lemons, the disease disappeared at once.

We conquered the Letaba River by means of a low-level concrete bridge, which – together with similar ones over the Sand River, and later on over the Sabie – was efficiently constructed by Mr Joubert, whose services we were fortunate to obtain from the provincial roads department. Thus, before the tourist season of 1933, the park was efficiently linked up from north to south and a straight run through from Pafuri in the north to Malelane in the extreme south could be accomplished easily in two days, as against three weeks of laborious trekking a few years earlier.

With this great extent of country now available to the public, it was necessary to maintain a staff of three instead of two rangers north of the Olifants River. Hitherto neither Botha in the north nor Crous in the south had been able adequately to supervise the middle country, which since Fraser's departure in 1920 had perforce been left nearly to itself. Another ranger was appointed, Kirkman, but the new section was placed under one of the older officers, Tomlinson, who was transferred from the south for the purpose. He found native poaching rife, as was to be expected, but some energetic police work on his part, resulting in several captures and convictions of the principal gangs of hunters, soon put a stop to it.

Shortage of funds remained our chronic handicap. We had no capital to draw upon and usually had to spend next year's estimated revenue in advance, though now and then government came to our aid with small grants. Our income increased annually until, by 1935, that derived from tourist traffic alone approached £20 000. It was amusing to reflect how no more than ten years previously I had speculated concerning all that might be done were only £15 000 a year to be available on which to run the concern – a sum then far outside my wildest dreams – and here we were in possession of over double that amount, including what we got from government for administration, and yet bewailing our poverty. Truly is eating said to encourage appetite. But of course our necessary expenditure increased even faster than our revenue. Always there was some new call. Each year something more had to be done for visitors. There seemed, indeed, at one time a danger that tourist traffic was going to absorb the whole of our estate. Fortunately, however, this did not occur; the welfare of the animals was not forgotten.

At the end of each dry season, away from the main rivers and a few permanent pools, the country was waterless. In consequence the game crowded down to such places, and for some miles back completely ate up all the grass, converting the veld into a bare and dusty expanse. Long distances away, where no water existed, there was, on the other hand, plenty of grazing unvisited by any wildlife. To adjust matters, and so far as possible to prevent the game from trekking away east and west, we at first built dams in suitable places. But the high rate of evaporation, combined with the quantity drunk by the game where no natural replenishment existed, always resulted in these sources of supply becoming dry just when they were most required. I had long entertained the idea of sinking boreholes, but hitherto the cost of hiring the necessary plant had been prohibitive.

Talking the matter over one day with a constant visitor – Mr Jearey of Cape Town – he offered to initiate a publicity campaign, which, if the public were to prove sufficiently interested, might permit of something being done. Mr Jearey first approached *The Star* newspaper in Johannesburg, and with its ready help the movement caught on and spread beyond wildest hopes. Public bodies and individuals all over South Africa eagerly and generously subscribed, with the result that in a short time about £5 000 was available towards better watering facilities for the animals. The immediate response made by the public was the most encouraging thing that had yet occurred in the history of the park. It showed that people were genuinely interested in it and its wildlife, to the extent of putting their hands in their pockets for its benefit – always the acid test – that they regarded it not only as an interesting holiday resort, but as a national asset which they were prepared to support. All the larger towns subscribed generously. Two ladies, Mrs Orpen and Mrs Armour Hall, each subscribed the money for a complete borehole. The Government provided a couple and agreed not to make any charge for failures to strike water.

The work began at Pretoriuskop about the middle of 1933, and with two machines working by the end of 1935 some twenty boreholes had been sunk, fourteen of which were successful. Water was struck at depths of three hundred feet and less, and delivery varied from three hundred to two thousand gallons per hour. The formation was mainly granite, and the water more or less salt, which, however, is no drawback where wild animals are in question – in fact they prefer it so. With the exception of those at Pretoriuskop, Rabelais and Malopene entrance gates and Satara, which were designed for camp use as well as for their original purpose, the boreholes were sited in otherwise waterless areas where the surrounding grazing was good. Windmills were erected as being the simplest method of pumping the water and that requiring the least attention an important consideration in a wild country.

There was some discussion as to the best mode of delivery; the irrigation department was insistent on concrete reservoirs with attached drinking-troughs – an excellent system for domestic stock, no doubt, but wild game has the bad taste not to appreciate clean drinking places. Some species, indeed, are not happy unless they can wallow in mud during or after the operation. However, lest we should be thought unduly assertive, two of the boreholes were equipped in accordance with the advice of the professionals – complete with reservoirs, drinking-troughs and ball-cocks. The game obstinately refused to go anywhere near the strange receptacles (though the windmills themselves did not seem to occasion much, if any, alarm), indeed, after having observed the water-troughs from a safe distance, wildebeest, zebra and impala preferred to travel for miles in search of some more familiar type of drinking place.

Not so the lion. Concrete drinking-troughs seemed to them the fulfilment of an unexpressed want. A family party would lie up the whole day by a trough, chins resting comfortably on the margin, while long tongues now and then lazily took a luxurious lap. In fact, so greatly did they appreciate the new arrangement, that I doubt even had the other animals eventually become reconciled whether they would have been permitted to participate, except at rarest intervals. So in the end I had my way; the troughs were cut off from the supply, and at these and the other boreholes the water was pumped straight into natural pools in which the game could splash and puddle to its hearts' content, while the muddy, trampled margins were less suitable for the midday siestas of the king of beasts.

Fourteen boreholes sunk in arid places were a great help, but of course, to provide anything like an adequate water supply all over so large a tract of country, ten times as many would hardly have sufficed. The provision of water in hitherto unaccustomed places brought out very strikingly the innate conservatism of wild animals, or rather, perhaps their instinctive subservience to custom. At the time of year when their experience taught them that all water had dried up within a given area, they left it, oblivious of the new source provided. The artificial supplies were used only when there was not another drop of moisture to be found anywhere within reach, and the slightest shower was enough to cause every beast to slake its thirst in the beds of the creeks, in tiny rain-pools, anywhere rather than at the really imposing sheets of water which, after the first year, the windmills supplied. In 1935 I noticed that up to the end of October, a herd of about a hundred buffalo were drinking at one of the puddle dams attached to a windmill, a place where in most years it was usual to find a little water until that time. Early in November this herd had in the past always been accustomed to trek to the Sabie River, and it carried out its programme exactly as usual. It happened that in 1935 the grazing at Lower Sabie completely failed; even the roots of the grass perished in the long drought and under the blazing sun. Numbers of the buffalo either died of starvation, or became so weak that they were easily pulled down by lion. About December, when things were at their worst, I visited the borehole in the vicinity of which the herd had been feeding six weeks before. Rain had fallen locally and any quantity of young sweet grass had sprung up, while the small pond had developed into a miniature lake. Not a single buffalo and hardly another animal was to be seen. The tracks showed that a few kudu and a stray duiker or two were using the water; nothing else, except, of course, the lion – animals which, in their wanderings, seldom miss anything and are never slaves of custom. The only move made by the starving buffalo, under extreme stress, was to the Crocodile River, where things were but little better than at the Sabie. In the past, grass and water had not existed at Hlambamaduba after October, and therefore it was useless, they felt, going there to look for it.

No doubt in due course the relatively unintelligent herbivorous animals will learn that water is to be found all the year round without fail at certain new places, and then the boreholes will adequately fulfil their object. In the meantime it seems as hard to overcome the prejudice of animals as it sometimes is that of human beings. Were the water supplies evenly spread over the whole park, it would be capable of maintaining many more animals than has been the case in the past, and I am inclined to believe that, although unfed dams are likely in all cases to dry up before the peak of the drought each year, yet they are of considerable assistance in that, if numerous enough, and especially if they are enlargements of already popular drinking places, they will tend to lengthen the period which the great herds of game take to exhaust the bush pools each year, and so retard the animal migrations. Time will, no doubt, show.

Prior to the excision of the western portion of the reserve lying between the Sabie and Crocodile Rivers in 1923, the game could trek freely towards the end of each dry season, to the better watered veld near the foothills, and yet remain within the sanctuary. After this country was shorn away, the animals still continued their long established usual movements, but were of course then lost temporarily to the park. It is always remarkable to note how, after the first rains, the more migratory species, such as zebra and wildebeest, suddenly appear in vast numbers in places where none have been seen for months. There is also – and always has been – a certain migration eastward annually into Portuguese territory where the country is relatively fertile, but the greater movement is westward.

It is unfortunate that the grazing and watering facilities within the park should be inferior to those of the immediately adjoining areas, but one has to remember that the park is only a wildlife sanctuary because it was deemed useless for any other purpose. Fortunately, a large proportion of the farms lying over the western boundary passed into the hands of good sportsmen and wildlife enthusiasts. Thus, although lost to the sight-seeing public, their stock of game remains in good hands. It may even be that, at a later date, some of these farms will revert to the sanctuary. By a small amendment to the Act passed in 1935, certain government farms in the same area were also added with the object of preventing their use as stepping-off places for illegal game destruction. In the meantime it is all to the good that so many farms adjoining the park should have become private game preserves, used for reasonable sport in the season and well protected during the rest of the year.

How, most fittingly, to commemorate the origin of the Kruger National Park and to place on permanent record the names of those to whose farsighted policy its existence was due, was a question which, for a considerable time, exercised the Board of Trustees. Ultimately it was decided that it should most appropriately take the form of a memorial stone, sited in such a position that, while easily accessible to the visiting public, it would still express some of the aloofness and natural grandeur which it was desired permanently to associate with the general conception of the sanctuary. Accordingly, a large granite boulder, prominent by the roadside some fourteen miles north of Sabi Bridge, now known as Skukuza, was selected. In it was imbedded a simple bronze tablet, bearing an inscription in both official languages to the effect that the Sabi Game Reserve had been first instituted in 1898 by President Kruger and that Mr P.W. Grobler had, in 1926, been responsible for piloting the National Parks Act through parliament. The

*Two bronze plaques, set into a granite outcrop near Skukuza
in 1933, commemorate those involved in the founding of the
Kruger National Park. They were unveiled by Hilda
Stevenson-Hamilton, wife of the warden, who is seen here
with Board Chairman W.J.C. Brebner on her left, Minister of
Lands P.G.W. Grobler and an African ranger.*

memorial was unveiled in September 1933 by the wife of the warden, in the presence of the chairman and the members of the board, the majority of the white staff and a few representatives of the public. Mr Grobler, who was himself present, made an admirable opening speech, and was followed by Colonel Reitz and Mr Papenfus. A picnic spot was later established at the place, and a ladder, placed out of sight behind the boulder, enabled tourists to climb to the top and enjoy the view to be obtained thence. In its solitude and simplicity this memorial seems to touch exactly the right note.

———— ❖ ————

CHAPTER ELEVEN

I COULD HARDLY RECOGNIZE my beloved and once battered Cinderella in her new garb and surroundings, and truth to tell, I did not admire her nearly so much in them. The whole atmosphere had changed. The Spirit of the Wild shunned the neighbourhood of crowded camps and roads. Only far from their bustle could her presence still be sensed, while for me at least, the ever-increasing work of decking out my charge in new articles of apparel and touching her up with various adventitious aids to supposed attractiveness, rendered such opportunities of contact ever less frequent. Even the seven months of each year during which the park remained closed to the public did not necessarily imply a general return to the primitive. Roads had to be made and renewed, rest-camps built or added to, bridges constructed, all implying a maximum of supervision and of office work, and a minimum of that which most appealed. Civilization had come to us and was not to be shaken off.

During the height of the tourist season processions of cars cloaked the roads in clouds of dust; on bank holidays merry trippers, packed on crowded lorries, shouted and discarded bottles and orange-peel as they careered along. At night the rest-camps resounded with the strains of broadcast music, of gramophones and of community singing. Even the animals seemed to have changed and, accommodating themselves to altered conditions, to have acquired an appearance of domesticity. Of course I was prejudiced. Conditions were not really so bad, or rather so changed, as my memories of the past caused me sometimes to deem them. In practice, the work of development proved extraordinarily interesting, and as I have inferred elsewhere

249

and was constantly telling myself, only persons who are in some way mentally deficient can possibly prefer discomfort, hard fare and chronic lack of companionship, to the ease, comforts and lively social surroundings of civilized existence.

Yet in moments of temporary depression, for instance during the impingement of a severe cold, or when recovering from an attack of malaria, I could not help contrasting Cinderella in her former rustic simplicity with the sophisticated town lady which, on such depressing occasions, she seemed to me in a fair way to have become. I reflected that I had been to a considerable degree responsible for the transformation. At such moments I was in danger of forgetting that had she not found her way into the palace and become the bride of the prince, my Cinderella would inevitably have been swept into oblivion, unregretted and unrecorded, except perhaps as a once undeserving recipient of charity, which might well have been devoted to better purpose. With her demise, too, the Spirit of the Wild would have spread wings, and with averted face would have fled forever from the lowveld. I suppose that a certain sensation of anti-climax is apt to follow the successful consummation of any kind of mundane effort. The trials and struggles, the disappointments and anxieties are forgotten and only the glamour of the past remains. Memories of difficulties overcome, of achievement, even of surroundings and a way of life which were commonplace enough at the time – in retrospect – are illuminated with a rosy glow which tends to deepen with the passage of time.

In the early days of the park the visitors were nature enthusiasts, people of simple tastes who were quite content, having been shown a camping place, to sleep on the ground, to draw water for themselves from the nearest spruit or pool, to cook their own food and to use the roughest of tracks for travelling: no one then complained. Ten years later, after the board had provided permanent buildings, adequately if plainly furnished, catering, stores where practically everything necessary could be purchased, bathrooms with hot and cold water laid on, motor repair shops, even at one camp, partial electric lighting and a telephone office, letters began to appear in the press voicing protests against the 'sordid conditions', the 'hard life unsuitable to civilized human beings', the 'utter absence of all comfort'.

Such complaints doubtless represented the views of a small, even a tiny minority of visitors. Yet there is no doubt that our early public, the nature lovers, had been reinforced – and to some extent supplanted – by the ordinary holiday-makers from the larger cities. These, apart from the desire to

Until high level bridges were constructed, vehicle crossings were made by pontoon, such as this one opposite Skukuza.

see a lion (which seemed a universal ambition) came to the park less because they were interested in what it had to display than because a visit thereto was becoming fashionable and formed a change from Durban and Muizenberg, whose amenities some resented not finding at their disposal in our rest-camps. No doubt their point of view was deserving of some consideration, even of sympathy. The absence of a cocktail bar, of electric light and a telephone in each bedroom, the necessity for walking across the open in order to reach the bathroom, of having to shout for an attendant, instead of merely being required to press a button, with a hundred other frustrations of reasonable wants, could not but bear hardly on any really up-to-date, twentieth-century citizen or citizeness.

On the other hand the style of dress adopted by some, which, except for the high-heeled shoes of the ladies, would have been eminently suitable for African exploration in the early days, was perhaps an indication that even greater hardships were anticipated during a motor run through the park than were in reality likely to be encountered. Many old-fashioned people appeared to think that up-to-date hotels on the American model would be out of place; would, in fact, tend to mar the character of the surroundings. It all depends on the angle from which the matter is studied. No doubt, were the necessary capital forthcoming, it should not be impossible to provide, in connection with the attached golf links and tennis courts at each rest-camp hotel, some kind of zoological gardens, after the Whipsnade model, wherein visitors who so desired might see the animals in comfort, without having to drive about the hot and dusty roads for the purpose. Perhaps it is best to go slowly in such improvements. In view of the astonishing changes which ten years have wrought, he would be a bold man who would even hazard a guess as to what another ten years may see.

I have always, myself, held the possibly mistaken view that, apart from the financial impracticability of doing anything else, the course hitherto adopted of doling out to the public each year some small fresh amenity is the correct one. Except for the absence of any facility for purchasing stimulating liquors on the spot, there is now really no vast difference between a 'luxury' rest-camp in the park and a South African country hotel. In fact, compared with some rural hostels to be met with not so many years ago, the average park rest-camp seems a paradise of amenity. Thus, step by step, and without prematurely scaring the old-fashioned people, who think a wildlife sanctuary ought to be a place wherein everything should remain so far as possible just as it has been from time immemorial, we may gradually attain to the ideal of a series of first-class hotels, connected by tarred roads and possessing all reasonable comforts, including cinema palaces, dancing halls and swimming baths.

Apart altogether from the vexed question as to just how far comforts and conveniences for visitors may be provided without damaging the character of such an institution as the Kruger National Park – a matter concerning which I have invariably attempted to maintain views as unprejudiced as are possible to a person of my antecedents – it may not be out of place to set forth, even at the risk of being considered by some old-fashioned, what, in my opinion, should be the ideals of a permanent wildlife sanctuary. There exist fundamental distinctions between the great South African national park and those of the United States of America, whose example first inspired in my mind the conception which later matured. In the latter, the attractions are mainly scenic, the animals play a secondary role and the various dangers of the primitive African bush are absent.

Were we to cover our own sanctuary with a network of roads and allow our rest-camps to become too numerous, the privacy which is so necessary for the wild animals would be seriously threatened, and during the open period they might tend to seek more complete seclusion in Portuguese territory or in other lowveld land less overrun by visitors. In fact, while the American national parks are rightly known as 'playgrounds for the people', the Kruger National Park may more fitly be designated as 'a sanctuary for the fauna to which the public is admitted'.

The situation therefore requires careful watching, since there is a natural and perhaps growing tendency to invert the relative importance of visitors and animals, leading ultimately and inevitably to the disappearance of the character of the park and its gradual conversion into a mere glorified zoological garden. So long as this is borne in mind, every possible consideration should be shown to the public and every reasonable facility provided. This should be done because on the continued popularity of the park depends the whole future of wildlife in South Africa, and to some extent elsewhere, so world-wide has become its fame and so greatly has it stimulated similar effort in many other countries.

The first object of the park should be to educate the public in the rudiments of natural history; to show people what the wild animals of their country look like, and how they act in their natural state, free from the terror of man. It should also cultivate a spirit of sympathy with them; to let it be realized that animals are more admirable alive, and in their natural setting – themselves in fact – than converted into the rags and bones of hunters' trophies, or confined, listless prisoners behind bars. As town populations increase and urban industries develop, life generally grows more and more artificial and it will no doubt become correspondingly more interesting – as well as scientifically valuable – to have retained one spot where nature remains unspoilt, where the public can form some idea of how the country looked before man intruded. It will be here in the forests and the streams, peopled by their wild denizens – just as they were during thousands of years in the far past – that a scene from the Pleistocene, within a few hours' travel of a great modern city, will be viewed at minimum expense and with no more hardship than may be involved in sitting quietly in an automobile.

But, in addition to its above popular objects, a wildlife sanctuary supplies the most favourable ground whereon may be sought the answers to many riddles of natural history, since the indigenous species are there permitted to live their natural lives unhampered by artificial aids and restrictions. Full answers to the various questions which suggest themselves cannot be expected now, nor perhaps at any time; a certain amount of artificiality is inevitable in any region where man is present, however firmly he may restrain his hand, and however honestly he may endeavour to leave nature to herself. But in the Kruger National Park there exists the opportunity of getting nearer the truth than is possible perhaps anywhere else in the world today.

For instance, we may learn how nature, left entirely alone, manages her own affairs in respect of limitation and increase of various species; how, in short, life went on in the world before man became a factor to reckon with.

What is the exact influence of the shortage or otherwise of some particular grass or tree food on each type, as affecting itself and others? How precisely does the balance between the preyers and the preyed-upon become adjusted? It has already been learnt that where carnivorous animals have been artificially kept down and the others allowed to increase unhindered by man, the first-named tend to multiply abnormally, since the relative ease with which food may then be obtained through lack of competition greatly encourages rapidity and extent of breeding.

In the days of the Sabi Game Reserve, when predatory animals were destroyed as a matter of routine, it was discovered that lion, for instance, could barely be kept static in numbers. So easy was it for them to catch their prey, that a lioness was accustomed to produce cubs at about twice the normal rate. In place of the usual two or three, she brought forth as many as four or five in a litter; while of these, instead of one or two only, probably all, or nearly all, were able to survive to maturity. When, after the inauguration of the Kruger National Park it was decided to permit nature, so far as possible, to take her course, the same accelerated rate of increase tended to persist, until prides of twenty or more, mainly cubs and half-grown animals, were by no means unusual. Presently, as the game began to lose the unnatural advantage which it had hitherto enjoyed, it was noticed that the younger lion were often in poor, even emaciated condition, that cubs were dying, and that the number of lion of all ages, especially young animals, slain by their companions, was greatly increasing. The reason, of course, was obvious. A large party of lion would kill, for example, a wildebeest. The older members would devour the whole of it at one sitting, while the younger would either have to stand aside still hungry, or pay the extreme penalty for trying to help themselves unasked. Lion, until about a year or more old, are unable to do their own hunting, and about that time their mothers cease to take any special protective interest in them.

Lionesses too, with small cubs, found it no longer so simple a matter as formerly to bring up a family. They often had to go hungry themselves; their supply of milk decreased, and only the sturdier youngsters were able to survive. When the game treks out of a certain district in search of food or water, the lion tend to follow, but this is not always possible in the case of females with young cubs often insufficiently nourished. A ranger once found no fewer than five young lion, their mature teeth not yet fully developed, slain by their companions round the remains of a kill. Another time seven cubs of about two months old were noticed, very thin and hungry, lying abandoned under the same tree, whence they did not stir for three successive days, their mothers absent, no doubt trying to find food. On the night of the third day the latter returned and removed their families, but one infant was too weak to travel at all, so was left behind, and would have died, had not Ranger Ledeboer picked it up and taken it home with him. It seems, there-fore, that nature is trying again to adjust her balance, temporarily upset by human effort.

There are a few fundamental rules which have to be understood before it is possible to form any opinion worth expressing about wildlife generally. Experience teaches that once a natural equilibrium has been established within an area of sufficient size, it can be upset only by exceptional causes. These are, firstly, man – the usual and chief one. Secondly, there is starva-tion, due to the giving out of the particular type of food essential to one or more of the indigenous species, each of which, among the herbivora, favours some special kind of herbage which is essential to its health, though it may not confine itself to that particular type. Thirdly, an outbreak of epidemic disease – a rare occurrence, usually communicated, as in the case of rinder-pest, to wild by domestic animals.

Herbivorous animals leave an area when the type of grass or herb favoured by the species becomes deficient, and will not thrive in one that does not contain it. To imagine that by artificially thinning out some species, which happens to be numerous within a certain locality, greater facility for numerical increase will be given to another which is less abundant there, is to betray ignorance of primary causes. Each species is plentiful or the reverse within any given area only in direct proportion to the suitability of the locality to its special requirements.

The extermination, under natural conditions, of one indigenous species by another – whether directly through carnivorous consuming herbivorous types, or indirectly by one herbivorous type proving too strong for its associ-ates in the same area – except as a final culmination, after man (or one of the other factors cited above) has first played the principal part, is unknown in natural history so far as our experience extends. It may safely be ruled out in any wildlife reservation of adequate extent where room exists for seasonal migration. Yet the notion that, in order to safeguard wildlife existing under primitive conditions, man must step in with his artificial aids – as though it were a pheasant preserve in England – is still widely held.

Excepting in an area maintained entirely for shooting purposes where the game is artificially confined within certain numerical limits, it is essential that its natural enemies be allowed to increase conformably with it. Otherwise, in the absence of any migration outlet, over-population, resulting if not checked in the outbreak of disease and famine – nature's own drastic remedies in overstocked areas – will ultimately result. Upsetting the balance of nature usually leads to unexpected and sometimes unfortunate results. The deliberate elimination of practically all the larger carnivorous animals from the Zululand game reserves resulted, within a few years, in the numerical increase of the big game to such a degree that the reserves could no longer support its needs, and the animals spread out far and wide over the surrounding settled country. Sooner or later, no doubt, this would have necessitated a serious campaign against them, entirely apart from the tsetse fly menace, which merely brought the matter to a head earlier than might otherwise have been the case, and condensed the period of destruction into a shorter time.

In a certain district of the Sabi Game Reserve, a season's intensive trapping of smaller carnivora – genet, mongoose, civet, wild cat and jackal – resulted in such a plague of bush rodents that the local natives lost most of their grain crop. The senseless killing of insectivorous and raptorial birds on

Even after the establishment of the Kruger National Park, Stevenson-Hamilton still toured the area regularly. The spectacular scenery in the gorge of the Olifants River made the Gorge rest camp, seen here, one of his favourite halts.

the part of the more ignorant farmers the world over must, in the aggregate, have resulted in immense financial loss. Among the originating causes of misfortune, many have of course been more or less fortuitous, and though emanating from man's presence, have not been deliberately designed by him. In a remote area of Portuguese East Africa the local natives had succeeded in completely exterminating, by snaring and otherwise, all the larger types of indigenous game. The lion, which had remained unmolested, in consequence were driven by hunger to become man-eaters, and for many years established such a reign of terror that the natives scarcely dared to venture into their fields and were even seized while sleeping in their huts. Instances of the same kind have been recorded from other parts of Africa.

In Southern Rhodesia, at the time of the rinderpest epidemic of 1896, large numbers of game and cattle died and their carcasses strewed the veld. The lion for a time waxed fat, and as usual under the circumstances, multiplied exceedingly. Presently this temporary source of food supply came to an end. Game and cattle were then relatively scarce, while the lion, on their side, had increased in numbers, and proportionately hungry, proved for a time a source of danger to human life in some parts of the country.

Two instances from America. A favourite feeding ground of wild geese was adopted for sheep farming. The numerous foxes which had been used to prey upon the geese now partly turned their attention to lambs. The farmers, rightfully incensed at this, set to work to exterminate the foxes, with the result that the geese multiplied to such an extent as to destroy most of the grass required by the sheep, and many more lambs died than had previously fallen a prey to the foxes. In the second instance, a small lake was well stocked with snapping turtles, and was also favoured by numbers of wild ducks. The banks were the haunt of a species of small fur-bearing mammal which kept down the numbers of the turtles by eating their eggs. A time came when the fur of these small animals acquired a market value, and consequently they were trapped to the verge of extermination. Freed from their enemies, the turtles increased enormously, and outgrowing and eventually finishing their natural food supply, acquired a taste for young ducklings. In consequence, the ducks forsook the lake and the turtles themselves then mostly died off from starvation. Wildlife was effectually evicted.

The ideal wildlife sanctuary should aim to be fully and accurately representative of the particular area, as it may have been before man had progressed sufficiently to disturb its ordered arrangement. All indigenous species of fauna and flora ought to be represented. The introduction of exotic types of either should be religiously avoided. They introduce a discordant element, and even should they succeed in assimilating themselves with the environment, they will generally appear incongruous, conferring an air of artificiality on the whole. Only by keeping such a place perfectly natural may the student acquire true knowledge and the ordinary visitor a real education in natural history. Where animals are molested or disturbed by human agency some links in the chain of their life economy will be missed and the relative value of observation to that extent marred.

Except in carefully guarded sanctuaries it is difficult to study wild creatures fully. Elsewhere, on man's presence being detected, all the little intimacies of animal life stop dead. His tyranny is to himself so much a matter of course, that, especially if he is of the great majority who live their lives divorced from wild nature, he views the frenzied terror which the creatures display on his approach as being their natural habit of life. From a place of concealment, you are looking over an African river scene. Tree-clad banks and green reeds fringe the water, which reflects the pure blue of the sky. Hippos splash and grunt; crocodiles float lazily about among unheeding fishes; otters protrude their heads, turn over in the water like seals, or lie lazily on stones by its edge. A pair of Egyptian geese are preening themselves on a sandbank; kingfishers poise and dive; bush pheasants strut about and call raucously to one another; a bateleur sails overhead; two fish eagles perch side by side on dead bough. A long line of impala makes its slow way towards the water, stealthily watched by a leopard extended along the horizontal limb of a great fig tree.

It is hard to realize that so peaceful a scene is all a part of the great process of eating and being eaten. And then, the moment you show yourself, what a change! The hippos and crocodiles dive; the otters disappear in water or burrow; the birds fly away; the impala snort and rush off; the leopard has simply vanished. In a few seconds not a sign of animal life is left visible to the human eye. Unvarying reaction to the recognition of wild nature's arch enemy.

If and when man should ever disappear from earth, there is no form of nature but would benefit by his departure. All his so-called improvements, his capture and drilling of natural forces, are designed solely for his own benefit. Viewed from any but the human standpoint they are mainly destructive. Wherever he goes he scars the face of the land, cuts down or burns the vegetation, exterminates the animals. In constructive mood, having wiped out some plant or animal indigenous to a particular locality from its natural habitat, he enjoys the experiment of introducing it to another, probably unsuited to its habits. Wasteful exploitation of natural products is inherent in the whole human race, and civilized man with his much enhanced powers of destruction, rises superior to the savage only by virtue of his possession of an occasional awareness of whither he is drifting.

There is an old Latin proverb to the effect that if you evict nature she will presently return armed with a pitchfork, and it has, throughout the ages, repeatedly been proved true in respect of man and his relations with his surroundings. Unfortunately, when he at last departs or ceases to be a force to count, it looks as though he will leave little, if any, other terrestrial form of life in existence, excepting no doubt the insects. The following – from an American periodical – not only points a warning but visualizes a condition of things in existence in some places even today.

> My boy! You are an American, of which you should be proud. I bequeath to you our great land, which we love so well. I hand the heritage to you, as my father passed it to me; but altered and developed a bit. Our forests of course have been cut to the last tree; the last head of game has been shot from the hillside; the last bird from the fields, and the streams no longer furnish fish and fur. Our vast public domain has been fed to the gravel, and is swiftly becoming a desert. The national parks are shot out. So stay in town my son, and don't stray beyond the pavements. But, if you do venture out, remember this – don't go near the water. Our once crystal streams are leprous now. Should you go to the old swimming hole, your feet will mire in bottomless slime and sewage, while the poisonous fumes assail your nostrils. All this is yours, my son – your heritage – the great outdoors of America.

Fortunately there is a brighter side to the picture. Within the last thirty years there has been apparent a steadily growing appreciation of what is due to nature. The enormous development of rapid communication, bringing the remotest places of the earth within easy reach, coupled with the competition to 'civilize' and 'develop' (in other words to exploit them as speedily as possible) has caused the more far-seeing to realize that if anything of the natural world is to be saved, immediate action is essential – hence the movement in the direction of government forest and wildlife reservations, in which America has the credit of having taken the lead.

It is obvious that the extinction of all larger wild animal life, even in the hitherto most secluded places, is only a matter of time and a very short time, unless special steps are taken to prevent it. Agricultural and pastoral industries, understandably, will not tolerate untamed nature on the doorstep. Ivory, horns, skins, all have a certain commercial value. The only hope is to set aside areas sufficiently large within which may be preserved inviolate the natural features, the native trees and the indigenous animals; not perhaps for 'all time' but for an indefinitely long period, at least until some war or revolution comes to wreak wholesale destruction. To secure permanence, or relative permanence, such areas must be popularized and made attractive to the visiting public of the world.

It is one of the most encouraging signs of the times to note how the people of South Africa have reacted to the opening to them of the Kruger National Park. The widespread educative influence it exerts has become abundantly apparent within the short span of years during which it has been accessible. Prowess in the slaying of wild animals is no longer envied as it was formerly. The camera is rapidly becoming the popular hunting weapon. Pictures of live animals arouse more interest than those of dead ones, and sympathy goes hand in hand with increased knowledge and understanding. There is inherent in nearly everybody some love of nature, an instinct inherited from remote ancestors, however blanketed over it may have become through artificial environment. The call of the wild usually appeals in greater or less degree, if it can only make itself heard. There must be thousands of people in South Africa now nature enthusiasts, who previously had little experience of other than town life and had never perhaps seen a wild animal of any kind outside a zoo. The immediate future of wildlife, here at least, is assured, and the remoter more hopeful than at one time seemed possible.

For this happy outcome the motor car must be allotted its due share of praise. As a means of rapid transport it has opened up all kinds of inaccessible places to the naturalist, and while wholesale massacres of animals and the acceleration of the extermination of wildlife may have resulted from its misuse, yet the motor car has provided the main influence for the popularity of the Kruger National Park. Without its aid, it is hard to see how our wares could have been adequately displayed, nor indeed how the vast majority of the people who are now regular visitors could have even become aware of the existence of the park. South Africa's main attraction could only have been viewed imperfectly and unsatisfactorily from the windows of a tourist train. Let us therefore salute the motor car!

*Izak Johannes Botha was appointed game ranger in 1929 and
in 1930 recorded the first nyala in the park. He is seen here
with Stevenson-Hamilton at Punda Maria in 1931.*

Every year the park drew more and more visitors to the lowveld, which
began to acquire a hitherto unknown prosperity from the presence in its
midst of an institution which, as the Sabi Game Reserve, some of its inhabitants had adversely criticized. Ramshackle iron erections grew into hotels
and new hotels sprang up. The roads leading from the larger Transvaal
towns were lined with directing notices 'To the Kruger National Park'.
People from the Cape Province, from Natal, the Free State, Rhodesia,
Swaziland and Portuguese East Africa, who might otherwise never have
dreamed of visiting the Eastern Transvaal, drawn by the lure of the park,
with the prospect it offered of seeing lion at close quarters in their wild state,
spent their money along the route, and incidentally became acquainted with
the magnificent mountain scenery in the neighbourhood of Barberton and
Pilgrim's Rest. These, but for Cinderella's promotion, might, and probably
would, have remained a closed book to many of them.

Recognizing the advantages which accrued from its presence at their
doors, a new and more friendly feeling towards the sanctuary began to be
apparent among local people. It was no longer a 'white elephant', a 'waste of
the tax-payers' money', or a 'freakish government conception conducted for
the benefit of a few favoured individuals'. Even the occasional irritating

261

depredations of its lion beyond its borders were regarded with a less intolerant eye and now called forth demands for restraint of the animals, rather than for the abolition of the source whence they came. It was amusing to note how some of those who formerly had not been the most backward in condemning the very existence of the reserve, under the changed conditions were eager to point out on every suitable occasion that the sanctuary had held its own in the past, and had ultimately achieved popularity and success mainly owing to their personal efforts and wholehearted support, and that, in consequence, special privileges should be accorded to them, and their suggestions for this or that addition or development receive preferential consideration.

Truly nothing succeeds like success! I have in my possession the copy of a report sent to the Transvaal Game Protection Association many years ago by one who later was known as a staunch supporter of the park and its objects, in which he eloquently recommended the 'abolition of the Sabi Game Reserve and the subsequent extermination of all the game in it'. He thought that in order to obviate the return of tsetse fly and the introduction of sleeping-sickness through crocodiles, there ought to be a zone of fifty miles west of the Lebombo hills denuded of all its wildlife.

Well! We change with the changing years, and I am sure many of those who wrote or spoke in the above strain are now pleased that their suggestions were not followed. Otherwise they would not today be in the happy position of being able to assume credit for what actually did take place.

Once Cinderella was securely established in the palace, she received of course nothing but flattery and unstinted praise. Her past was quite forgotten. In fact she was generally assumed first to have seen the light in 1926 when the National Parks Bill was passed. The newly appointed postmaster at Skukuza, when I told him I had lived at that place for thirty-four years, registered surprise and asked me if I had been farming there before the park was opened. Such is fame! Perhaps it is best that Cinderella's lowly past should be forgotten in her glorious present. The park was now 'a splendid national asset'; 'a worthy heritage to be passed on to our descendants'; 'a magnificent example to the rest of the world'; 'a glorious achievement ensuring the safety of our unsurpassed fauna and flora for all time'. I have always felt about this last panegyric that 'all time' must imply a very long time. Indeed, I should hardly conceive that even an act of parliament is capable of conferring immortality.

Such minor criticism as was heard was now directed against the administration. Was the splendid heritage getting the expert attention which it merit-ed? Did its local management do it justice? I could at times imagine myself back in 1903 or 1904! Yet, allowing for changed conditions, the general policy followed was still fundamentally that which had proved not unsuccessful in reviving the fauna from the anaemic condition into which it had fallen by the beginning of the century. I have always felt that nature is able to manage her affairs better than man can do it for her, and when possible, I have worked on that conception. It may have been a mistake to try to keep down the carnivorous animals in the days of the Sabi Game Reserve, but it was a policy forced upon us by circumstances. It has been indicated elsewhere how nature held her own in respect of the lion, and how our attempts to weight the balance too much in favour of the game reacted ultimately in an unexpected manner. Another lesson to leave the Great Mother alone.

Inevitably there are many who are convinced that they know better how things should be done than does the man on the spot. Few amateurs would, for example, risk telling a lawyer, an engineer, or an editor, how to conduct his business. Yet the two callings which it has been my lot to follow happen to relate to matters upon which any layman with some superficial knowledge conceives his opinions to carry more weight than those of the professional who has made a special study of the subjects.

Whatever else may or may not be the case, it is quite certain that any serious attempt at present to reduce the number of lion in the park would spell the end of its popularity with the public. The lion is among the most intelligent of the lower animals. In a hostile environment, where he realizes that at any time of the day a man with a gun may be on his track, he is careful, as I explained in the last chapter, to choose only the most secluded spots for his siesta. Only when it has become dark does he venture into the open. Any hunter who has made it his business to track or stalk lion on foot will have noted how, every few seconds, one or other of the sleeping group will sit up and look carefully round for signs of danger, and how at such moments almost the flicker of an eyelid will serve to betray the watcher. Lion were but rarely seen by visitors for some time after the park was opened. It is only latterly that they have returned to what probably are their natural habits and become largely diurnal, walking about unconcernedly stalking their prey in broad daylight and sleeping peacefully in the open even by the roadside, regardless of the chatter of tourists and the din of motor traffic. It would take but little to alter all this and to drive the lion back once more to his daytime fastnesses and former habits. In the few parts of the park where it has recently been necessary to shoot a certain number of lion, their habits appear markedly different from those which they have adopted in localities where, from experience, they have learnt themselves to be perfectly safe.

I sometimes wonder what the effect on the popularity of the park would have been, if the people who from time to time in the past used to advocate the extermination of lion as 'useless vermin' had had their way, and if we, for our part, had persisted in our previous policy of trying to keep down lion numbers. It ought to be realized that lion, leopard, wild dog, jackal and other predatory creatures, great and small, and whether of the earth, air or water, have their full place in nature, just as much as the animals on which they are accustomed to prey, and are entitled to equal respect.

I doubt if at any time there has been a dangerous disproportion between our predatory and other animals in favour of the former. In the early days of the Sabi Game Reserve game was undoubtedly relatively scarce and lion more numerous than they appeared to be. Our farmer neighbours were insistent that they ought to be exterminated, and throughout the country there was a general feeling that they were useless and dangerous encumbrances – the worst type of vermin in fact. There was the further consideration that for many years past the game had been relentlessly killed by hunters, white and native, without regard to its age, sex, or general future, while lion had been specially sought by only a very few. It was therefore felt that the herbivorous animals should be placed in a position of some relative advantage.

But even had we left the carnivora severely alone, I do not now believe that anything serious would have happened to the game. Lion in those days were far less prolific than became the case later. Wild dog (animals which no one previously had troubled to hunt) were present in considerable numbers. Yet the impala, on which they mainly preyed, seemed to be fully holding their own. Of recent years, probably because they were affected by some canine disease, the wild dog have almost disappeared from the southern regions of the park, while the impala have increased so much that they have, in many places, completely out-run their food supply and have spread into areas formerly considered to be unsuitable to them. I have heard the virtual disappearance of reedbuck from most of the Sabi reserve between 1914 and 1920 attributed to the depredations of wild dog. But this theory bears its own refutation, since there were in 1902 many more of these than in 1914, yet reedbuck were in the former year exceedingly abundant in their favourite localities and continued to increase up to about 1916.

The Shingwedsi portion of the reserve when first proclaimed in 1903 contained very little of either game or carnivora. So far as could be ascertained at the time there were no eland nor nyala. The only hunting of predatory animals which took place there before 1933 was while Major Fraser was at Malunzane, when he killed quite locally – along the Tsende River within a radius of ten miles and nowhere else – perhaps twenty or thirty lion and a few score of wild dog during twelve years; not enough to make any difference. Therefore, through the greater part of the Shingwedsi, where, after 1905, there were practically no resident natives, nature may be said to have worked unaided, and such interference as there was on the part of native hunting parties from outside the reserve, who killed game animals only and left the lion and other beasts of prey severely alone, militated of course against the game. After thirty years, during which there was, therefore, practically no control of carnivora, it was found that eland were present almost everywhere, sometimes in quite large herds, nyala were well established and all other game increased so greatly that it was found feasible to open the area to the public for sightseeing purposes. Lion, on their part, had multiplied to such an extent that when a ranger assumed charge of the central area in 1933, he expressed the fear that they would soon exterminate all the game!

The above and other experiences seem to demonstrate quite clearly – if indeed demonstration is required – that lion and no doubt other beasts of prey increase exactly in proportion to the animals on which they live, and as has been previously pointed out, if artificially reduced while there is abundance of food at hand, they make up for it by becoming increasingly prolific. Today in the park lion are probably not relatively more numerous to the game than was the case thirty years ago, but they show themselves by day without fear and so people acquire an exaggerated notion concerning their proportionate increase in relation to other animals.

In point of fact, all species, with the exception of the reedbuck, are many times more numerous in the lowveld than they have been within the memory of living man. But unfortunately the eastern portion of it, including most of the Kruger National Park, suffered from an exceptionally long period of drought between the years 1925 and 1935, during which the summer rains were scanty and badly distributed. The grass roots died in some places and only weeds grew instead after rain had at last fallen. Elsewhere the game, especially in the vicinity of permanent water, ate the whole veld bare. The result was that during the drier months of each year, which happen to be exactly those in which the park is open to the public, the seasonal migration of game in search of pasture – always to some extent a feature, as I have elsewhere pointed out – was greatly accentuated. There is a striking divergence between the total number of animals found within the park in summer and winter respectively, and were it possible to count them (which of course it is not), I would not be surprised to find that of the larger and more migratory species, such as wildebeest and zebra, there were five or six individuals in January for each one present in the months between June and October.

Yet in spite of this, during the last three months of the dry season, the park is undoubtedly in many places over-stocked and not under-stocked. The condition of many species, notably of kudu, impala, and to some extent waterbuck, all less migratory in habit than some other species, clearly demonstrates this. One need only look at the veld in the vicinity of the perennial rivers and permanent pools and note the condition of the local animals, to wonder how it is possible they can live at all. The browsers have stripped every tree for as high as they can reach of every possible kind of food and the grazers have bared the earth till it looks like a roadway. The older and weaker die. Many females, when the calving season arrives, either abort or are unable to nourish their young. Still their numbers increase – it is amazing. Were it not for the carnivora we might find ourselves faced with some kind of epidemic. If wild dog still existed in the numbers they did thirty years ago I believe the impala would be in better condition – if less plentiful than they are. Their chief enemies now are leopard and cheetah, and as the former have many other smaller beasts and birds on their dietary roster

Wildlife drinking at a waterhole. A photograph taken by P.W. Willis whose pictures were used widely as publicity material for the Kruger National Park.

and the latter are relatively scarce, they have no appreciable effect on the total, while lion take no serious toll, preferring the larger types of game. Accordingly, nature has to rely on another of her weapons – in this case starvation, with its consequent elimination of the weaker – once more to adjust her balance.

It is a difficult question concerning which I would not like to commit myself to any definite opinion, but at least it is possible that the over-stocked position today – which of course would not have occurred had normal rains fallen after 1925 – might have been considerably ameliorated, and lion and other beasts of prey no more numerous than they now are, had we refrained during the long period of twenty-five years from conducting the thinning out process. The natural boundaries of the Kruger National Park are those which confined the old Sabi Game Reserve before 1923. These allowed adequate room for seasonal migration westward to the better watered and more fertile country, now partly in the possession of private owners and partly to be established as a reserved area for natives. The park retained the eastern and more arid tracts of country, only limitedly suitable for the rarer species of antelope, such as sable and roan, and incapable of supporting to the square mile nearly so many even of the commoner animals as the land under the foothills. However, one cannot have everything, and once a cycle of adequate rainfall has returned, there will certainly come a pause in seasonal migration. The large tracts of good grassland, now deserted owing to lack of water, will hold their proper quota of animals, while the areas now overstocked in winter will cease to be so.

❖

CHAPTER TWELVE

CASUALTIES AMONG THE STAFF; WOLHUTER AND THE LION; DEATH OF
MAFUTA AND OF MPAMPUNI; MUBI; PLAYFUL ATTRIBUTES OF LION; THE
CONTROL OF THE PARK; EUROPEAN AND NATIVE STAFF; LABOUR,
CONSTRUCTION WORK AND REPAIR; ROUTINE OF ADMINISTRATION;
CONCLUSION

WHEN THE DUTIES OF any body of men involve their living year after
year in a wild country replete with dangerous animals, and when they
have in addition to protect it against encroachment by human enemies of the
game, it is inevitable that they must at times incur considerable risk to life
and limb. This is true not only in respect of the European, but also of course
of the native rangers of the park. Trouble with white poachers has been rare
and of a minor kind, but almost ever since the reserve was proclaimed, it has
been subject along all its borders to encroachment by native hunters, sometimes appearing in large bands and provided with firearms. These poachers
belong in most cases to the same tribes from which our own native rangers
are recruited and sometimes are even their blood relations. It is a high tribute
therefore to the natural courage and the loyalty to authority which is characteristic of the lowveld Bantu, that few of our police have ever hesitated to
carry out their duties even at considerable personal risk to themselves. Since
1904, when the first serious affray was recorded, four have been killed and
more than a dozen seriously injured while effecting or attempting to effect
the arrests of armed poachers.

Some years ago, there happened to be serving in the police one Mfitshane
so far in his physique below the ordinarily approved standard that only his
obvious eagerness to join had permitted his enrolment. One day, while he
and another were on patrol, they happened upon a party of natives from
Portuguese territory who had just killed a waterbuck. Mfitshane called upon

them to surrender themselves, upon which they attacked the police with their assegais. His companion thought it prudent to depart and seek assistance, but so energetically did Mfitshane defend himself, that the poachers, fearing also no doubt the imminent arrival of reinforcements, took to their heels. Determined that they should not thus escape, the redoubtable man pursued, and had just seized the hindmost when unfortunately he tripped and fell, upon which his opponent stabbed him through the lungs as he lay on the ground and then made good his escape. Mfitshane was soon found and was duly carried back to his picket, where he lay for some time at the point of death. Ultimately, however, he recovered sufficiently to return to duty and continued to pursue poachers with unabated zeal. One day the chase led him up the stony and thorn-covered slopes of the Lebombo hills, and the exertion proving too great, he ruptured an artery near the seat of his old injury, collapsed and died.

In 1926, a patrol of three native rangers near the Portuguese frontier came on a gang in the act of killing a kudu and succeeded in capturing one of them, the others escaping. It was a considerable distance to Satara, whither they intended to take their prisoner, and that night they slept in the veld near a pool of water. At early dawn the following morning the camp was surprised and rushed by a party of some twenty of the prisoner's friends. One of the police was killed on the spot and the corporal, his head smashed by a knobkerrie, was left for dead on the ground. The third man, though hotly pursued, managed to escape and gave the alarm. The raiders then stripped the two fallen police of their uniforms and equipment, freed the prisoner from his handcuffs and made their way back to their own country. Some hours afterwards, when help arrived, the corporal – Cement – was found to be still alive, and his skull being the most resistant portion of his anatomy, he entirely recovered from his injuries. Once they have escaped across the frontier, Portuguese natives consider themselves safe; but on this occasion some of the assailants had been identified and the Portuguese authorities were duly informed. With the readiness to assist which I have always found Portuguese officials to display, if properly approached, the local commandant took the case in hand and the majority of the offenders were eventually brought to trial and sentenced to penal servitude.

In 1934 a solitary native ranger was set on by a gang and also left for dead. Next day he was found dragging himself along the road on his hands and knees, having rather miraculously lain out all night in the veld without having been devoured by some marauding beast of prey. This man, though he seemed to have made a good recovery, never completely regained his mental powers, and was unable to give any clear account of what had happened to him.

Although it is exceptional for any native poacher to become aggressive should it happen that a white ranger is present, yet in 1911 Ranger Siewert with two police 'boys' became involved in something like a pitched battle with a large armed party of Portuguese natives. About fifty shots were fired and eventually the ranger considered it best to withdraw. Ranger McDonald also had a serious encounter among the Lebombo hills, in which shots were fired on both sides, but it seems one or more white men were involved in this affair, which resulted in the retreat but not the apprehension of the intruders. Until we, perforce, had to equip our frontier patrols with rifles, the poachers were accustomed to open fire as soon as they saw a native policeman coming, and the reason we did not suffer more casualties may perhaps partly be attributed to the fact that the less sophisticated type of native, seldom shooting at game from a greater distance than thirty paces, likes to break off his rifle sights as useless encumbrances. Ranger Wolhuter was once fired at point-blank by a native poacher and the bullet passed just over his right shoulder. The man then turned to run, when Wolhuter instantly covered him with his own rifle, but fortunately had the presence of mind to restrain himself at the last moment from firing.

Notwithstanding the considerable trouble they have given from time to time, these Portuguese native poachers are simple, straightforward souls and one knows where one stands with them. If caught red-handed, they cheerfully admit their guilt and take what comes to them without complaint or malice. They display, in fact, a sporting spirit, and I confess to some unofficial sympathy with them. Some of the Transvaal natives along our other borders, who have had the advantage of living in close proximity to the white population, are more erudite, and however clearly guilty, now and then seek the services of an attorney to find for them, haply, some loophole of escape. Whether, ultimately, even though the verdict be in their favour, they are always better off, financially at any rate, is another question. One, whom I knew had got off on a certain charge, assured me he had been found guilty. 'Certainly it was so,' he said, 'otherwise why did the white man make me pay £5?' He was referring, of course, to his defending lawyer.

Casualties through encounters with wild beasts have unavoidably occurred from time to time, though the only member of the white staff ever personally injured was Wolhuter. I have referred to the incident already and related its details in full in my book, *Animal Life in Africa*, but that work being now long out of print and forgotten, I may be pardoned for repeating myself and telling again the story of an exhibition of courage and self-possession which, so far as I know, is unique of its kind.

One day, Wolhuter, in the course of his return home from the Olifants River, having broken up his camp at the Nwanedzi, set out to march to a place called Metsimetsi where he intended to sleep at the permanent picket established there. He was accompanied by several native police and some pack donkeys. But the pace of this form of transport being a slow one, and the afternoon already well advanced, he rode on ahead, accompanied only by his dog. While still some eight miles from his destination, the sun went down, the short twilight soon passed, and in the bed of a small dry watercourse, which he found himself presently crossing, it was nearly dark. Suddenly, the dog barked, and he saw an animal, which, from its dimly discerned colour, he took to be a reedbuck, apparently approaching him from his right front. He was just thinking this rather an unusual proceeding on the part of an antelope, when he all at once realized that the animal was, in fact, a lion, and that it was coming straight at him. He pulled his horse round sharply to the left, by which action he evaded the full force of the rush. However, the assailant's claws caught the horse's quarters, and as the latter bounded forward Wolhuter – unseated – was shot straight into the jaws of a second lion, which had been coming up behind. This animal unhesitatingly picked him up by his right shoulder and dragged him off. He found his face pressed against its chest, while his legs dragged underneath its belly. He was thus hauled over rough ground for some way (I paced the distance a few weeks later as ninety-four yards), his spurs catching continually until they were pulled off. At first, he says, he gave up all hope and merely reflected rather bitterly what an ignominious end for an experienced hunter his was likely to be. Then he remembered his sheath-knife, which he was wont to carry on the back of his waistbelt. On every recent occasion when his horse had come down with him, this knife had fallen from its case, and it was with little hope of finding it still where it ought to be, that, getting his left (and free) hand behind and under him as he was being dragged along, he proceeded to grope for it. To his surprise and relief it was miraculously still there, and grasping it tightly, he pulled it out, and got it into a convenient position. He knew that this knife represented his very last chance of saving his life and he held on to it, he says, as a drowning man grasps a floating plank.

Then, with his one available hand, which it will be noted was the left, he felt, very cautiously, round the lion's chest to the point where he judged its heart ought to lie. He had to exercise the greatest caution in his movements, for his best hope lay in simulating death and thus lulling the lion into a sense of security. The slightest attempt at a struggle, even any noticeable movement, would have invited a savage worrying from the animal, and, of course, the end. Presently at the base of a small tree, the lion stopped and let go its hold on his shoulder. This was Wolhuter's chance, and he took it.

With desperate back-handed strokes, he twice drove his knife – which luckily happened at the time to be sharp – into its side and then a third time upwards into its throat. It sprang back, deluging him with its blood as it did so. Wolhuter scrambled to his feet and for a few moments man and beast faced one another a few paces apart, the former anticipating nothing but a fresh attack. Calling to mind the frequently stated influence of the human voice, he desperately shouted every opprobrious epithet which occurred to him at his adversary, which to his astonishment and relief, presently turned round, and walked slowly away into the darkness.

One of the classic wildife adventures of southern Africa concerns the attack on Harry Wolhuter in August 1903 by two lion. Many years later, Wolhuter points out the Lindanda tree into which, though badly mauled, he had climbed to escape further attack.

Wolhuter lost no time in scrambling up the small tree by which he was standing and managed to reach a branch some eight feet above the ground. Hardly was he ensconced in its fork with the trunk, when he became faint and fearing he might fall to the ground, he loosed his neckerchief, and with it tied himself as securely as he could to the tree. While thus employed he heard the lion groaning a short distance away and for the first time it dawned on him that he might have killed it. Presently the other lion, which had unsuccessfully been pursuing the horse, came trotting back. Wolhuter's plucky dog, which had never left it, and to whose efforts the horse no doubt largely owed its own escape was still barking at its heels. Having apparently first stopped at the spot where the attack had taken place, this lion followed the spoor of its mate and that of Wolhuter to the foot of the tree, around which it continued to patrol, making occasional and cleverly avoided rushes at the dog.

At the end of what seemed a long time, voices were heard and, by shouting, Wolhuter attracted the attention of his men who, greatly perturbed, released him from the tree and supported him along the path towards camp. It was a terrible walk for the wounded man – appearing to him to be eighty miles, rather than a mere eight. During the first part of it, the lion, concealed by the bush but close to the track, followed the party, probably hoping for a chance to get hold of one of the donkeys. Even when camp was at last reached and he was able to lie down, there were no medical aids available, except some permanganate of potash, with which an attempt was made to wash his injuries. But after a few efforts, Wolhuter says he stopped his attendants from trying any more, on account of the excruciating pain which any handling of his shoulder or arm caused him. By the morning he was running a temperature. There was of course no skilled assistance, nor indeed another white man anywhere within reach. He was able, however, to give directions to the 'boys', and on a rough improvised litter of branches was carried for a long two days' journey to Komatipoort.

Arrived there and the district surgeon happening to be absent at the moment, he was sent, still without attention, by train to Barberton, where for the first time – nearly three days after the accident – his wounds were properly dressed. The shoulder was badly lacerated and blood poisoning of course supervening, his arm became black and swelled to an immense size. At first the doctor did not think he could live, and later was sure he must inevitably lose the injured limb from the shoulder. However, a wonderful constitution, and the fact that at the time of the accident he was in the hardest of condition without an ounce of superfluous flesh on his body, ultimately pulled him through. In a far shorter time than seemed possible under the circumstances, he was discharged from hospital as convalescent. But so terrible an experience could not leave anyone quite scatheless, and his right shoulder became permanently stiff, with consequent inability to raise that arm higher than the horizontal – quite sufficient, however, for the trigger hand of a rifle!

Some years after his recovery, Wolhuter paid a visit to England, and while in London bethought him of the firm which had turned out the knife that had served him so well. He thought he would like another of the same kind and also believed the story would excite a certain pleased interest if related to the vendors. He therefore proceeded to London, and having discovered the warehouse entered, and interviewed one of the intelligent young men he found there. A replica was duly produced and the attendant having eulogized it sufficiently, Wolhuter said, 'I know it is a good knife, I once killed a lion with one like it'. 'Oh, yes,' brightly replied the other, 'I am sure you could kill a lion with it – it will kill a sheep!'

One of our native rangers named Mafuta was less fortunate in the issue of his adventure, and this story, too, is something of an epic. Early in 1926 the ganger stationed at the point on the Selati railway line afterwards known as 'Kemp's Cottage', complained that lion were nightly visiting his native compound and frightening his labourers. Having to go to Pretoria for a few days on official business, I was obliged to defer any pursuit of the animals until my return. I therefore detailed an old and experienced native ranger, named Mafuta, as a guard, arming him with a Martini-Henry rifle and a few rounds of ammunition. Mafuta was known to be a good shot and had himself killed several lion while employed on grazing guard and while serving with Ranger Duke at Lower Sabie. His instructions were, in addition to protecting the labourers at night should the lion appear dangerous, to find out if possible where this particular troop was located, that on my return I might not experience too much difficulty in tracing it. He was not to disturb the animals.

The first news that greeted me on my coming back three days later, was that Mafuta had been killed by a lion. It appeared that early on the first morning some were heard roaring a few miles away in the bed of the Nwatimhiri Spruit north of the line. Mafuta, although I had detailed a labourer to assist him in any tracking he might have to do, set out alone with his rifle and a hand-axe, saying he would be back in an hour or two. As by midday he had not returned, two natives set out to look for him, but being unsuccessful, went on to Sabi Bridge about thirteen miles from Kemp's Cottage. Arriving in the evening, they reported him as missing.

The following morning a large search party started out, and at a point about three miles from Kemp's Cottage saw vultures on the trees. Hurrying to the spot they found, in the middle of an open piece of ground, the body of the missing man. Jackal were gathered round, but both these animals and the vultures had seemingly been afraid to come close and the corpse had been practically unmolested. It showed some claw-marks. One thigh was badly bitten, and was bound round with the man's puttees, which had thus evidently been used as a rough bandage. His rifle was found lying under a tree about twenty yards distant.

In order to discover exactly what had happened I set out early on the morning after my return, accompanied by the best trackers, and using the point where the body had been found as a centre, sent them out in all directions in search of clues. The first thing we noticed was a great deal of blood at the foot of the tree where the rifle had been lying. Thence, tracing a fairly clear blood spoor for about four hundred yards, the searchers came on the carcass of a lioness, of which the vultures had left little but the bones. Underneath it lay Mafuta's sheath-knife, stained up to the hilt with dried blood and close by was a small tree, the trunk and lower branches showing claw-marks as well as those of nailed boots. From this point were clearly seen the pug indentations of a charging lion, and forty yards away in a thick patch of scrub, the blood-stained 'form' in which a wounded animal had obviously been lying. The tracks of a lion and those of a following man were then traced back to a point nearly a mile distant, where Mafuta's axe was discovered with his jacket and a few small articles which he appeared to have laid down as encumbrances to be retrieved later.

Pieced together by the bush signs the story soon became as clear as if one had witnessed all the details in order of occurrence. Mafuta had duly discovered the lion lying up for the day, but instead of obeying orders had decided to do a little hunting on his own account, and had fired at and wounded a lioness. Unable to accompany her companions, which had fled hurriedly in another direction, she had still made off at a pace sufficiently rapid to distance her pursuer, who had been obliged to follow slowly on the trail. At length exhausted, she had laid herself down in the middle of a thick patch of low scrub, and on Mafuta's appearance later had charged out upon him. He had fired one shot, whether a hit or a miss it was impossible to say. Then, dropping his rifle, he had sprung into the lower branches of an adjacent thorn tree. The lioness had, however, easily followed him and both had fallen to the ground together. During the struggle which ensued Mafuta had managed to stab his adversary to death with his knife, but not before she had – besides tearing him badly with her claws – inflicted a severe bite in the thigh which had severed an artery. His enemy disposed of, Mafuta had bound up his terrible wound as well as he could with his puttees, picked up his rifle and endeavoured to make his way home. Before he had gone a quarter of a mile, he found himself too weak to proceed further and had sat down in the shade of an evergreen tree.

From the relative position of the sun with regard to the blood pools found there, it seemed that he had first sat down about eleven a.m., and as the sun moved round had shifted his position until about two p.m., after which there had been no further movement on his part. He had evidently died about that hour. All had then remained peaceful until night fell. Then the other lion had returned to seek their companion and having found its remains, had followed on the blood spoor of Mafuta, until they came on him dead under the tree. They had inspected and walked all round the body and then a lioness, apparently in anger, had seized and dragged it about twenty yards to the place where it was found next day. They had interfered no further with it and we saw their tracks as they had walked quietly away. Lion are never man-eaters by ordinary habit. Mafuta had fired certainly two, but not more than three shots in all. (He had been given six cartridges.) After taking his original shot, he had pocketed the shell in accordance with a routine order, for it was in the pocket of the jacket he had later discarded. Under the tree by which the remains of the lioness were found was another shell, no doubt representing a shot which he had taken as she was charging. Lying around the tree where he had died were three live cartridges fallen from his pocket as the lion had dragged away his body during the night. The sixth cartridge was never recovered and he may either have fired or dropped it accidentally. The only other item of his equipment remaining undiscovered was his hat, which it is quite possible a jackal may have picked up and taken away.

It is a remarkable thing that with all his experience, both alone and in accompanying white rangers when after lion, this man should in the final event have displayed so little caution in following what he must have known was a badly wounded lioness. Yet when Mafuta faced death, it was in a spirit of dour courage that demands the highest admiration. To be dragged from a tree by an animal so immensely powerful and so infuriated, and then mauled by it on the ground, might have proved too severe a trial for the resistive powers of many and reduced some indeed to screaming surrender. But Mafuta, armed only with a sheath-knife, fought so determinedly that he actually emerged victorious from the struggle, and, his terrible adversary dead at his feet, bound up his own wounds, collected his rifle and made a desperate effort to walk home. It was sheer ill luck that his wound happened to be of such a nature that nothing but expert attention could effectively have staunched the blood flow. One can imagine him staggering along, becoming weaker at every step, and then sitting down in the shadiest spot he could find, pathetically anticipating the arrival of a search party which never came. One can only regret that all his gallant struggle and subsequent effort was of no avail.

Mpampuni was a corporal and one of the oldest in point of service among our native rangers. He had long experience of lion under all circumstances, and had himself killed a good many. Yet he lost his life, I believe, through temporarily losing his nerve. One afternoon from the door of his hut, which stood on rising ground, he noticed vultures sitting on a tree some five hundred yards away. Carrying only a stick, he walked towards the place, and having crossed a small dry stream-bed, found himself in more or less open ground about two hundred yards from the large fig tree in which the vultures were sitting. A lioness, probably accompanied by her cubs, was at the kill – whether otherwise alone or not is unknown. Anyhow, she suddenly appeared at the edge of the patch of bush amid which the tree stood, her tail waving and making a great noise; displaying in fact the usual indications of wanting to scare away an intruder. Mpampuni, doubtless thinking under the circumstances he had better not pursue the matter further, turned to walk away, on which the lioness left covert and bounded in his direction.

A woman who was at work in the grain-fields close to her village, situated on another little rise opposite to that occupied by Mpampuni's picket, was an eye-witness of the whole affair. She shrieked, 'Look out, the lion is after you!' Hearing this, Mpampuni, instead of turning and facing the animal when it would in all probability have stopped and eventually turned back, or alternatively climbed into one of the numerous large trees around (which he had plenty of time to do), took to his heels and ran for home. The lioness at once also accelerated, and though he had long legs and was a good runner, she caught him just as he had crossed the little spruit, seized him by one leg, pulled him down, and inflicted a couple of severe bites, one in the groin. Mpampuni, for his part, slashed her on the nose with a small pocket-knife, upon which she left him. Noticing the woman on the rise who had been shouting all the time at the top of her voice, she then made a demonstration in that direction – but intimidated by the number of people who had by then run down from the kraal, she thought better of it and returned to her cubs. Mpampuni had meantime picked himself up and walked to his hut where he was attended to by his wife. He then sent a message by a passing tourist car to Ranger McDonald who, arriving within an hour, took him to Komatipoort and dispatched him by the first train to Barberton hospital. The injury to the groin, however, proved fatal, and he died a couple of days later of the shock. Thus was another good policeman lost.

Natives do not believe any such accident can happen naturally; the lion must always have been sent by some enemy, who has worked a spell. The same superstition holds good in relation to stock which fall victims to lion or leopard. In the present case Mpampuni's wife was generally assumed to be the culprit. It was known that relations had been at times strained, and that the week before she had paid a visit to Newington, some fifty miles up the Selati line, in the neighbourhood of which place lived a well-known keeper of lion, a woman who, for the sum of £5 in cash, was always willing to 'lend' one of these animals for the purpose of getting rid of some undesirable person, or of killing his cattle. It was known, too, that the wife had returned home on the very morning of the day on which her husband met his death. Proof positive, in fact. A few weeks later some cattle were killed in the neighbourhood. When the 'lion-keeper' was remonstrated with, she explained that having once let the creature loose, she had no power to take it back unless another £5 was forthcoming. Consternation, therefore, reigned for some time, until Ranger McDonald shot an old lioness in the vicinity, which may or may not have been the guilty animal. The power of what is known as *umthakathi* entirely rules the native mind and directs much of his course through life.

I have known only one native who was quite free from this superstition. He was for many years one of our police 'boys' and merits a few descriptive words. Rather darker in complexion than the average east coast native, his straight features, full beard and hard mouth indicated an Arabic or other Semitic strain in his ancestry, and though he was slightly below the middle height, his slim wiry figure was capable of the greatest feats of endurance. He was completely fearless, resolute to ruthlessness, and utterly unscrupulous – a strong character, in fact. I first got in touch with Mubi under – for him – rather unfortunate circumstances: to wit, when he had been arrested for having shot a zebra. Some time later, on the principle of setting a thief to

In 1941 there were eight African corporals (one in each section of the park) and over one hundred police. Stevenson-Hamilton greatly admired their sense of duty, particularly in view of their poor pay and lack of promotion incentives.

catch a thief, and impressed besides by the influence he seemed to exercise over most natives with whom he came into contact, his knowledge of the country and of bush lore, I had him enrolled in the police. In this capacity he had a long and varied career. For some years, during which he attained the rank of corporal, he exercised his special talents with great success in the cause of law and order. Then the Old Adam triumphed and he began to get into trouble, being accused, among other things, of having tried to get rid of someone he disliked by setting fire to his hut at night. For this he stood his trial, but stoutly denying his guilt, was acquitted of the charge. However, taking one thing with another, it seemed desirable to allow him to lapse again into civilian life.

At a later date he was once more taken on the strength, and did such excellent work as again to find promotion. So his career proceeded – periods of exceptionally good service varied by lapses – until at length, the balance appearing to lean too much towards the wrong side, on the recommendation of the ranger of his section he was finally discharged. He was a dead shot with a rifle, even at considerable distances, an unusual characteristic in a native. And though it was suspected, probably with truth, that he took his own toll of the animals he protected, on the other hand poaching on the part of anyone else absolutely ceased within his sphere of control. So, under our then primitive conditions, it seemed the best policy to be a little blind.

The following story told of him is characteristic. Arriving on patrol at a village one day, he learnt that a leopardess with cubs had taken up her quarters in a thicket not far away and was in the habit of carrying off almost nightly goats and fowls from the pens. The women of the kraal began to laugh at him and to dare him, for all his reputation, to go in and deal with the animal single-handed. He did not say much, but picking up his assegai and calling a small dog which was accompanying him, he walked quietly into the thicket. An uproar followed, and presently he emerged dragging the dead leopard after him by its tail. Slightly helped by his dog he had speared it through the heart as it came at him, so coolly and expertly that he did not himself sustain a single scratch. I know of but one similar case in the reserve, and that involuntary, when another native ranger, Office, while searching about for the spoor of a wounded leopard, suddenly came right on the animal which charged, and was dispatched by him in similar fashion. But on this occasion the beast had been pretty badly wounded and my little fox terrier bitch, Polly, had attached herself firmly to its tail.

Possessing many admirable qualities, I am afraid Mubi was hardly up to our civilized conception of a good citizen, though had he lived in earlier days, I have no doubt he would have made history as the famous (or infamous) leader of some predatory tribe. Perhaps, had he belonged to another race and lived in another country, he might even have become a celebrated gangster. He spoke little of his exploits previous to the South African War, but it was whispered that highway robbery had figured to no inconsiderable extent among them. I am sure he did not esteem a human life as of greater value than that of a buck; in fact, I understand he used to admit as much. Withal, he was a man who, once he had been allotted some definite duty to perform, would carry it out against any odds and with complete indifference to the consequences as affecting himself or anybody else. One might add that no cross-examination, no matter how subtle, was ever able to shake his evidence in the witness-box! Eventually, having become too old for serious poaching, and police work, the only form of legitimate activity which had ever appealed being closed to him, he settled down (not in the park, *bien entendu*[12]) until his death to a peaceful life with his five wives, only, it was hinted, occasionally breaking the law indirectly by hiring out one or other of his carefully concealed firearms to any would-be hunter prepared to pay him his price.

Excepting Wolhuter and Mpampuni, no members of the staff have in all these years become casualties from lion or leopard, save when following up or coming suddenly upon them when wounded or otherwise injured. Nor have such accidents, I think, exceeded those incurred at the hands of native poachers. During the long period when they were assiduously hunted, lion systematically avoided the neighbourhood of human habitations so far as was possible, and in those days a single small boy by shouting could usually rely on scaring them away from a kill or from the neighbourhood of grazing domestic animals. Later, when they had acquired confidence from immunity, they developed playful tendencies which, if sometimes exasperating, were seldom inimical towards human beings.

When the irrigation mechanics were sinking boreholes in the park, their work necessarily took them into areas where the only water for miles round was that which they were able to pump up in the process of drilling. Lion used to come round nightly, often in considerable numbers, to drink from the puddles and from the half-empty buckets which had been left lying about after the day's work. They were never aggressive, and after a while the men became quite accustomed to their presence and paid little attention to it. One party related how on a moonlit night when everything could be clearly seen, some lion were thus engaged in satisfying their thirst. While one big male was trying to get the last drop of water from the bottom of a bucket, the handle fell back behind his ears and so held him prisoner. With the utensil jammed tightly over his head he dashed frantically round in circles, muffled roars coming from the depths. His companions, apparently thinking it some kind of game, rushed round after him loudly voicing their interest in the proceedings, until the whole procession disappeared in the bush, whence the bucket was next day recovered a quarter of a mile away and somewhat damaged. The lion were also greatly interested in the bags of shot used in drilling. One would pick up such an article and run off with it in his mouth pursued by the others, until the bag burst open, when they would all roll themselves about among the scattered shot, a proceeding which seemed to afford them considerable satisfaction.

Sanderson, our coloured workman, was once employed on some task which took him into a lonely part of the bush, where he slept in a tent with two native assistants. There was a pool of water about forty paces away to which lion came nearly every night. Sometimes the younger ones would come closer to have a look at the tent, and when they approached unpleasantly near Sanderson used to throw stones at them. This seemed not to annoy but to amuse them, and on a stone striking or falling near an animal, he would pick it up and run off with it, drop it and pick it up again, the others joining in the game, each one competing for possession of the missile. On this being reported to me, I thought it a bit dangerous and so provided the party with a stock of ordinary crackers, which, tied like rockets to light sticks and energetically hurled, have generally proved completely effective in scaring off too inquisitive beasts of prey.

Ledeboer relates how, late one night he heard the small gong which was pendent just outside the gate of the fence surrounding his house and was used to summon his 'boys' to work each day, being energetically struck.

It was Leonard Henry Ledeboer, seen above, who, in 1903, alerted the colonial authorities to the merits of the Shingwedsi region as a game reserve. Later, in 1921, he joined the reserve as a ranger, replacing Major Fraser in the northern area.

282

Having opened his door, he saw in the moonlight a young lion hitting the gong with his paw, while others sat round interestedly looking on!

Instances such as the above do not fit in with the accepted idea of the lion's character, but they are nevertheless true, and many more could be quoted. I think there are few places in Africa outside the park, where it has ever been possible to observe the true mentality and habits of lion in their wild state when free from human menace and with plenty of their natural food at hand. They seem not only to be among the most intelligent of lower animals but also to possess a well developed sense of humour. When the usual condition of active warfare exists between beast and man, no true conception can possibly be obtained of what the former is really like or how it acts when it knows there is nothing to fear. But of course lion vary in temperament, just as do human beings. There are bold and timid, excitable and placid, good natured and irritable individuals among them. Being what they are, and since there is no means of gauging beforehand the individual temperament of each, it is wise to take nothing for granted in respect of its possible conduct. I once reared four cubs from early babyhood until they were some four months old. All of the same litter, each differed markedly from all the others. Samson was high-spirited, rough, boisterous and something of a bully; Sandow was good-natured and greedy; Mary a perfect little lady in every respect, while her sister, Sarah, was irritable, peevish and unreliable. Had it been their fate to have grown up in their wild state, the last-named would probably have become a dangerous animal to disturb. As with human beings, it is often a matter of general health. One should never generalize.

CHAPTER THIRTEEN

PROSPERITY OF THE PARK; TOURIST INCIDENTS; THE FOOT-AND-MOUTH
DISEASE OUTBREAKS OF 1938 AND 1944; THE SECOND WORLD WAR AND
HOW IT AFFECTED THE PARK; EPILOGUE

CINDERELLA WAS NOW A Great Lady. Praise and bouquets were continual-ly showered upon her. Year by year her fame grew and spread far beyond the limits of South Africa, while within the palace itself events had proceeded with reasonable smoothness.

The era of exciting incidents had by this time largely passed away, but one which occurred just before the opening of a tourist season, may be worth recording. Early one morning it was reported that two big lion had, during the previous night, got into the visitors' camp at Skukuza and had scared away the native workmen who had gone down to prepare for its opening. Naturally, no one would venture near, and as the work, which was urgent, seemed likely to be held up for the day, I went down with my rifle, and find-ing the animals disinclined to shift, shot one of them. The other, escaping through a wicket gate which led into the compound, tore through the latter at full speed, scattering natives and dogs in all directions. Amid a babel of barking and shouting, it then charged into the boundary fence at the back of my office, nearly meeting on the way Sergeant Cartwright of the South African Police, who was on his way from the charge office with some papers to sign. Unable to get through or over the fence, the lion – looking and sounding uncommonly nasty – crouched near it. There, having followed as quickly as possible, I managed to dispose of him before any damage was done. Lion had frequently before and since got into the compound, where of course the domestic animals were kept, but always had been persuaded to leave quietly. In this case the animal had become frightened and angry, and so had arrived at the dangerous stage.

From time to time we found it necessary to destroy individual lion, which from old age, injuries or other cause, were becoming a menace to human life. There were no casualties either among the staff or the public, and very few among the natives, all of which were speedily avenged.

The only change in the staff for some years was the appointment in 1938 of Captain (later Lieutenant-Colonel) M. Rowland-Jones to the rangership of Punda Maria district in place of Ranger I.J. Botha. Captain Rowland-Jones had for many years previously been in control of the Pretoriuskop entrance to the park. This was a peculiarly exacting post, demanding not only constant tiring work but boundless tact, and one which he had filled with conspicuous success. After little more than a year in charge at Punda Maria, he went on active service with his regiment, the Natal Carbineers, and later with the staff of the Union Defence Force, returning to us only at the end of the war, having meantime been decorated with the Order of the British Empire.

The year 1938 was, in terms of tourist traffic, by far the most prosperous so far in the history of the park. Some ten thousand cars, carrying over forty thousand visitors, passed through the entrance gates during the twelve months. Our overseas guests also reached a hitherto unattained numerical peak, though unfortunately, owing to the fact that the season when the whole park was open to the public coincided with the summer in northern latitudes, few visitors came from Europe or America during our best months.

Luckily, Pretoriuskop, the only reasonably healthy area during the summer, was well stocked with animals representing most of the indigenous species, and the passengers from the various 'luxury' liners which used to visit us at intervals generally expressed satisfaction, often mixed with relief, because some of them had been previously warned of the extreme discomfort and uncleanliness they were likely to encounter. Therefore when they found comfortable sleeping quarters, clean sheets, electric lighting, hot and cold water laid on in bathrooms, and satisfactory catering, their minds were proportionately relieved.

Various amusing incidents were related about overseas visitors. One well-to-do citizen, having hired a car from a local garage, was being driven round Pretoriuskop when the chauffeur, noticing a big lion asleep by the roadside, stopped the car and pointed out the animal to his fare. The latter's immediate reaction was one of indignation. 'You can't fool me like that. In my country we think nothing of putting out stuffed bears for tourists to see!' Just then the lion woke up, rose, yawned and stretched himself. 'Driver,' shouted the visitor, 'put your foot on the gas and drive like hell!'

Among the 'luxury' cruisers came a large German one. This was about the time of the height of Nazi power; the passengers were strictly controlled by a Gestapo man and were very well behaved. All their expenses were pre-paid and they were allowed to carry little or no money, obtaining curios and other things they wanted by bartering personal belongings. Some of them having – probably unknowingly – broken the regulations by getting out of their car, were reported to their leader, who paraded and reprimanded them severely for having brought discredit on the party.

Towards the end of 1937 delegates to a veterinary conference at Lourenço Marques discovered foot-and-mouth disease among some cattle at Momba, a Portuguese station on the railway near the border. Not long afterwards the disease was identified among native cattle on the Transvaal side. Far-reaching consequences to the park, and the lowveld in general were later to result.

At first all infected herds and possible contacts from the Union border to near Hectorspruit were destroyed. These, though mostly native cattle, did include a few which were the property of white farmers, and the old agitation against the game revived. After this, matters quieted down for a time, but frequent veterinary examinations of all lowveld stock, including that within the park, were instituted.

At this time the natives living along the western border of the latter owned a good many cattle. Elsewhere within it there existed only a few small and isolated groups of from ten to twenty head each, widely separated and unlikely to make mutual contacts, the danger from lion discouraging movements of livestock. Some of the European rangers owned a few milch cows, and there was a herd of about thirty oxen and breeding stock on the Sand River, seven miles north from Skukuza, the property of the parks board. At the last-named place I kept three Friesland cows, stall-fed.

For some months the park was reported free from disease, a happy state of affairs soon to be rudely disturbed. Ranger Ledeboer owned at Satara a few milch cows which had no outside contacts so far as was known, but on one of his visits, the local veterinary officer diagnosed foot-and-mouth disease among them. At once Satara became the focus for numbers of senior veterinary officers and their attendants. The herd was destroyed, and that motor vehicles should not spread the disease (it then being the height of the tourist season), all cars on leaving Satara, had to drive through a specially constructed concrete drain filled with disinfectant.

Then came another lull, which proved to be the last before the storm. Late in November a disturbing rumour spread of foot-and mouth disease having been discovered among native-owned cattle at the farm Toulon, only five miles outside our western boundary, and the same distance from my headquarters. A few days later I was sitting in my office, when suddenly there drove up amid a cloud of dust, a whole fleet of cars and lorries from which poured a stream of government veterinary officers, stock inspectors, police and native attendants. The party included some top ranking members of the veterinary department from Pretoria, who explained that a serious outbreak having occurred on Toulon and neighbouring farms, and there being no proper accommodation there, they required the use of our tourist rest-camp for sleeping purposes, whence they would move daily to their duties outside the park. It being the off-season, and in consequence no visitors being present, this was quite feasible, and I offered the senior officers accommodation at my own headquarters. All being satisfactorily settled, the army dashed off in more dust, and did not reappear till evening.

Next day, one of the Dip Inspectors on his return from work at Toulon, announced that he had to inspect my three stall-fed Friesland cows, which of course involved examination of their tongues. He remarked at the time that he had, prior to the present crisis, no experience of foot-and-mouth disease, and asked me if I was well acquainted with the symptoms. I noticed that while all the white officers employed on examination work were carefully provided with rubber boots, gloves, and long coats, some of the native attendants, who occasionally were called in to help, were arrayed merely in the exceedingly dingy cast-off European clothes customary among town natives. Nor did they always, like the white officials, systematically wash their hands with disinfectants. It was doubtless pure coincidence, but three or four days later, my wife came to the office in some agitation to announce 'Rhoda has got foot-and mouth!' I held an inspection at once and found that two out of my three cows were showing the tell-tale mouth ulcers, though they had contacted no other cattle, and had not been outside the enclosure. Well, that was that!

Meantime the disease outside had spread. Ever-widening cordons were established, and a systematic slaughter of all cattle and other cloven-hoofed domestic animals within their limits was carried out by shooting.

I have no doubt that the compulsory dipping of all stock against the various tick-borne diseases had much to do with the spreading of the present highly contagious malady. Some hundreds of native cattle were wont to assemble weekly at a single dip, and if any infected animals happened to be among them, the sickness would spread among the others like wildfire.

Instead of at once suspending these periodical gatherings, some of the local veterinary officers at first had all the cattle in their districts ordered to the same spot for examination, and Ranger Wolhuter nearly got into trouble for refusing to allow the natives in his area to comply.

The summer of 1938 to 1939 proved one of the wettest for many years. The rain commenced about Christmas and continued steadily and sometimes heavily for nearly two months. The whole country was flooded. Some hundred of native-owned cattle had been shot a few miles up the Sabie River from Skukuza, and for quick disposal of the carcasses a bulldozer was used to push them into a dry ravine or donga, and subsequently to cover them more or less with earth. As it happened this donga opened out within a short distance into the Sabie River and some weeks later, the heavy rain having converted the hitherto dry donga into a roaring torrent, all the decomposing remains were washed into the river, not far above our drinking water supply, which was pumped from it!

A further four or five hundred head were shot around a cattle dip a few miles from us, and in the absence of a bulldozer were left just as they fell. Naturally, for a considerable time the surrounding atmosphere for a mile or two told the tale. But it was a remarkable thing that this enormous mass of self-advertising carrion was not visited, so far as we could ascertain, by a single beast or bird of prey and was left to dissolve entirely by natural means. I have never heard of the same thing happening in other than cases of mass slaughter, and as a naturalist have been curious as to the reason, for which I have heard no adequate explanation. Having completed the extermination of all native cattle outside the park as far as the Drakensberg foothills on the west, the veterinary authorities suddenly sprung on me that it was designed also to destroy all the ruminant domestic animals inside as a 'precaution', though it was admitted that all except my three cows were free from the disease and were entirely isolated. So far as I could gather, the pretext was that if the cattle happened to contract foot-and-mouth disease they might infect the game.

I pointed out in writing to the Director of Veterinary Services, that by eliminating all those isolated groups we were likely to lose a useful means of discovering the presence of any communicable animal disease in the park, since such would certainly first be noticed among domestic stock. With the game alone remaining it would be much more difficult to discover, especially were it of the nature of the tsetse fly-borne nagana to which wild animals are immune. I also offered to get the park's herd, which was certified clear of the disease and was in excellent condition, placed at the disposal of the veterinary authorities for experimental purposes. Admittedly they knew very little about the pathology of the South African form of foot-and-mouth disease, and it seemed to be a unique opportunity for endeavouring to find out whether recovered cases were reinfective, how milk supply and future calving were affected, and many other things which would no doubt occur to the scientific mind – and of which I, as a mere layman, would naturally be ignorant. However, it was no good: the *fiat* had gone forth, and the slaughter had to proceed to the last beast. They even shot all Ranger Tomlinson's small private herd, though it was sited nearly two hundred miles from the nearest known case of sickness.

It was assumed that the disease originated from Portuguese East Africa, where it was said to be rampant. But having occasion to visit the Portuguese station at Mapulanguene just over the border, I asked the local veterinary officer whom I happened to meet there, why all the cattle I had seen were in such fine condition, in spite of the foot-and-mouth disease. He registered some surprise, and said, 'We never had any here, but until we heard you had killed all your cattle, I was considering moving all ours back from the border for fear of infection'.

During the height of the campaign I was asked to allow some experiments on wild game to be conducted with the object of discovering if and how far it might prove to be susceptible to the disease. I therefore captured, uninjured, four impala ewes for the veterinarians. Two of these were inoculated with virus from an infected cow, each with a specially strong dose. The other two were kept as 'contacts' in the same small enclosure with those which had been inoculated. After a longer period than that usually required for the symptoms to appear in the case of domestic animals, one of the inoculated impala showed signs of foot-and-mouth disease in the clefts of the forehoofs, the other one and the two contacts so far remaining healthy. Unfortunately, before this interesting experiment could be satisfactorily completed both, the inoculated ewes developed a dangerous and highly contagious form of sepsis, which necessitated the immediate slaughter of all four animals. Thus, the only tangible knowledge gained was, first, that impala were liable to contract foot-and-mouth disease and second, that they were seemingly more resistant to it than domestic ruminants.

No doubt were the disease widely spread among the antelope populations, and were it as severe among them as even it is in its mild form among South African cattle, it would hardly escape notice through the general deterioration in condition and even deaths from starvation, owing to difficulty in masticating the dry, hard herbage. But in spite of careful observation and the shooting of suspected cases, we were never successful in coming upon a single instance. Therefore it would seem that even if present sporadically, foot-and-mouth disease is not either readily contracted by, nor easily inter-communicable among wild game.

At the beginning of February the whole lowveld became flooded and at Skukuza we were nearly marooned, with roads impassable and the main railway line to Pretoria blocked by a fall of rock in the Crocodile River gorge. I had to attend a meeting in Cape Town and wondered how I could get there, road and rail being alike debarred. Finally I managed to get to Lourenço Marques by the last train to get through before that line, too, was washed away. On arrival, I was just in time to climb on to a small Portuguese plane going to Johannesburg, there being only the pilot, his assistant and myself on board. We left in rain but did not strike mist till we crossed the Transvaal border. This got worse and worse. We could no longer see the railway track which we had been following and must have gone far off our course, for suddenly a fortunate break in the mist showed us to be surrounded on three sides by high mountains, and apparently heading for a *cul de sac*. So when the pilot called back to me 'I think we go home' I was definitely relieved. Next morning I embarked on a big four-engine Junker which was able to fly high over mist and cloud. It landed me safely at Johannesburg, whence in due course I reached Cape Town in time for my meeting.

On my return I found the elimination of all native stock, cattle, sheep, goats and pigs nearly complete. I visited the place where the park's herd had stood. In one day a 'green and pleasant valley' covered with sleek healthy animals had been converted into a stinking repulsive Golgotha. Such is man! By the courtesy of the chief veterinary officer, my own three cows, all in full milk, were left till the last and I therefore had the unusual opportunity of observing the disease run its full course. It was very interesting and instructive. In less than a week from first showing, the ulcers between the forehoofs and in the mouth had begun to heal. In three weeks they were gone, and after a month it was possible to tell only by close examination that anything had been wrong. The cows lost no condition and continued to give their full quota of milk throughout. Of course, having been fed on soft food, bran mashes and mealie meal chiefly, they suffered little inconvenience from mouth-sores while eating. No doubt the prime cause for grazing animals losing condition is the difficulty in masticating grass, especially when dry and hard, and the few deaths during the mild South African form of the disease are due simply to weakness from inability to take food. At any rate, when my three cows with their calves at last faced the executioner all were in prime condition.

Some three thousand native cattle in the park were destroyed, none reported to be infected. For the natives the loss was serious. Besides being used for ploughing among them, cattle to a large extent represent currency. When six hundred head were shot at Nyongane's on the western border, the native owners stood by in absolute silence, though I was told that it was only the chief's influence that prevented a demonstration.

Further, the killing of all small stock, except fowls, deprived the natives of their meat supply (for in the sanctuary they might not kill game) and so many of them emigrated.

Compensation in money, not at a highly generous rate, was paid later, which I had the duty of distributing. As one headman remarked when I handed over to him £70 in notes, 'What is the use of all this paper money? Probably it will get burnt or eaten by white ants, and even if not, it will quickly be spent at the stores and soon be finished, while the cattle would have been increasing every year.'

Having thus been cleared of domestic stock, the park was declared an 'infected area' and no animals, such as equines or dogs, might be moved from it without permission from the veterinary department, and then only after disinfection of their feet under official supervision. The natives asked how it was while they might not send a donkey to the store a mile outside the park to get a bag of meal, the zebras and wildebeest could travel backwards and forwards at will! 'Can they not then also carry infection on their feet?' Henceforth there was no fresh milk in the park, which came rather hard on young children, and it was not always easy for the natives to buy artificial substitutes.

The year 1939, however, had not yet finished with us. In September the second great war burst upon the world. Up to then the park had been enjoying a nearly record tourist season, but of course after the beginning of September traffic almost ceased. Luckily it was nearly the end of the season, and during the following summer, Pretoriuskop, which as usual remained open all the year round, did well enough with South African visitors, though the overseas stream had dried up.

The only small excitement which came our way during the rest of the year happened a few weeks after war was declared. A certain Count von

Starenberg (popularly conceived to be the prospective Gauleiter for the Eastern Transvaal after the German occupation, and for some time resident near Tzaneen), anticipating arrest and accompanied by two others of his countrymen – one of them – quite a lad – bought a donkey from some natives and set out to cross the forty miles of the park into neutral country. The police were a bit slow off the mark in telephoning me and a day was lost before I could get in touch by wireless with the ranger concerned. So our effort was not likely to be more than a gesture, the fugitives having a forty-eight hours start. However, he followed their tracks and found they had taken immense trouble to avoid all footpaths and slept at night without a fire, which with lion all round and a donkey as bait, must have been rather wearing. Had they but known, it would have been quite simple to have entered as ordinary tourists by car, driven to the nearest point of Portuguese territory, and then walked for a few miles to the nearest white habitation, since at that time there were no special controls of any kind. As it was they had a pretty hard time and arrived at the first Portuguese post much exhausted. One of our natives coming back from leave and still some distance inside Portuguese country, came on three white men hiding in a donga, who at once covered him with rifles and told him to run, which he lost no time in doing. I heard these men got away in the last German ship to leave Delagoa Bay, but that it was captured by a British cruiser off the west coast of Africa.

Surprisingly, the following year, 1940, was a fairly prosperous one. Petrol had not yet been rationed. Large military camps had been formed at Barberton and elsewhere, and their occupants were wont to visit the park in considerable numbers. Nor did the shattering events of May and June in Europe have much if any apparent effect on the visiting public.

Early in June, I received an urgent wire to go to see the chief of the General Staff in Pretoria at once. I went by train the same day and was met by a Staff car, which whirled me off to headquarters of the Union Defence Force. Here I found the whole General Staff assembled in a state of considerable agitation. It appeared that an alarmist report had been received to the effect that some two thousand armed Germans were concentrated on the Portuguese side of the Kruger Park border, and that they had established landing grounds for aircraft within a few miles of it. I could not help feeling a little surprised. Living, as I did, almost on the frontier, which was regularly patrolled by the white rangers, and with native police of the park constantly in touch with natives from beyond it, and knowing – as everyone who lives

During the Second World War the Kruger National Park was closed to visitors and many of the rangers enlisted for active service. Stevenson-Hamilton, pictured here in 1943, had to content himself with providing regular reports on suspected German agents using the park as an access point for Mozambique.

among tribal natives must know – that the arrival of even one strange European in a purely native area would, within a couple of days, be discussed for fifty miles round, I was convinced that some kind of misapprehension must exist. Moreover, the Witwatersrand Native Labour Association maintained a chain of posts within a few miles of the frontier on the

Portuguese side, with whom I was in frequent communication. It seemed most unlikely that had such an enemy gathering taken place they would not have known all about it; nor was it probable that the Portuguese would have permitted anything of the kind. It showed how remote and unknown this part of the country still remained. A land of mystery, where anything might happen, as indeed had been the case in far-off days!

I therefore asked for a good map showing both sides of the frontier, and after some delay, one was found. I then, with its help, endeavoured to explain the position, and after a time a measure of calm was restored. Eventually, after having scouted some rather unrealistic suggestions, one of which was that I should raise a corps for border defence (a kind of up-to-date Steinacker's Horse), it was agreed that I should act as chief intelligence agent for such part of the Portuguese frontier as adjoined the Kruger National Park, and should furnish the names of any persons recommended as reliable assistants. Having been provided with the necessary written authority, I suggested that the Intelligence Department might establish contact with the Witwatersrand Native Labour Association, whose local manager, Mr H.S. MacKay, had his headquarters at Soekmekaar in the Eastern Transvaal. I knew that Mr MacKay frequently visited Portuguese territory on duty, that he and his European employees were in a position to know all that went on there, and could be relied upon to furnish early and trustworthy information of any unusual happening.

After rather a hectic, but not wholly unprofitable day, and having promised to traverse the border and furnish regular reports, I departed the same evening, feeling rather perturbed at what seemed the complete lack of military information, nine months after the beginning of the war, as to what was taking place in an adjoining foreign country.

On the other hand, German intelligence – though, to it, the matter must have appeared of very minor importance – had without doubt succeeded in obtaining against eventualities a tolerably accurate knowledge of all the country on both sides of the border. For a long time before the war its agents had been at work. A single German, stated to be a prospector or trader, had been camping and travelling about the Portuguese side for over a year. Some months before the war a party of five, travelling in one car, had entered Portuguese territory by a route north of the Limpopo. Stating themselves to be a hunting party, according to the Portuguese *chef de poste* who told me, they carried only one firearm but plenty of surveying instruments!

Sometime in July 1939, while on my way south from the Olifants River, I noticed a car drawn up by one of our windmills and two men standing near it apparently making notes. Driving up to them I explained that by the regulations visitors were supposed to remain in their cars. The two young men, on my telling them who I was, came smartly to attention and, apologizing profusely, explained that being thirsty, they were trying to pump a little water from the mill. They did not give the Hitler salute, though I half expected them to do so.

But whatever intelligence might have been gathered by the enemy for possible future use, that was a very different thing from an actual armed concentration, and before leaving defence headquarters, I managed to gather the source of their startling information. Apparently it emanated from 'a reliable agent' who had been doing 'private intelligence work in Portuguese territory'. I even learnt his name, and on hearing it my surprise at the nature of the report was largely dissipated. Indeed, had the bubble been not thus early pricked, he might have been nearly as successful as was the late Colonel Steinacker with the military authorities, though in the latter's case there really was an existing, if quiescent, enemy to contend with. It really seemed a pity to have spoilt such an exciting story. Not that it was at first by any means disbelieved. In fact, only a few days after my interview, a fleet of army lorries descended on Komatipoort, the border village, and out of them poured a mass of young and excited soldiery, who, greatly to the astonishment of the inhabitants of that sleepy little dorp, immediately began asking 'Where are the Germans?' Indeed, the authorities were even then not completely satisfied. The troops took up covering positions, and it was only after some weeks and, it was said, an outbreak of malaria among them that they were withdrawn.

As soon as possible after my return from Pretoria I communicated with Mr MacKay, the local Witwatersrand Native Labour Association manager, who readily agreed to take me to his posts in Portuguese country near the frontier. We made three expeditions in all at various times during 1940, and I was able to see all *chefs de poste* as well as the provincial administrator at Magude, with whom we lunched. I took the opportunity of asking him what he knew of the person who had so disturbed the Union General Staff, on which he laughed and said, 'Oh, yes, we knew all about him; there was trouble with the police about illegal native recruiting and a few other things, so he left in a hurry'. It appeared that with the exception of the few persons who, before the war, had been 'prospecting' and 'hunting' near the border, there had been no Germans nearer than Lourenço Marques, where in addi-

295

tion to the small local colony, refugees from the Transvaal had gathered. There, under the leadership of a member of the Gestapo, they set up an efficient system of intelligence, passing on the news they received from sympathizers in the Union (where various secret wireless sets were believed to be in operation) to Germany and to U-boats operating in the Mozambique channel. There does not seem to have been much sympathy for their cause among the Portuguese. Indeed, the border officials made no secret of their sentiments, and one of MacKay's staff, on the strength of some connections with the Union, even succeeded in joining its forces.

The landing-places for aircraft which the Germans were said to have made were of course Portuguese and long established; but for possible benefit of the Union Defence Force I sent a description of them. At the latter's request we also enlarged and put in order the two small landing grounds at Satara and Punda Maria, constructed some years previously by the Johannesburg light plane club with the idea of attracting 'businessmen in a hurry', which they had failed entirely to do. As a matter of fact they were never used during the war either, except by General Smuts on two occasions, which perhaps was just as well for the animals.

Besides the air landing strips, the defence force wanted the road through Satara to Sweni made into an all-weather one and continued to the Portuguese frontier. The roads department undertook this, and with the aid of bulldozers and other mechanical monsters completed the work in several months. But when finished it was difficult to see how the new road, which must have cost a lot of money, improved on our old one, while the new bridges over the small streams and dry watercourses which supplanted our own concrete level crossings were mostly washed away during the first summer floods. I had to use some tact in explaining to the Portuguese authorities over the border that an invasion by Union forces was not imminent, as they had been told by the German wireless was the case.

Shortly after getting back from Pretoria, where I had been told to organize a scheme for military intelligence about happenings on the Portuguese border, an event occurred which, though rather comical in itself, might have upset this plan as well as disorganized all the park service. Owing to the difficulty of communicating with the northern sections, especially when road communications were cut by floods, we had been supplied with wireless transmitting sets to connect Skukuza with all stations north of the Olifants River.

While in my office one afternoon, I was told that a man wanted to see me.

On being shown in, he introduced himself as a post office employee, and said he had instructions to remove my wireless transmitting set. Asked why, he said he did not know, but that every station in the park was being visited at the same hour that afternoon, and all wireless sets were being removed. I told him that I held the set for the National Parks Board and had no intention of surrendering it without the authority of that body. Moreover, since he was unable to produce any written credentials or authority I had no means judging him not to be an enemy agent or a gangster emissary. I then got on the telephone to the chairman of the board in Pretoria, whom I fortunately contacted, and on his instructions formally refused to allow my visitor to touch or go near the set. At the same time I allayed his injured feelings by telling him that privately I did not believe he came under either of the heads I had mentioned, but that this did not affect my official attitude. At the usual hour next morning I called up all stations and told them on no account to give up their sets except by my instructions, having surmised – correctly as it proved – that even if their transmitting sets had already been taken, they would be listening in on their private receivers.

Afterwards I heard what happened. Satara, possessing no transmitting set, and Ranger Ledeboer being away on patrol, his wife, under protest, allowed

During the war those rangers who did not enlist contributed to the war effort by improving airstrips and road communications within the park. Camps such as Satara, shown here in the 1940s, were renovated at this time.

297

the house to be searched. When they had quite finished, Mrs Ledeboer suggested that they might have confused Satara with Letaba, and so, having agreed that this might be the case, they dashed off to cover the fifty miles in record time, but arrived late enough to be fined ten shillings each. Rather crestfallen, they seized Ranger Crous's set, but on getting my message next morning, he took it back, threatening them with arrest. Unfortunately for us, before handing it back they managed to render it useless. At Shingwedsi all had gone according to plan, and the raiders were already on the road with their booty when Ranger Tomlinson, having received my message, pursued at breakneck speed, overtook them and, accusing them of being enemy agents, held them up at the point of his rifle, on which they held up their hands and surrendered! He then took them to the police post at Punda Maria, where it was arranged to leave the set pending further enquiries.

Punda Maria proved easy. Captain Rowland-Jones was with the troops in Abyssinia, and his wife, not having got my message, unprotestingly surrendered the set. This party thus departed in triumph taking away the wireless mast as well. So it might be called a drawn battle, with two points to us, one to them, and one (Letaba) indeterminate in their favour.

The struggle was then shifted to Pretoria, where it raged for some days. The board's chairman was Mr Chief Justice de Wet, later to become Acting Governor-General, so he carried a good deal of weight. In fact the matter was taken as far as the Prime Minister, General Smuts, and ended in the Postmaster-General having to restore all the sets, without cost, to us. Some 'face' was saved by no mechanic being sent to restore the Letaba set to working order.

Some little time later, however, the defence force provided every station in the park, free of cost, with an up-to-date transmission set, and agreed to keep them in working order for us, which eminently satisfactory arrangement continued until the close of the war.

I never discovered exactly what prompted the Postmaster-General's action in our case; but at that time, as a precautionary measure, all private transmission sets were being called in. For us a kind of military operation seems to have been planned. Four post office vans left Pretoria for the four stations in the park known to possess transmitting sets. They were instructed that zero hour was 4 p.m. on the same day, and precisely at that hour all sets were to be seized, presumably before mutual warning could be given.

Of course, with the war in Europe having so far gone badly, and with a good deal of openly expressed sympathy for, as well as some hidden activity present in the Union on behalf of the Axis, it was understandable that many people should have suffered from nervous strain and have been prone to impute improper action to any whom they considered not properly supervised. In fact, 'distant fields' were among such people apt to appear 'murky'. Nor were there wanting disguised enemy agents, sometimes employed in good positions, who lost no opportunity of sowing mistrust and friction.

The year 1941 found us a little short-handed, as Rangers Rowland-Jones and Kirkman had joined the forces overseas, but fortunately, Mr W. Lamont, our irrigation expert, was available as a substitute and functioned with great success for the next few years.

We had a busy year. The public had largely settled down with the comfortable feeling that South Africa was going to suffer neither from invasion nor from civil war, and there being as yet no restrictions on travel, the park had an excellent season, to the extent of justifying a small bonus to all employees. Outside the park the year was also a good one for the game, all firearms having been called in by the Government – though out of no consideration for the animals! The members of the park staff, after some correspondence, were allowed to retain their weapons, it having been pointed out that a ranger's duties still involved a certain amount of risk.

In July 1941 His Majesty King George of the Hellenes, accompanied by most of the Greek royal family and a retinue of about forty people (including police), paid us a three-day visit. The King had been in Crete during its recent capture by the Germans and had escaped thence only some six weeks previously, so that the rapid change from the surroundings there to the peaceful scene of the Sabi, must have been – and was in fact – admitted to be most refreshing. Not that the first day at Pretoriuskop could be called entirely peaceful. A large crowd of tourists happened to be in camp, and the King was so mobbed by amateur photographers and autograph hunters, that at last he said, 'I feel like a bear in the zoo, except that no one offers me a bun!'

Next day a still larger crowd had to be faced at Skukuza rest-camp, but on this occasion he took the precaution of appearing hatless and arrayed in khaki shorts and a brown pullover, with the happy result that no one took the slightest notice of him; whereas Colonel Baston (head of the Transvaal police and an imposing figure clad in full uniform with belts and medals) being taken for royalty, was persistently followed everywhere by the click of cameras.

On the last day of the visit I happened to be with His Majesty in the leading car, well ahead of the procession. Having somehow been 'mislaid' by the rest of the party, we spent a most interesting forenoon traversing various by-ways free from other cars, and besides many other animals, seeing lion at close quarters on three occasions. Upon rejoining the main party, rather after the luncheon hour, we found that there had been some uneasiness at our prolonged absence, and poor Colonel Baston, who was responsible for royal safety, was really perturbed, thinking the King had got lost in the wilds!

The party during their visit slept in the Governor-General's special train, parked at Huhla siding, and after dinner on the night of departure, we all joined hands round a huge bonfire and repeatedly chanted 'Auld Lang Syne' at the top of our voices. Then the engine driver blew the whistle and the party had to embark. I walked over to the train with the King and as he said 'Good-bye' he added rather plaintively, 'Can't you hide me behind a bush till the train has gone?' I really believe he wished it could have been possible. It made one reflect how lucky one was to have no greater responsibility than the care of wild animals.

Towards the end of the year came the first petrol rationing; but as people could still draw twenty gallons per month, visitors (from the Transvaal at least) had sufficient to allow one visit to the park in the season. It was too far for those from other provinces, however, and so for the 1942 season it was decided to open only so far north as the Sabie River. Though for official duties the staff was not rationed, we cut down services considerably.

Although there was some uneasiness about the Japanese during the early part of the year, it came to an end when our troops occupied Madagascar, and thereafter my connection with the war mainly consisted of endeavours to answer hectic official enquiries about Nazi infiltrations. For instance, I was once instructed to enquire into and report on information to the effect that many lorry-loads of machine guns were being smuggled into the Union from Portuguese territory through Sabie poort. Since at and near this point the stony Lebombo hills were passable only by an active foot passenger, and with some exertion, and since we maintained a native ranger post on our side at that exact place, I ventured to ask for the source of the information. The reply came in due course. A young flying officer, heading north and flying some distance seaward from the coast, had noticed the tracks of lorries crossing the Lebombo hills at a distance of not much under two hundred miles!

However, thinking it well to calm possible misconceptions so far as possible, I spent some days on foot and horseback making a rough map of the

Lebombo from the Sabie to the Crocodile Rivers, showing all native tracks, kraals, and any other details likely to be useful, for which I received a letter of thanks and heard no more about Nazi smuggling of machine guns. Matters concerning the border had by now been transferred from the defence force to internal security, and I had the advantage of dealing with Colonel Verster, the Deputy Commissioner of Police, who was always most helpful and patient under the stress of what must have been extremely harassing work.

Individual enemy agents did, of course, now and then slip across the border in both directions, principally south of Komatipoort where it was not very difficult to do so, but generally speaking, secret wireless transmission could probably supply all information needed about the departure of convoys and other matters of interest.

With the occupation of North Africa by Allied forces, enemy activity, such as it had been, came to an end. The Nazi intelligence group, hitherto luxuriously quartered in the Polana Hotel at Lourenço Marques, unable to draw further funds, gradually faded away.

Thus our practical interest in the war was concluded; but for park administration hard times were just beginning.

Early in 1943 the petrol ration was again cut down, this time to five gallons a month, a curtailment which naturally prohibited any but local people from visiting the park. Accordingly, it was decided to close the latter entirely to the public, except Pretoriuskop, which was within comparatively easy reach of places like Nelspruit and White River. The expense of maintaining a special tourist staff at other camps was not justified under the circumstances. Therefore from the beginning of 1943 until May 1946, east of Pretoriuskop our lion had to abandon their annual diversion of gathering by the roadside to watch visitors passing by in their cars.

So far as the animals generally were concerned, the absence of the public seemed generally beneficial. They could now wander freely, no longer, as they had been at the height of the season, driven away from the main roads by noise and clouds of dust. Although they had learnt to pay little attention to motor traffic, and certainly showed no nervousness of it, yet constant noise was probably disturbing, while the passage of the cars, by coating the grass and trees near the roads with thick dust, made the herbage unpalatable. Travelling in the early morning during the tourist season, the herds of game would be noticed slowly feeding away from the roads towards the quiet of the bush. During those three undisturbed years, although the increase of game was in no way beyond normal, a good deal more was visible close to the roads than there had been during the tourist seasons in recent years. Of course, transport had to be cut down drastically and lorries used as little as possible. Upkeep of deviation roads was abandoned and only main communications were, so far as possible, kept in repair. In fact, for the time, nothing but the most essential work could be undertaken.

Although beyond the camp at Pretoriuskop there was no accommodation for the general public, each winter numbers of official people found their duties called them to visit the park. Air Force personnel came to visit our two landing grounds, officers of the police made periodical inspections of the post at Skukuza, a few members of the National Parks Board sometimes stayed on after the conclusion of the annual joy-ride through the park, and many others arrived on all kinds of missions, which seldom were found to be necessary after the end of the cool weather. There was, of course, plenty of accommodation in the empty rest-camp at Skukuza. Also, it was convenient for relatives and acquaintances, who came as private guests of members of the staff, to find the park roads free from traffic. The warden's telephone was kept busy receiving and answering requests for privileged entry for one reason or another. It was indeed quite remarkable how far many people seemed to be capable of making their cars travel on five gallons of petrol per month.

But for most of the time the roads were bare of any traffic and the rest-camps silent. So much so, that availing himself of the general quiet, an elephant spent most of one afternoon taking his siesta in the shade of the clock tower just outside the entrance gate to Skukuza rest-camp.

In 1944 there was a recurrence of the foot-and-mouth disease scare. This time it was discovered among the farmers' cattle in the neighbourhood of Hectorspruit, to the east of which place all stock had been eliminated in 1938. But when the veterinary authorities proposed to continue the process of liquidation, the farmers this time said firmly and unanimously 'hands off'. When, at a meeting, one of the experts explained how serious and lasting were the effects of the disease, how a cow, once affected, could never regain condition, give milk, or even produce a healthy calf again, a fat Jersey cow was produced, accompanied by a vigorous-looking calf a few weeks old, and it was affirmed that she had contracted and not long ago had recovered from the disease. The farmers, in fact, remained unconvinced of the necessity for slaughter, and since they not only commanded a good many votes, but exercised a considerable amount of political influence otherwise, the rifle was laid aside, and a cordon system substituted, with the result that the malady faded out in a relatively short time.

The question of the origin of this fresh outbreak aroused much discussion. The farmers were convinced that foot-and mouth disease was endemic among the game animals in the park, and that it had been brought by them to the cattle on the adjoining farms across the Crocodile River. Although at the time of the previous outbreak the veterinary authorities had given as one of their reasons for liquidating all the native cattle in the park the fear that if these cattle should happen to contract foot-and-mouth disease it might spread to the game, now began to think it might after all be endemic among the latter. Therefore, as on the last occasion, any animals appearing to be ill or lame, were, by request, shot and examined, but always with negative results.

It was then decided to place a 'test' herd of cattle in the middle of the game country, to discover whether or not they would become infected. Accordingly, a small number (twenty-four) of Afrikander *tollies* (half-grown oxen) under charge of a veterinary officer from Onderstepoort and a native assistant, were sent from Pretoria by train, disembarked at Huhla siding and placed in the same camp which, prior to 1939, had been occupied by the park's herd of cattle. The site was on the Sand River, close to favourite drinking places of large numbers of impala, waterbuck and kudu. The cattle went to graze daily in the bush and an armed escort was provided as a protection against lion.

At the end of about three months, the young oxen having remained perfectly healthy except for one that died of redwater, it was decided by the veterinary authorities to end the experiment and shoot all the animals, since having once been within a proclaimed infected area they might not be removed from it. The cost to the Government (i.e. to the taxpayer) was twenty-four oxen at £14 each, plus their railage and the salaries, fever, and cost-of-living allowances of the European overseer and native assistant, added to the park's charges for native labour and escort. I could not help reflecting how this experiment could have been equally well tried, and would have cost the Government nothing, had the suggestion made in 1939 to spare the small native herds, or at least the park's own herd, been followed. They had all been living barometers as regards disease among the game. As it was, no one was satisfied. The park was still considered an infected area, donkeys still had to get permission to leave it and had to have their hoofs washed before doing so and we were not even permitted to dispose of thatching grass to neighbouring residents.

During 1945, the European war being over, we saw a procession of distinguished visitors. General Smuts came by air, bringing with him the Crown Prince and Princess of Greece, and at various times there arrived Air Marshals Tedder, Harris, Garrod, the Governor-General of the Sudan, the Governors of Kenya and Northern Rhodesia, the British High Commissioner, Sir Evelyn Baring, and many of our own cabinet ministers with their families, so we were kept busy socially. The animals on the whole rose well to the occasion.

We also pushed on with various repairs and improvements in anticipation of the reopening of the park in 1946. A concrete causeway over the Crocodile River, just below the railway bridge, was completed, displacing the old pontoon, which thus was distinguished by having been the first installed and the last to go. A large reservoir was constructed by damming the Nwaswitsonto River at the narrowest part of its gorge through the Lebombo hills, and what was hoped would prove a much needed permanent water supply was laid on to Pretoriuskop camp.

It was indeed time for some revenue from the public to come to our aid. The board had, fortunately, a little capital in reserve from the prosperous years before 1943, and this, with the subsidies paid by the Union government and the Transvaal province, just saw us through. But only just. By the end of 1945 our capital was exhausted and the subsidies, together with the small takings from Pretoriuskop, would no longer have sufficed to cover even the salaries and wages bill. Probably with no financial improvement, it would have been necessary to reduce the staff in 1946 and so follow the disastrous precedent of 1914, with similar lamentable results to the animal population. Fortunately it was not necessary. Petrol rationing ceased and therefore the public would be able to come to the park freely, bringing the wherewithal to make the wheels go round again.

The end of the war seemed to indicate the end of my long guardianship of the erstwhile Cinderella. The park was now recognized as one of the main – if not the main – attractions of South Africa, and had attained world-wide celebrity, less from propaganda and advertisement (which on the whole had been of poor quality) than from what returning visitors had said and written about their own experiences. It was an attempt – and not an unsuccessful one – to keep alive, and render it possible, especially for those accustomed only to artificial surroundings, to see a little bit of Africa as it had existed before man arrived to upset its economy.

So, it seemed quite time I handed over to someone younger. Also, the

*Stevenson-Hamilton (c.1927) surveys his beloved lowveld
from Shirimantanga koppie, the highest point in the southern
part of the Kruger National Park. As early as 1928 he
expressed the wish that on his death he be interred at this
spot. He died in 1957 and his wife, Hilda, in 1979. Their
daughter, Anne Doyle, scattered the ashes of both parents at
this spot at a ceremony held on 10 April 1979.*

park had been for so long practically a 'one-man show', administered along
certain well-defined lines, that it was probably ripe for some more demo-
cratic kind of control, and for experiments in various administrative directions other than those to which it had been accustomed.

Harry Wolhuter, who had been my colleague from the beginning and had
helped the neglected little Cinderella to become what she had become,
retired at the same time, as did Ledeboer, who had served for about twenty-
five years. Chief Justice N.J. de Wet, who had officiated as the highly successful chairman of the National Parks Board of Trustees for some ten years
after the much regretted death of Senator Brebner, resigned his office about
the same time, his place being taken by Mr A.E. Trollip, who was Deputy-
Speaker of the House of Assembly.

The board made an obvious choice in appointing Wolhuter's son, Henry,
in place of his father at Pretoriuskop. Henry Wolhuter had been born in the
Sabi Game Reserve and had spent most of his boyhood there, thus being

already an expert both in regard to wild animals and native administration. On his return from active service overseas, he gave up the promising post he was filling in Johannesburg under the Chamber of Mines to take up his father's work. D. Swarts, who had been storeman at Skukuza for some years, took Ledeboer's place.

Regarding the filling of my own vacancy, more than a year previously the chairman of the board had introduced me to a Colonel Sandenbergh, then in charge of the large military air force depot near Cape Town, and suggested that he might be a suitable man to replace me some day. I found Colonel Sandenbergh, who was in the middle thirties, to be very keen and energetic, and with some previous experience of wildlife, both from hunting expeditions and from owning a large and well-stocked game farm in the lowveld. I was therefore gratified when the board selected him as my successor.

Of the original members of the board appointed in 1926, only Mr W.A. Campbell remained, while with the departures of Wolhuter and Ledeboer, the senior ranger was Tomlinson, appointed in 1926, followed closely by Crous, MacDonald and James; then came Steyn (1929), Kirkman (1933) and Rowland-Jones (1938). The temporary staff – that is, those officers whose duties were concerned with visitors only, and who were appointed annually, but who often returned year after year – was of course disrupted by the war. Only Captain Tucker, a wounded veteran of a past conflict, and, like Rangers Tomlinson and James, a New Zealander, remained throughout in charge of Pretoriuskop gate.

Nearly all the old native ranger staff, some of them with over thirty years' service, had already died or left. My native ranger-sergeant Njinja, who had been in the service since 1910, died from tuberculosis in 1945; Kukise and Office, two very old faithfuls with equally long service, had passed on some years previously. It was time for me to leave.

I had at least brought up Cinderella and launched her on her career. I loved her best when she was a pathetic and dust-covered little wench, derided and abused. Always I felt that, given her chance and her attractions recognized, unlimited possibilities lay before her. Now that she had become a Great Lady it was fitting she should be provided with custodians perhaps better suited to provide her new requirements.

Might her success, and the gifts increasingly showered upon her, not at last permanently affect her character and transform her into a dame so bedecked by human art that her natural loveliness would be hidden and her simple nature spoilt. Might those holding her future in their hands, realize the true nature of their trust, and not, by estimating her worth at artificial values only, cause her to languish and ultimately perhaps to perish. *Absit omen.*[13]

And so, after a kind farewell meeting held for me by the park staff at Skukuza (which I like best to remember by its older and more familiar term of Sabi Bridge), I finally, on 30th April 1946, severed my connection with the place that had been my home for almost forty-four happy years.

NOTES TO THE TEXT

1. When it was proclaimed in 1898 and re-proclaimed in 1902 the Sabi Game Reserve was not officially named. In early official Transvaal colonial documents, however, it is referred to as the 'Sabi Game Reserve' (not 'Sabie'), and as this is the term James Stevenson-Hamilton uses in *South African Eden*, it has been retained. Officially the northern game reserve was known as the 'Singwitsi' but this spelling was rarely used other than in official documents. Because it is unfamiliar to the public, it has been decided to retain the officially incorrect 'Shingwedsi' employed by Stevenson-Hamilton. The names of the rivers referred to have, however, been corrected in accordance with modern practice to 'Sabie' and 'Shingwedzi'.

2. Let the experiment be made upon a worthless body.

3 Now Mozambique.

4. This is not correct because, in fact, many game protection laws were by then in existence in the Transvaal. Given the troubled political times, however, they were impossible to enforce.

5. Pleasant idleness.

6. In 1899, the same year as the South African War began, the British became involved in a costly war against Muhammed Abdille Hassan of British Somaliland, the 'Mad Mullah'. In 1903 Hassan sued for peace and received favourable terms, retaining his autonomy and being permitted to remain in Italian Somaliland under the protection and control of the Italians.

7. So passes away the glory of the world.

8. Appetite comes with eating.

9. There is considerable documentary evidence to suggest that the public of the Transvaal, far from being apathetic, was enthusiastic about game protection.

10. The end crowns the work.

11. Let now [thy servant] depart. (Luke 2:29.)

12. Of course; it must be understood.

13. Perish the thought.

BIOGRAPHICAL LIST

Andersson, Sir Llewellyn, was the son of C.J. Andersson, a famous explorer of Central Africa and Namibia. After his father's death Andersson settled in Johannesburg, becoming a wealthy accountant and speculator. In 1895 he joined the Reform Committee, was implicated in the Jameson Raid and was imprisoned in Pretoria. Later he had a distinguished military career. He was also a sportsman and keen hunter.

Bolton, W.N., had seen service in Pietersburg during the South African War as a military prosecutor, and remained in the district as a civilian magistrate for many years thereafter. Bolton was an enthusiastic member of the Transvaal Game Protection Association and was instrumental in having the Singwitsi (Shingwedzi) Game Reserve proclaimed in 1903.

Botha, Izak Johannes, was appointed game ranger at Punda Maria in the Kruger National Park in 1929. He took charge of various sections of the park until his resignation in 1938.

Botha, Louis (1862-1919), was a famous Boer general and South African statesman. His parents were Voortrekkers and settled in the Orange Free State. Young Louis moved to Natal, settling in Vryheid as a surveyor, farmer and businessman. In 1896 he was elected to the Transvaal Volksraad and during the South African War of 1899 to 1902 was an extremely competent general. He continued his political career after the conclusion of the war and was leader of the Het Volk party which won the 1907 election in the Transvaal. Botha became the first prime minister of the Union of South Africa in 1910, a post he held until his death.

Brebner, W.J.C. (Jack) (1866-1945), was educated in Bloemfontein and by 1897 had become government auditor of the Orange Free State. He fought in many parts of the country during the South African War of 1899 to 1902 and was a signatory to the Peace of Vereeniging. He shared the political position of his close friend, J.B.M. Hertzog, after Union in 1910, joining him in the formation of the National Party and advocating neutrality for South Africa at the outset of the Second World War. Brebner was the first chairman of the National Parks Board, a post he held until September 1935.

Brent, Ranger, Brent's first names are not known nor is the date he was appointed as a game ranger at Rolle station in the Sabi Game Reserve. He was employed in the reserve some time in 1923 and resigned in February 1924.

Buxton, Edward North (1840-1924), spent his life advocating conservation causes. He was one of the first promoters in England of the idea of public open space and forest reserves, and for many years was involved in the Society for the Protection of the Fauna and Flora of the Empire as its president, as well as with other organizations sharing similar aims.

Caldecott, Harry Stratford (1886-1929), trained as an artist in Paris and was greatly influenced by Impressionism. Landscape was his major interest and his love of nature and wildlife is evident in his South African work. A close friend of Stevenson-Hamilton, he was the major publicist for the Kruger National Park legislation, rallying newspapers and giving lectures in support of the scheme. He was also influential in other national projects, particularly in the establishment of the organization which later became the Wildlife Society of Southern Africa and on the commission which decided upon the new South African flag.

Campbell, W.A. (1880-1962), generally known as 'Wac', was the son of a Natal settler and prominent politician. The owner of extensive sugar estates, with an interest in hunting and wildlife, Campbell became the Natal representative on the National Parks Board on its establishment, remaining until 1950. This involvement sparked a love of the lowveld and he bought the farm 'MalaMala', adjoining the Kruger National Park, from the Transvaal Consolidated Lands Company in 1929.

Charter, A.E., who was the Transvaal provincial secretary in 1928 and a member of the National Parks Board from 1926 to 1927, had immigrated to the Transvaal after the South African War to join Lord Milner's 'kindergarten'.

Coetser, J.J. (1872-1935), was the first Afrikaans-speaking game ranger employed by the Kruger National Park. Coetser was born in Lydenburg and fought in the South African War of 1899 to 1902 and in East Africa during

311

the First World War. He was a good linguist and spoke many African languages fluently. In 1928 Coetser resigned from the park and was later killed by an elephant in the northern Transvaal.

Coetzee, S.H., was the member of the Provincial Council for Lydenburg, one of the constituencies adjoining the Sabi Game Reserve. It was he who proposed in the Provincial Council in March 1916 that the Government reduce the area of the Sabi Game Reserve to allow the grazing of domestic stock, thus initiating formal official discussion on the matter.

Colenbrander, Johannes Wilhelm (1857-1918), had a restless and adventurous life. Born in Natal, he soon became involved in colonial and Zulu politics. He was a trader and travelled in Swaziland, the goldfields of the Transvaal and into present-day Zimbabwe, where he befriended the Ndebele chief, Lobengula, although he later fought against the Ndebele in the rebellion of 1896. During the South African War of 1899 to 1902 he was a scout for the British and colonial forces and thereafter became a treasure hunter and estates manager. He then returned to Natal where he assisted in the suppression of the Bambatha rebellion. He drowned crossing a flooded river on horseback while playing the part of Lord Chelmsford in the shooting of an early South African film, *Symbol of Sacrifice.*

Crous, Gerhardus Christoffel Snyman (d. 1975), joined the employ of the Kruger National Park in 1928 as the first permanent ranger at Tshokwane. After a career of travel in the United States merchant navy and as a hunter and explorer of the northern Transvaal and Swaziland, he became stationmaster at Komatipoort. In April 1929 Crous was accused of murdering a poacher in the Kruger National Park but was acquitted. Crous shot the first white lion in the park.

De Jager, Petrus Lafras, a game ranger at Rolle station from 1919 to 1929. De Jager had been a professional soldier, serving with distinction during the South African War of 1899 to 1902 and in the First World War.

De Laporte, Cecil Richard, was appointed as game ranger in May 1903 and retired in 1929. He moved around the reserve, acting as warden in the absence of Stevenson-Hamilton on occasion.

De Souza, E., represented Lydenburg on the Transvaal Provincial Council.

De Wet, Nicolaas Jacobus (1873-1960), a champion of the Afrikaans language and its literature, was chairman of the National Parks Board from 1935 to 1945. He was military secretary to General Louis Botha during the South African War of 1899 to 1902. After a long and distinguished legal and parliamentary career – he was minister of justice from 1913 to 1924 – De Wet became chief justice of the Union of South Africa in 1939. He declined to become Governor-general, a post which was offered to him on the death of Sir Patrick Duncan.

Duke, Thomas (1860-1934), game ranger at Crocodile Bridge and Lower Sabie, was employed in 1902 and retired in 1923. He was born in Ireland and came to South Africa with his parents who settled in the eastern Cape. His son also became a ranger in the Kruger National Park.

Duncan, Sir Patrick (1870-1943), was born in Scotland, the son of a crofter. He studied Classics and law at the University of Edinburgh and joined Lord Milner's team for the reconstruction of the Transvaal after the end of the South African War. Duncan was active in politics throughout his life, holding various cabinet posts, and in 1937 became the first South African citizen to be appointed Governor-General of the Union.

Erasmus, Jacobus Abel (1845-1912), the child of Voortrekkers, grew up in Ohrigstad. He was a farmer and minor civil servant and he fought in the wars of resistance of the Venda and Pedi. After the Transvaal War of 1880 to 1881, Erasmus became native commissioner for the Lydenburg district and was greatly feared by the Africans of the area. After gold was discovered Erasmus became a wealthy speculator in land.

Francis, H.F., had been a hunter in the lowveld before the outbreak of war in 1899, collecting material for museums as well as for trading purposes. After assisting in the relief of Ladymsith and Mafeking, Francis joined Steinacker's Horse. His interest in game led to his appointment in 4 July 1901 as 'game inspector', or warden, of the Sabi Game Reserve, a position he had filled informally since 18 May 1901. He was killed in a skirmish with the Boer forces on 7 August 1901.

Fraser, Affleck Alexander (1855-1929), a retired professional soldier, was appointed warden of the Pongola Game Reserve in 1903, but was moved to the Shingwedsi reserve as warden not long afterwards. He retired in 1920 and died in Johannesburg.

Fuller, Claude (1872-1928), entomologist and veterinarian, was born in Australia and joined the Cape Department of Agriculture in 1897. After 1910 he was transferred to Pretoria and became head of the Division of Entomology. Fuller was interested in a variety of entomological problems, including plant diseases, termites and tsetse fly. The research into tsetse fly disease led to an interest in the route followed by Trichardt's party of Voortrekkers. As Fuller's duty was the protection of the domestic stock of South Africa, he was not an ally of the game protection movement, fearing that diseases of wildlife would transmit themselves to livestock.

George II, King of Greece, together with his family and government, spent their exile from Greece during the Second World War as the official guests of the South African Government.

Gill, Edwin Leonard (1877-1956), trained in zoology and geology in England, and was involved in museum work there and in Scotland before his appointment as Director of the South African Museum in Cape Town in 1924, a post he held until his retirement in 1942. Gill's special interest was in avifauna, but he was extremely knowledgeable about southern African wildlife generally and advocated its conservation in all possible ways.

Glynn, Henry T. (c.1824-1894), 'the elder', emigrated from Ireland to the Cape in 1838. He made many trading trips into the interior of southern Africa and later became a diamond digger. In 1873 he settled near Lydenburg and subsequently acquired a farm near the present town of Sabie. Glynn was a great hunter and acted on many occasions as a guide for hunting parties into the lowveld.

Glynn, Henry Thomas (1856-1928), 'the younger', was the second son of H.T. Glynn. Glynn found gold on his farm near Lydenburg, floated a company and settled later on the site of the present town of Sabie. He left South Africa during the South African War to avoid being called up on the Boer side and afterwards was one of those responsible for establishing the White

River Estates Company. Like his father, Glynn was a keen hunter but also a conservationist: in 1896 he advocated the establishment of a game reserve in what is now the southern part of the Kruger National Park.

Gorges, Edmond Howard Locam, was born in 1872 in King William's Town. He joined the civil service in the Cape and moved to the Transvaal after the South African War. After a spell in the office of the colonial secretary, he became secretary to the prime minister, assistant colonial secretary, and then chairman of the Public Service Board. After Union in 1910 Gorges was secretary of the interior and during the First World War, chief censor. In 1915, when the Union took over German South West Africa, he became administrator of that territory.

Grant, A., represented Pretoria East on the Transvaal Provincial Council.

Gray, Edward George (Gaza), was born in the eastern Cape but spent many years in the lowveld. Gray applied to replace Francis as warden of the Sabi Game Reserve but he was rejected. Stevenson-Hamilton was later impressed by his knowledge of the area and made him an honorary game ranger in 1902. For many reasons his relationship with Stevenson-Hamilton deteriorated and he left after a few months.

Grobler, Pieter Gert Wessel (1873-1942), whose mother was President Paul Kruger's niece, was born on the president's farm and lived with the president in Pretoria. He became a clerk, then a journalist, and during the South African War of 1899 to 1902 was Kruger's private secretary and went into exile with the president. In 1910 Grobler entered politics. A committed republican, he was involved in the 1914 rebellion, for which he was imprisoned. He was minister of lands from 1924 to 1933, and was a firm believer in apartheid, for which he campaigned all his life.

Gunning, Jan Willem Boudewijn (1860-1913), trained as a medical doctor but taught zoology. He became director of the State Museum in Pretoria, and later raised sufficient funds to establish the Transvaal Museum. Gunning was also instrumental in the foundation of the National Zoological Gardens in Pretoria.

Haagner, Alwin Karl (1880-1962), was appointed to the staff of the Transvaal Museum in about 1906. Haagner published widely on South

315

African birds and in 1911 succeeded Gunning as director of the National Zoological Gardens, a post he held until 1926. He was an active protagonist of the idea of national parks in southern Africa, and was chairman of the Wildlife Protection Society at the time of the establishment of the Kruger National Park. He served on the National Parks Board of Trustees in 1926 and 1927. Thereafter he lived in Beira but returned to South Africa in the late 1940s.

Hartog, G., was born in 1880 on the Kimberley diamond fields and later became an advocate. In 1917 he joined the Transvaal Provincial Council and was a member of its Executive Committee until 1920. Hartog wrote important books in the legal field.

Havenga, Nicolaas Cristiaan (1882-1957), was born and educated in the Orange Free State. He fought on the Boer side during the South African War of 1899 to 1902 and afterwards studied law. Politics was, however, his first love. Havenga was a great friend of Hertzog and a staunch republican. When the Pact government came to power in 1924, Havenga - by then a leading figure in the National Party - became minister of finance, a post he held from 1924 to 1939 and again from 1948 to 1954. He was disappointed not to have succeeded Malan as prime minister and retired from politics. He was a keen hunter and founder member of the Veld Trust movement.

Healy, Guy Rambont ('Tim'), an Irishman, first joined the staff of the Sabi Game Reserve as the South African Constabulary assistant to Stevenson-Hamilton in his work as justice of the peace. In 1903 one of his duties was to oversee the northern extension of the reserve and he formally became a game ranger in 1908. Healy was killed in action in Tanganyika in 1916.

Hertzog, James Barry Munnik (1866-1942), was a lawyer, Boer general and statesman. An early supporter of the Afrikaans language movement, by 1895 Hertzog was a judge on the Free State bench. During the South African War of 1899 to 1902, Hertzog at first acted in a legal capacity. In 1900 he became a general, and was one of those who recommended using guerrilla tactics in order to continue the war. At the Treaty of Vereeniging he was the representative for the Orange Free State, a leader thereafter in the revival of Afrikaner politics and a delegate to the National Convention at the foundation of the Union of South Africa. Hertzog broke with the political ideals of Louis Botha, founding his own party, which came to power in 1924 with Hertzog as prime minister. He was therefore prime minister of the Union at the time of the establishment of the Kruger National Park. Under his leadership other important issues which were resolved included the promotion of Afrikaans to an official language, the adoption of a new national flag, and the loosening of ties with Great Britain. In 1929 Hertzog again won the general election and after 1933 entered into a coalition with and then fused with the party of Jan Smuts. After losing the vote for South African neutrality at the outbreak of the Second World War, Hertzog retired from politics.

Hoare, F.R.G., a member for many years of the Transvaal Game Protection Association, was appointed to the National Parks Board in 1930s as the representative of the Wildlife Protection Society. He remained on the board until 1941.

Hockly, Robert Ainslie, who was on the National Parks Board from 1926 to 1944, was member of parliament for Fort Beaufort from 1929 to 1938.

Hofmeyr, Jan (Frederik) Hendrik (1894-1948), was extremely gifted as a child, matriculating at the age of twelve and qualifying at Oxford while still a teenager. He was the first principal of the University of the Witwatersrand and later chancellor of that institution. In 1924 he was appointed administrator of the Transvaal and in 1929 entered parliament. Hofmeyr held numerous cabinet portfolios and was chief advisor to Smuts, but his liberal attitude to race relations led to his resignation from the cabinet in 1939. During the war, however, he held the portfolios of finance and education, frequently acting as prime minister in Smuts's absence.

Hornaday, William T., was the director of the New York Zoological Park for many years. He took a great interest in the conservation of the fauna of Africa, was a member of numerous international protection societies and published widely in the field.

Howe, Elliott, made his career in the police force, joining the South African Constabulary during the South African War of 1899 to 1902 and later serving in the Orange Free State and Cape Town. In August 1923 he was transferred to headquarters in Pretoria. When Stevenson-Hamilton was on leave in Britain, Howe was seconded to the post of warden of the Kruger National Park and held this position for a year until the return of Stevenson-Hamilton in June 1929.

Hoy, Sir William Wilson (1868-1930), began his association with railway administration in his youth when he became a junior clerk in the Scottish railways. In 1889 he joined the Cape railways and during the 1890s was involved in solving tariff disputes between the Cape Colony and the Transvaal. During the South African War of 1899 to 1902 Hoy supervised the military rail network in the Orange Free State and Transvaal, and after 1910, as general manager of the South African Railways, his achievement was to unify the railway systems of the four provinces.

Hull, Henry Charles (1860-1932), an attorney first in Kimberley and then on the Witwatersrand, became counsellor to Lord Milner at the outbreak of the South African War and subsequently took an active military role during the war. In the first cabinet after the Union of South Africa in 1910, Hull became minister of finance and consolidated the four provincial financial systems. His political career ended in 1912 after a dispute with a colleague.

James, Thomas Llewellyn (1886-1971), enjoyed a long career as game ranger in the Kruger National Park from 1929 to 1952. James was born in New Zealand and before entering the service of the park had been a farmer and tin miner in the Waterberg.

Kirkman, Walter Henry (1899-1989), was born in the Cape Colony and joined up for military service in East Africa during the First World War. Afterwards he returned to the family farm but later moved to the lowveld as manager for the Transvaal Consolidated Lands Company with responsibility for a group of farms known as the Toulon Block, later a portion of the Sabi Sand Game Reserve. During the drought of 1933 James joined the employ of the Kruger National Park as a roads foreman, returning to the Toulon farms on his retirement in 1959. An account of his life is to be found in *Game Ranger*, a book by Hannes Kloppers. 'Harry's Huts' in the MalaMala Game Reserve are named after Kirkman.

Kretschmar, G.H., an advocate, was a member of the Transvaal Provincial Council representing Vrededorp.

Lagden, Sir Godfrey Yeatman (1851-1934), began his Transvaal career as a clerk in the post office when the British annexed the Transvaal in 1877 but was soon promoted to more senior posts in the civil service. When the Transvaal regained its independence in 1881, Lagden became an administrator of Basutoland and Swaziland. After the South African War of 1899 to 1902 he was appointed commissioner of native affairs in the Transvaal and in this capacity administered the game reserves of the Transvaal for some years.

Lamont, William Henry (1884-1974), was born in Scotland, joined the navy and then served during the South African War. He remained in South Africa after the conclusion of the war, attempting prospecting and farming. In 1937 he became a tourist officer at Shingwedzi camp in the Kruger National Park and was also involved in road and dam construction. While others were away at war, Lamont acted as a game ranger and retired in 1950 to live on the Chobe River in Botswana.

Ledeboer, Leonard Henry (1868-1959), came from a Natal family. During the South African War of 1899 to 1902 Ledeboer joined the South African Republic Police, but after his surrender to the British forces in May 1901 he changed sides and became an intelligence officer for the British in the northern Transvaal. Ledeboer's knowledge of African languages proved very useful in this work. He became involved in some of the escapades of the notorious Bushveld Carbiniers and gave evidence at the courts martial of 'Breaker' Morant and others. After the war Ledeboer remained in the northern Transvaal, and his association with what is now the Kruger National Park began in 1903 when he suggested to the magistrate, W.N. Bolton, that a game reserve be established in the north-eastern Transvaal. Ledeboer joined the staff of the Sabi Game Reserve as a ranger in 1921 but despite his early interest in game protection, he seems not to have been a very enthusiastic game ranger, having at times to be goaded by Stevenson-Hamilton into carrying out his duties efficiently.

Lloyd, William Walter, who had been farming near Kiepersol, was appointed a game ranger in 1919. A Welshman, Lloyd came to South Africa after the conclusion of the South African War. He died of a lung infection in 1922.

Lounsbury, Charles Pugsley (1872-1955), was born and educated in the United States and emigrated to the Cape Colony in 1895 as an entomologist after the *Phylloxera* epidemic had affected the vineyards of the Cape. His interest in those insect pests which attack fruit crops was augmented by a study of animal diseases spread by ticks. After 1911 Lounsbury joined the Department of Agriculture. He proved to be an able research scientist and the results of his findings were widely published.

Loveday, Richard Kelsey (1854-1910), a surveyor, civil servant and politician, was born in Pietermaritzburg but moved to the Transvaal and helped defend Pretoria against the Boers during the Transvaal War of 1880 to 1881. Afterwards he became a Transvaal citizen and between 1891 and 1900 represented the constituency of Barberton on the Volksraad. During this time he acted as a thorn in the side of the Kruger government, opposing or contesting almost all the legislation which came before the Volksraad. He also campaigned actively for social and economic reforms. In 1895 Loveday introduced a motion in the Volksraad for the establishment of a game reserve in the eastern Transvaal which met with favour from his colleagues. However, it took three years of Loveday's cajoling before President Kruger finally signed the game reserve into law. After 1902 Loveday remained active in civic affairs.

Lucas, Frank Archibald William (1881-1959), was an advocate who had studied law at Oxford and in Holland. In 1924 he became chairman of the Wage Board and was later appointed a judge. Lucas was interested in politics, particularly working class issues, and was leader of the Labour Party in the Transvaal Provincial Council. He represented Troyeville in the Provincial Council and was a member of the Game Reserves Commission of 1918.

Ludorf, Joseph Francis, born in 1918, represented Pretoria South in the Transvaal Provincial Council. Chairman of the 1918 Game Reserves Commission, Ludorf was a member of the National Parks Board from 1930 to 1951, acting for that period as vice-chairman, and he was chairman in 1951.

Maberly, C.T. Astley (1905-1962), was born in Bristol and emigrated to South Africa in 1924. Maberly was a writer and illustrator and his work appeared in books, periodicals, brochures and on items of porcelain. From 1925 to 1936 he spent almost half of each year in the Kruger National Park, sketching and writing. He held group and solo exhibitions.

Mbandzeni (Umbandine), became king of Swaziland in 1875. During his fourteen-year reign, he granted land and other concessions in Swaziland which involved that country in boundary disputes with its neighbours.

McDonald, Hector, born in 1886, was appointed to the post of game ranger in the Kruger National Park in 1929. For many years prior to that date McDonald had explored and hunted in the lowveld and knew the area extremely well. He retired in 1951.

Papenfus, Herbert Boshof (1865-1937), was educated in the Orange Free State and was called to the English Bar in 1896. He was a member of the Reform Committee and supported the Uitlanders but he did not join the Jameson Raid. He was one of the first councillors of the Johannesburg municipality and served with distinction during the First World War. A supporter of Botha's policy of conciliation between British and Afrikaner, Papenfus's major interests were in education and the welfare of animals. He was a member of the Transvaal Game Protection Association after 1902 and served on the National Parks Boards from 1926 to 1937, as well as holding office as president of the Wildlife Protection Society of Southern Africa from 1930 to 1937. He was the member of parliament for Hospital from 1915 to 1929.

Pirow, Oswald (1890-1959), was of German parentage and earned a medical degree in Germany before reading law in England. From 1929 to 1933 he was minister of justice and from 1938 to 1939 minister of commerce and industries. In Parliament he represented Zoutpansberg from 1924 to 1929 and Gezina from 1929 to 1943. Throughout his life he kept alive his relationship with Germany, meeting Hitler and being influenced by his personality and his doctrines. Pirow considered that South Africa should support Germany at the outbreak of war. In 1940 he founded the New Order, an organization devoted to furthering national socialism in South Africa. His political career ended with the war and he began writing, principally accounts of hunting and wildlife experiences. Through his books, Pirow came into contact with the Stevenson-Hamiltons and the men became firm friends.

Preller, Gustav Schoeman (1875-1943), was a great champion of the Afrikaans language and of Afrikaner nationalism. He took part in the South

African War of 1899 to 1902 as a war correspondent and also in a military capacity as an artilleryman. After the war, Preller became a leading journalist and critic, founding his own periodical and promoting the use of Afrikaans as a literary language. Although not an historian, Preller wrote many historical works with the aim of providing an heroic past for the nascent Afrikaner nation. Owing to his role as an interpreter of the Afrikaner heritage Preller was given a place on the first National Parks Board from 1926 to 1939.

Price, Sir Thomas Rees (1848-1916), was educated in Wales and Australia and trained as a railwayman. On coming to the Cape Colony in 1880, he advanced rapidly in railway management, becoming in 1901 general manager of the Cape railways and playing a significant role in co-ordinating the railways systems of the various colonies at the time of Union in 1910.

Prince of Wales. The Prince of Wales who visited the Sabi Game Reserve in 1925 was Edward (David), the eldest son of King George V and Queen Mary. Between 1919 and 1925 Edward toured the British Empire and for three months in 1925 travelled extensively in southern Africa. He acceded to the throne as Edward VIII but abdicated on 11 December 1936 in order to marry Mrs Wallis Simpson.

Reitz, Deneys (1882-1944), was the son of F.W. Reitz, president of the Orange Free State. During the South African War of 1899 to 1902 he joined the Boer forces and was a member of the Smuts commando which raided the Cape Colony. After the war Reitz refused to take the oath of allegiance and only returned to South Africa in 1905. He became an attorney and began a political career, acting on Smuts's staff during the First World War. He was elected to parliament, firstly for Port Elizabeth Central and subsequently for Barberton, and was minister of lands from 1921 until 1924. After fusion in 1933 he was again in the cabinet as minister of lands until 1935 and was deputy prime minister in the early years of the Second World War. In 1943 he was appointed high commissioner to London. Reitz recorded his experiences in numerous books, of which *Commando* remains enduringly popular. Reitz was a great supporter of the idea of national parks and paved the way for the legislation which was passed by his successor as minister of lands, Piet Grobler, in 1926. Reitz was a member of the National Parks Board from 1926 to 1942.

Reitz, Hjalmar (1877-1946), was the brother of Deneys Reitz and thus also a son of F.W. Reitz, a former president of the Orange Free State. He practised law in South Africa and then in England and, like his brother, fought on the Boer side during the South African War of 1899 to 1902, becoming a prisoner-of-war in India. Afterwards he continued his legal career in the Transvaal. His political career differed from his brother's in that Hjalmar was a republican, a member of the National Party and a disciple of Hertzog, rather than of Smuts. In parliament Reitz represented North Rand, Brits and Jeppe. He was interested in Afrikaans literature and published legal works and novels.

Rissik, Johann Friedrich Bernhard (1857-1925), was the surveyor who inspected the Witwatersrand goldfields, and Johannesburg was probably named after him and Christiaan Johannes Joubert. He fought under Louis Botha during the South African War of 1899 to 1902 and, although prepared to assist in an advisory capacity, refused to hold public office until the Transvaal was granted responsible government in 1907. He then served as minister of lands and native affairs, and after Union was administrator of the Transvaal. On retirement from the post of administrator in 1917, he became commissioner for railways and harbours and also public debt commissioner.

Rood, Willem Hendrik, was the member of parliament for Barberton from 1924 to 1929 and for Carolina from 1929 to 1938. He was a member of the National Parks Board of Trustees from 1927 to 1941.

Rowland-Jones, Maurice (1899-1959), emigrated to South Africa after a military career and joined the staff of the Kruger National Park as a gatekeeper in 1931. He was promoted to game ranger in 1938 and was responsible for many construction works in the Punda Maria section. Rowland-Jones compiled the first official list of birds of the Kruger National Park. He lived in Haenertsburg after his retirement.

Sandenbergh, J.A.B., had a distinguished military career, on the basis of which he was appointed to succeed Stevenson-Hamilton as warden of the Kruger National Park in 1946. He held the post until 1954.

Schoch, Dr Arnold, was a senior law adviser to the Government. He was born in Rustenburg in 1883 and obtained a doctorate in law from Leiden University. In 1919 he was appointed as assistant attorney-general of the

Transvaal. Throughout his life Schoch supported wildlife conservation and it was he who drew up the legislation which became the first National Parks Act in 1926.

Selby, Paul (1877-1940), a mining engineer, was born in the United States. He came to South Africa in 1902 and was employed as general manager on various gold mines. He took a keen interest in game protection and his excellent wildlife photographs promoted the conservation cause, together with his lectures and fund-raising ability. Today his pictures are classics of their kind. He was president of the Wildlife Protection Society from 1927 to 1930.

Shaka (Chaka, Tshaka) (c.1787-1828), was a son of the Zulu chief Senzangakhona. He spent some years in exile with his mother and became a leading warrior in the Mthethwa army. On his father's death Shaka succeeded to the Zulu throne, and as king of the Zulu he furthered centralization and the militaristic nature of the Zulu state. He expanded the Zulu kingdom greatly, destroying or dispersing groups and clans that resisted him. He was assassinated in 1828.

Siewert, Paul, was appointed a game ranger in 1911 after having been a shop-keeper. Siewert was born in Germany but raised by an American family. He was ostracized during the First World War because of his German background.

Smuts, Jan Christiaan (1870-1950), became state attorney of the Transvaal in 1891 after reading law at Cambridge. He wrote an important book about the causes of the South African War of 1899 to 1902, *A Century of Wrong*, and took part in many military campaigns. After the war he entered Transvaal politics in order to counteract Milner's policies, and after Union in 1910 became prominent on the national stage. Smuts played a major role in drafting the constitution of the Union of South Africa and was later prime minister from 1919 to 1924 and again from 1939 to 1948. He was involved in South Africa's campaigns during the First and Second World Wars and was active in international affairs. Throughout his life he was interested in nature, especially botany. He established the Rustenburg Game Reserve in 1909 when he was colonial secretary of the Transvaal and supported the national parks idea from its inception to its fulfilment in 1926.

Sommerville, James, was born in Scotland in 1877. In 1900 he was appointed Lord Milner's confidential clerk and rose up the civil service ladder to become secretary for lands in 1921, a position he held until 1932.

Soshangane (Manukosi) (c.1790-1858), was a Zulu chief and the conqueror of Mozambique. The leader of a clan whose territory was in northern Zululand, Soshangane was defeated by Shaka in about 1820 and fled with a small group of followers to the vicinity of Delagoa Bay. He then raided and conquered the smaller Tsonga groups of Mozambique and provided a haven for fugitives from Shaka. Although mostly Nguni in origin, Soshangane's followers were given the name 'people of Gaza' and their descendents have become known as 'Shangaans'. Soshangane pursued a reign of terror in Mozambique, clashing with Shaka's impis, with the Shona, Tsonga and whites.

Steyn, Louis Botha (1901-1962), after working as a government auditor, was appointed a game ranger in the Kruger National Park in 1929. He was interested in Voortrekker history and traced the route of the Trichardt party through the national park. From 1954 to 1961 Steyn was warden of the Kruger National Park.

Stoffberg, T.C., the representative for Ventersdorp, was a member of the executive of the Transvaal Provincial Council.

Swarts, Dawid Hercules (1904-1970), joined the police force at Louw's Creek and was sent to Skukuza as clerk of the court. He also acted as a game ranger in various sections of the park. Keen on history, Swarts identified the locality where the Van Rensburg Voortrekker party was murdered.

Theiler, Sir Arnold (1867-1936), was born in Switzerland. He emigrated to the Transvaal in 1891 as the only veterinarian in the country and became renowned in the field of livestock diseases. He established an experimental farm and founded a research station, and after the South African War of 1899 to 1902 (in which he fought on the Boer side) became ever more active in the field of research.

Tomlinson, Herbert Ernest, was the first game ranger appointed after the proclamation of the Kruger National Park, having been farm manager of the

Toulon farms owned by the Transvaal Consolidated Lands Company. Tomlinson worked at Malelane and Shingwedsi and built the rest camp at Shingwedsi.

Trollip, Alfred Ernest, was the member of parliament for Brakpan from 1938 to 1953 and for Bezuidenhout from 1953 to 1958. He was active in the Wildlife Society of Southern Africa and was a member of the National Parks Board of Trustees from 1945 to 1950.

Trollope, Stephen Harold (1881-1949), a member of Steinacker's Horse and a well-known hunter and shot, was appointed a game ranger at Malelane. He left the service of the Kruger National Park in 1928 and in 1931 became the first warden of the Addo Elephant National Park in the eastern Cape.

Van Oordt, Herman Frederick (1862-1907), left Rotterdam in 1881, and first taught in Namaqualand before establishing himself as a trader, hunter and explorer. In 1888 he settled in the Transvaal, worked in a shop and then joined the Native Affairs Department. In the latter he acted as tax collector and secret agent for the Transvaal on the troubled boundary between that country and Swaziland, Zululand and Mozambique. He was appointed warden of the Pongola Game Reserve in 1895 and left the district to fight in the South African War in 1899. After his release from St Helena, where he was held as a prisoner-of-war, Van Oordt lived in what is now Namibia.

Viljoen, P.R., born in 1889, was appointed secretary for agriculture and forestry in 1939.

Wade, C., represented Germiston on the Transvaal Provincial Council.

Warren, Ernest (1871-1946), joined the staff of the University of London as a zoologist but emigrated to South Africa in 1903 on being offered the post of first director of the Natal Museum in Pietermaritzburg. Warren was in favour of national parks, advocating a park at St Lucia in Natal, and was one of the few scientists to argue that game destruction would not terminate the outbreak of nagana during the 1920s.

Willis, Percy ('Pump' – 1876-1959) and his brother *Bertram ('Clinkers')*, were born in Natal and in 1899 took up elephant hunting and prospecting in

Mozambique. When the South African War broke out they returned to the Transvaal and joined Steinacker's Horse at Komatipoort. After the war they became farmers and storekeepers on a large scale in the lowveld. 'Pump' became well known for his wildlife photography and many of his photographs appeared in early editions of *South African Eden*.

Windham, W., was born in 1864 in Natal and became a prominent civil servant in the field of native affairs in Zululand and the Transvaal. Between 1904 and 1905 he was commissioner of native affairs in the Transvaal.

Wolhuter, Henry Charles Christoffel (1876-1964), was born in the Cape and joined Steinacker's Horse during the South African War of 1899 to 1902. From 1902 until his retirement in 1946, Wolhuter was the game ranger in charge of the Pretoriuskop section of the Kruger National Park. His memoirs are chronicled in *Memories of a Game Ranger* which he wrote after his retirement.

Wolhuter, Henry Charles Junior (1920-1964), grew to love the life of a game ranger while living with his family near Pretoriuskop. After a spell in the Middle East during the Second World War and a short career with the Chamber of Mines, he was appointed to his father's post when the latter retired in 1946.

Woolls-Sampson, Sir Aubrey, was a member of the Reform Committee and was jailed after the Jameson Raid in 1896. At the outbreak of the South African War in 1899, Woolls-Sampson founded the Imperial Light Horse and had a distinguished military career. He was active in Transvaal politics after the war and was member of the Union parliament for Braamfontein from 1910 to 1915.

INDEX

Italicized numbers = illustrations